MIKE WEIR

MIKE WEIR

THE ROAD TO THE MASTERS

LORNE RUBENSTEIN
FOREWORD BY MIKE WEIR

M&S

Cloth edition published 2003
Trade paperback edition published 2004

Library and Archives Canada Cataloguing in Publication

Rubenstein, Lorne
Mike Weir : the road to the Masters / Lorne Rubenstein.

ISBN 0-7710-7572-3 (bound).—ISBN 0-7710-7574-X (pbk.)

1. Weir, Mike. 2. Golfers – Canada – Biography. I. Title.

GV964.W435R82 2003   796.352'092   C2003-903969-2

We acknowledge the financial support of the Government of Canada through the
Book Publishing Industry Development Program and that of the Government of
Ontario through the Ontario Media Development Corporation's Ontario Book
Initiative. We further acknowledge the support of the Canada Council for the
Arts and the Ontario Arts Council for our publishing program.

Typeset in Minion by M&S, Toronto
Printed and bound in Canada

This book is printed on acid-free paper that is
100% recycled, ancient forest friendly (100% post-consumer recycled).

McClelland & Stewart Ltd.
The Canadian Publishers
481 University Avenue
Toronto, Ontario
M5G 2E9
www.mcclelland.com

1   2   3   4   5   · 08   07   06   05   04

To my mother, with thanks

Contents

Foreword

It was early in the spring of 2003 when Lorne Rubenstein told me that he was going to follow me in the year's majors and write a book about my quest to win one. He'd been watching me since my amateur days, and I knew he would provide a close-up look into what life had been like for me as I made my way in golf. I was glad to help him out with the book, and looked forward to reading it myself. We had had many conversations with each other, and I believed Lorne had a unique perspective on my career.

I've enjoyed talking with Lorne over the years, because we always cover so much ground. It's not unusual for us to start discussing a particular round, or a shot that I had hit, and then to veer off into other matters: swing theories, the life of a pro golfer, the ways in which other players have managed themselves so that they could play their best. I've had to learn how much there is to improving, what it takes to be more consistent so that I could be competitive, and what's involved in being a tour player. You'll learn in this book about my development as a player, and how I got to the point where I felt I could contend in – and win – majors.

Lorne watched me grow up as a player on the Canadian Tour. I remember those days when I was considered the young Canadian hopeful, and he believed in me. He was on the board of directors at the National Golf Club of Canada when he suggested that the club offer me an honorary membership as a show of support. The club did that, and the gesture made me feel good. Then there was the night that Lorne and his wife, Nell, invited me to dinner at their place in Florida. I was a young kid trying to get into PGA Tour events, and I'd made it to the Honda Classic. The PGA Tour can be a lonely place for a young player, so it was nice to be with them that evening. But I won't go into the time they invited me to meet them at a restaurant with some other people, and gave me the wrong directions. It took me two hours to find the right place.

I had my struggles in the game, not only on the Canadian Tour but also on mini-tours in the United States and in tournaments in Australia and Asia, and in my early PGA Tour events too. But I always felt good about my chances of getting ahead. Lorne was there when I won my first tournament as a professional, the 1993 Tournament Players Championship on the Canadian Tour, and when I hit a shot into the water on the last hole of the 1996 Greater Vancouver Open (which was later renamed the Air Canada Championship), when a birdie would have gotten me into a playoff for the tournament. He was there when I lost a playoff for the 1997 Canadian PGA Championship, and when I shot 80 the last round of the 1999 PGA Championship. I was tied for the lead with Tiger Woods after three rounds, and played with him that day. A lot of people figured I'd have a tough time rebounding from that round, but I took it as a learning experience, and that's how Lorne wrote about it. I won the Air Canada Championship three weeks later. It was my first PGA Tour win.

I've been fortunate to grasp some wonderful moments in golf. It's hard for me to put my finger on why I felt so many years ago that I would win the Masters one day, but I did. I had the dream of winning the tournament when I was a kid, and I never wavered from that vision. I always kept the dream alive, even while it was taking me years to get to the PGA Tour. I had my critics and I had my well-wishers, but mostly I had my belief in myself. I dreamed of the day when I'd have a putt to win the Masters, and I practiced for that moment. By reading this book, I think you'll sense the passion I had, and still have, for the game.

– MIKE WEIR

Acknowledgements

Golfers and non-golfers read various drafts of this book, and contributed their comments. In the non-golfing category, I'd like to thank my dear aunt Ruth Waterman from Winnipeg, and my wife, Nell, who so generously offered her observations, while realizing that I was involved more in Mike Weir's life than in ours during the few months in which I wrote about his road to the Masters. As for my golfing pals and colleagues – Harvey Freedenberg, Michael Grange, Howard Ganz, and Michael Savoie – well, thanks, guys. Your comments helped me understand what I was doing here.

I also appreciate Chris Goodwin and John Drake, the owners of Redtail Golf Course in St. Thomas, Ontario. They provided me with a retreat where I wrote some of this book. A writer couldn't work in more inspiring surroundings. Thanks also to my terrific editor, Pat Kennedy, who fit this book into her already busy schedule, to Kristi Perras of <mikeweir.com> for her help with photographs, to Brennan Little and Dan Cimoroni, also for photos, and to Mike Weir's family, especially his brother Jim and his father, Rich, for always answering my questions in a timely manner.

Finally, thanks to Mike himself for his cooperation since I met him ten years ago, and for the way he plays the game. He has a lot to teach us about determination, and the deep pleasures that the game offers, whether one is a novice or a master.

The Putt

Alone, but not isolated, he stands on the 18th green at the Augusta National Golf Club. This putt is for par on the 72nd hole of the Masters, the putt to force a playoff, to give himself a chance to win his first major. It's only seven feet, the length of putt he's made thousands of times on practice greens and in tournaments around the world and, years ago, in the evenings at the Huron Oaks Golf Club in Brights Grove, Ontario, where he learned the game. How long is seven feet anyway, when measured in years and practice balls and dreams?

This is where Mike Weir is, now, on an early evening, with the sun shining on this last green at this famous club. He has rolled his first putt from forty-five feet short of the hole to this point. He has come up short, but he has made this length of putt all day. Seven feet. He's holed one must-make putt after another from this range. He has been alone for the last hour and a quarter, his fellow competitor Jeff Maggert, who was leading the Masters – and Weir – by two shots after three rounds, having faded from contention, and Len Mattiace, tied with him at seven-under-par for the tournament, finished. Mattiace has played a beautiful round of golf, marred only by a bogey on this last hole. But he has shot seven-under-par 65 in the last round of the Masters, and he, too, has not yet won a major championship.

Rich Weir looks on. The golfer's father has followed his son every hole this week. He has followed every hole of this and the three previous Masters his son has played. The golfer's mother, Rosalie, is watching at home in Brights Grove. She would have liked to be here, but could not attend because of a stress fracture in her foot. She is at home, alone by choice, because she gets nervous while watching her son in tournaments and tends to pace the room.

There's hardly a sound around the last green. Mike Weir's wife, Bricia, is here. His eldest brother, Jim, is here, behind the green with his father and Bricia. Officials have allowed them to stand near the green to get a clear view. Jim and Craig, the middle brother of the family, drove their younger brother to tournaments when he was a kid. They, or their dad, flew to Brigham Young University in Provo, Utah, after school ended so that Mike didn't have to drive home alone to Brights Grove. (Craig isn't at this Masters because he's home in Sarnia, where his partner, Tammy Brodeur, is expecting twins.)

Rich Weir says something to himself. "Michael, you've made this putt for the Masters thousands of times at Huron Oaks." Inside, during this final round, Rich Weir has churned, but he wouldn't let this show. His son has noticed him in the gallery. He's always felt that his father was level-headed, easygoing, and, looking at him today, he has felt his calmness.

Mike Weir has left himself a putt that he wouldn't wish on anybody to get into a playoff for the Masters. He walks up to his second putt on this last green. "It's not going to end this way," he tells himself. There's another word in there too. "It's not . . . going to end this way." You can guess the word. It is not a word you would use at a family dinner.

He is feeling some anxiety as he studies the line of his putt – just a little, but he is aware of it. It will take only a little anxiety at this moment to introduce a wrinkle into what has been a smooth stroke all afternoon and evening. His anxiety is understandable. This putt is for the chance to win the Masters, and he has worked so hard to get here, spent years in the golfing trenches. He has *designed* himself for this moment, this putt. Rebuilt his swing with his instructor, Mike Wilson, who was here until Wednesday and who is watching at home in Palm Springs. Refined his golfing mind with his mental coach, Dr. Rich Gordin, who watches from left of the green. Converted his body into a golfing machine under the guidance of exercise coaches. Studied the methods and the minds of the best players: Ben Hogan, Jack Nicklaus, Nick Price, Tiger Woods.

He takes a few deep breaths while examining his putt. Brennan Little, his caddie since 1999, his friend since they played junior golf in Ontario tournaments, and a professional golfer himself, stands nearby, holding the flagstick. Now Weir moves into his stance. His routine is identical on this ultimate putt to the one that he used on the first green, some sixty hours ago. "Make the complex simple," Dr. Gordin has advised him since they met six years ago. He has taken the same amount of time to study the line of the putt, to read the speed of the green, to feel the stroke he wants to make, as he did on his first putt in the first round. Nothing has changed, but everything has changed: this is for the opportunity to win the Masters.

"It's not going to end this way."

Was it so many years ago that he stood over a putt of this length at Huron Oaks and pretended that it was for the Masters? Alone on the practice green there as night fell, a thirteen-year-old putting for the Masters. A fourteen-year-old. A fifteen-year-old. He saw himself here. He's always felt he would get here.

Now he is here. He pretended at Huron Oaks that he was putting for the Masters. Now, at the Masters, he pretends he is at Huron Oaks. Time collapses. His thoughts echo his dad's. He reminds himself of all the putts he has made this week. Inside him are the putts he has made at crucial times, real and imagined, so many times over so many years. All those repetitions. Those drills. Those evenings. "Let's make another one."

Settling into his stance, he suddenly feels calm. That anxiety he felt a moment ago? It's gone. Passed through him. Past. He gets focused, and tells himself, "It's up the hill, left center. I know it's firm. Okay, on the left side of the hole." He tells himself one last thing: "Hit the putt right in the sweet spot. Hit a really, really solid putt." He is all process. There is no thought of outcome.

The stroke is pure. The roll on the ball is pure. The ball drops, dead center of the hole. Mike Weir is tight-lipped. There's a small fist-pump. There's more work to do. The playoff for the Masters will begin in a few minutes. On the way to the 10th tee to start the first playoff hole, he thinks: "Okay, if I could handle that putt right there, if I could get myself to react like that, to be calm, I can handle whatever happens now."

Thirty minutes later, he has won the playoff against Mattiace on the first extra hole, and defending champion Tiger Woods places the green jacket that goes to the winner over his shoulders. Mike Weir is the new Masters champion.

CHAPTER ONE

Monday

April 7, 2003

Rain, nothing but rain. The Augusta National Golf Club is turning into a quagmire. The practice areas were closed soon after eleven this morning, and then reopened just after three o'clock. The course has been closed because of lightning and standing water; it's the first time in twenty years that officials have closed the course to players for a practice round. The rain's been coming down since six in the morning, and the course is inundated, while the walking areas for spectators are too slippery for safety. The vast lawn that sits between the back of the clubhouse and the course, so festive and colorful most days, full of people drinking iced tea and chatting about this, that, and every other golf and non-golf matter, is empty. There's nobody under the massive oak tree with the limbs that hang out almost to the 1st tee; normally this would be a busy spot, teeming with people who have arranged to meet here: "See you under the tree at eleven." It's teeming here, true, but with rain. The more than thirty thousand people who hold tickets for today won't be able to see any golf, but the club will refund the twenty-one-dollar cost of a practice-round ticket. These tickets are so popular that the club holds an annual lottery for them; the Masters is the only tournament where this happens, and the people who couldn't get in today will get priority assignment for next year's lottery. But many won't be able to come back. Some have driven hundreds, or even thousands, of miles, to get here. Nori Alai, who lives in Atlanta but is returning home to Japan next month, certainly won't be returning. His visit here was to be a once-in-a-lifetime occasion, during which he hoped to purchase souvenirs to take back to Japan.

The weather system that's parked itself over Augusta today is called – wouldn't you know it? – a wedge, because, spatially, that's what the colliding forces resemble on weather maps. In this case, cold air from the north has been trapped on the east side of the Appalachian Mountains a couple of hours to the northwest, and has met warm air rising from the Gulf of Mexico to the south. The result is the overcast conditions, early blowing rain, and lightning in the area today. It's perfect weather for storm-chasers, but not for golfers.

Meanwhile, Mike Weir has managed to get in some practice off the course. He and his swing coach, Mike Wilson, spent forty minutes on the practice range and twenty minutes on the putting green before they closed. Weir got in last night and is staying in a hotel, though he's rented a house for family and friends who are here, or who are yet to arrive.

Things seem off-kilter. There's the unremitting rain, for one thing. Then there's something rather more significant, away from planet golf. The United States has sent seven hundred troops into Baghdad today for the first time, trying to take the city as part of its mission to depose Iraq's dictator, Saddam Hussein. Back here, a protest against the Augusta National Golf Club's male-only membership stance looms for Saturday; Martha Burk, the chair of the National Council of Women's Organizations, sent a letter to club chairman William "Hootie" Johnson – everybody calls him by his nickname – last June 12. She insisted that the club open its membership "to women now, so that this is not an issue when the tournament is staged there next year." Now it's next year, and who knows what will transpire come Saturday?

Meanwhile, dogwoods and azaleas brighten the sodden course on this gloomy Monday. They're everywhere in the area, equally at home in gardens surrounding mansions that line the streets behind Augusta National and beside trailer homes. And a sign beside the road into Augusta from the south proclaims, "The biggest lie: When I get what I want, I will be happy."

．⁀

Mike Weir wants a major. The trajectory of his career suggests this is his next logical step. But what's logical about golf? He's won two PGA Tour events this year, but missed the cut in the BellSouth Classic in Atlanta last week. The BellSouth is one of some forty-five tournaments on the PGA Tour's traveling road show that starts in January in Hawaii and ends in early November this year in Texas with the Tour Championship. It's the longest season in pro sports, because it's always warm somewhere, to make golf possible. The tour moves from Hawaii to Arizona to California and, in March, to Florida, before sliding slightly north to Georgia. The Masters, which started in 1934, is the first of the four majors that are played each year and in the same months each year. The roving band of 150 to 200 golfers who make up the roster of PGA Tour players play the spring tournaments that follow the Masters in the Carolinas, Louisiana, and Texas, before heading north as the weather warms up there.

Tournaments in Ohio and Maryland precede the U.S. Open, the second major, which is in June, and will be just south of Chicago this year; the first U.S. Open was held in 1895. Four more PGA Tour events are on the schedule prior to the British Open in July, at the Royal St. George's Golf Club in Sandwich, England. This third major is the oldest of the four; it was first played in 1860.

Following the British Open, the PGA Tour conducts three tournaments in New York and Michigan, after which the fourth major, the PGA Championship, which started in 1916, is held in August. The PGA Tour resumes with a series of northerly events, including the Bell Canadian Open in the first week of September, before turning south again in the fall to its early-November finale at the Tour Championship, a limited-field event for which the top thirty players on the year's money list are eligible. While the Tour Championship will be played this year in Texas, it does move around, and has been held recently in Georgia and Oklahoma as well. A variety of special events is held through the rest of the year, but the Tour Championship is the last official tournament on the PGA Tour's calendar.

Weir can play wherever and whenever he wants, because he has done well enough in recent years that he's eligible for just about every tournament on the schedule, including the majors. He won the 2001 Tour Championship, which gave him "exempt" status through 2004; he's exempt from having to qualify to get on the PGA Tour through that year. Weir plays about twenty-five tournaments a year, including each of the majors, and has been traveling by private plane since 2001. He doesn't have his own plane, as golfers such as Arnold Palmer, Jack Nicklaus, Nick Price, and Greg Norman do, but he buys time that allows him access to private planes. This way of traveling allows him to get home after a tournament ends on Sunday from wherever he is in North America. Weir and his wife, Bricia, have two daughters, five-year-old Elle and three-year-old Lili, so Weir can spend that much more time at home by flying privately rather than commercially. It's one of the better perks that can come with playing well.

Weir has said that the most difficult aspect of tour golf is the time he has to spend away from his family. He stays in pleasant, often luxury hotels, or rents a private home where possible, but he likes being in his own home more than anywhere else. Weir and his family live in a modest, three-thousand-square-foot house that's partway up a mountain, and they can see downtown Salt Lake City, twenty miles from their front door. He loves Utah's open spaces, as does Bricia, which is one of the reasons they choose to live there. They have a cabin in the mountains, where they go as often as possible, because they enjoy skiing. Weir has also taken up fly-fishing, and likes going out in the early morning to a remote river when the mist is hanging like a curtain over the water. Bricia ran the Los Angeles Marathon in March, and enjoys following her husband at tournaments.

This year, 2003, Weir started his season in Phoenix, in the third week of January, where he tied for ninth. He won the Bob Hope Chrysler Classic in Palm Springs the next week, and was in contention to win the AT&T Pebble Beach National Pro-Am the following week, where he tied for third place. It was time for a rest after his excellent start, so he took a week off and went home. But he came right out the next week and won the Nissan Open at the storied Riviera Country Club in Pacific Palisades, just outside Los Angeles. His form wasn't as sharp in his next three tournaments, but he did win his first match in the Accenture Match Play Championship following the Nissan, and tied for fourteenth and twenty-seventh in the two Florida tournaments that he played before the BellSouth. Missing a cut the week before a major is not exactly the way a player wants to come into one, but Weir isn't too concerned. He's excited about returning to Augusta for his fourth Masters, and believes that his play last week was an anomaly in what he is sure will be his best season on the PGA Tour since he first qualified to play on it in 1998.

Still, the pundits who wanted to worry about Weir's form could look beyond last week, past his wins earlier in the year, settle on what he did – or didn't do – in 2002, and argue that his terrific play this year won't continue. His two tournament wins this year, they might argue, came after an inferior 2002 season, when he didn't have a top-ten finish in twenty-five tournaments and finished seventy-eighth on the PGA Tour's money list after finishing eleventh in 2001, sixth in 2000, and twenty-third in 1999. He had won a tournament in each of 1999, 2000, and 2001 – and winning, or at least contending, are what matter to Weir. Though he continued to refine his swing and his approach to the mental side of the game in 2002, the results he sought weren't there. Weir felt he had let himself down, and also disappointed Canadian golf fans, who had come to expect that he would be in contention regularly. Some people said that they were such fanatical Weir fans that they wouldn't watch tournaments on television unless he had a chance to win. Some decided that Weir, at thirty-two, was past the best days of his career.

Weir didn't feel that way. He had thought things over during the off-season, and realized that the same characteristic that had led to his PGA Tour wins – his drive to improve – had hurt him. Who knows where the fine line lies between seeking improvement and expecting perfection? Can the golf swing be mastered? Depending on how you look at it, golf offers either the promise or the illusion of steady improvement.

At home in Draper, Utah, with his family, he concluded that he had tried too hard during the 2002 season. Dr. Bob Rotella, a sports psychologist who works with many tour players, wrote a book called *Golf Is Not a Game of Perfect*. Weir had been trying to be perfect, and had stopped enjoying the game. Where was the kid who loved to stay out until dark at Huron Oaks, chipping and putting the night away?

It was a good question. Any player, even a successful one, can lose the sense of golf as a *game*. It's his business, after all, and aren't businessmen always interested in increasing their profits, their return on investment? If he wins once or twice, the player wants more. Weir's swing had gotten tight and efficient by 2001, but he decided he wanted to get some more rhythm into it, and so, for much of 2002, he had removed his trademark waggle (or rehearsal, as he prefers to call the move) from his pre-shot routine. He had incorporated this preparatory move to remind him where he wanted to have the club during the first part of his backswing. Taking it out would, he thought, introduce more rhythm into his swing, and more flow and rhythm would mean more distance. Golf's a power game now, or so goes the refrain anyway: juiced-up golf balls; large-headed drivers that send the ball three hundred yards in the air; space-age shafts that allow a player to swing as hard as he can without losing control of the club; golf courses manicured more painstakingly than the White House lawn. The ball goes forever, so a player has to keep up. A player has to be a long hitter to compete in the modern era. So goes the thinking, and Weir had bought into the idea. It made sense to him that he could remove his waggle and be a more fluid golfer, while not losing control of the club, the flight of the ball, and himself.

But the plan didn't work. Weir rethought the changes, and decided on what he had to do to play well this year. He had put the rehearsal motion back into his swing two-thirds of the way into 2002, because he felt disoriented on the course without it. Back it came, for good. That was step one to finding the game that had won him three tournaments since he became a full-time PGA Tour player in 1998: the 1999 Air Canada Championship, the 2000 World Golf Championships–American Express Championship, and the 2001 Tour Championship.

There were more steps. Weir considered other modifications he had made in 2002, and decided to stay with an important one. He had altered his grip to reduce the chances of his hitting a troublesome, out-of-control hook. Changing one's grip is tricky, because it alters a player's feel of the golf club. But Weir was determined to make the change, and he saw the benefits in the last six tournaments in 2002, when he hit no more than one or two hooks. In fact, he and Wilson had been working on his grip for years, but the subtle adjustments that they made in 2002 were proving the most troublesome.

"I wasn't fiddling with my swing and grip for the sake of fiddling," Weir says. "I was expecting to get better. I'm secure enough in myself as a player that the fact that I didn't do as well as other years won't hurt me in the long run."

But Weir's most significant alteration was internal, and not visible in his swing or grip. He needed to enjoy golf again, because it had become burdensome to him. Expectations in Canada, as well as his own, were high, and he wanted to meet them. Now living in Utah, Weir wasn't always privy to what Canadians were saying and writing back home. His agents at the International Management Group in Toronto maintain files of articles written about him, but they don't send him every one. Still, he knew that many Canadians were down on him, and skeptical that he could return to form, let alone win again on tour, let alone contend in major championships, let alone win his first major. "It's not fun to hear some of what I hear," Weir said toward the end of 2002.

To enjoy golf again, Weir needed to put more creativity back into his game. He had emphasized trying to hit the ball longer and higher in 2002; his ball flight was fairly low, and the thinking about how to play Augusta National in particular, but also U.S. Open and PGA Championship courses, was that they required a higher, softer flight. It was possible to run the ball into the greens at British Open

courses, where the ground was firmer and the greens weren't protected in front by deep bunkers. But Augusta National's greens are
protected by bunkers and by mounds that kick errant shots away,
while U.S. Open and PGA Championship courses are defended by
bunkers and also by high rough.

By focusing on hitting the ball longer and higher, and on
removing the waggle from his pre-shot routine while continuing to
refine his grip, Weir had neglected his short game. He prided
himself on getting the ball up and down from anywhere when he
missed a green – and a player will always miss greens. Even after
putting the waggle back into this game later in 2002 – having
endured the disappointment, and rebuke, of missing the cut in the
U.S. Open – Weir didn't concentrate on his short game. During his
off-season he decided that he would again relish the challenge of
getting the ball into the hole in as few strokes as possible, whether
or not his ball-striking was reliable. He would put a renewed effort
into his short game and putting.

Weir approached the 2003 season with a fresh attitude. He
committed to enjoying the game, to better balancing the need and
desire to improve with an acknowledgement of the difficulties inher-
ent in golf. He would accept bad shots, not blame his swing. Making
mistakes, he decided, was part of the game. Weir would just keep
hitting shots, doing his best, and taking what the game gave him.

"I was trying to have a perfect swing last year," Weir says of how
he handled the game in 2002. "A perfect stroke, perfect everything.
I was just trying to be too perfect, more than anything. I was trying
to do a few things that just didn't work out. But the time I took away
from the game after the season allowed me to think about what I
wanted to accomplish with my game. I think sometimes when you're
playing week to week, you don't really see what's going on and what's
wrong with your game. You need time to assess what went wrong

and also what went right, to build on things that were actually pretty good. My ball-striking was pretty good last year, but my short game wasn't very good, not only my putting, but my wedge game and bunker play. So I assessed these things and worked on them in the off-season. This year, whatever happens, I'm trying to figure it out, to say, 'This is what I have for this shot,' and I try to figure out a way to get it in. I didn't have that attitude last year."

Weir's plan transformed his attitude to the game, and his time away from golf helped rekindle his enthusiasm for it and rejuvenated him for the new season. Although he had won the season-ending 2001 Tour Championship, he wasn't among the top thirty money-winners and so wasn't eligible for the 2002 edition. Weir missed being there, but he still felt the need to hit balls. He did that in the snow near his home prior to the Tour Championship, even though he wasn't playing in the tournament. His passion for the game had returned.

Weir was ready when his 2003 season began. After his tie for ninth in the Phoenix Open in the third week of January, he traveled to Niagara Falls, Ontario, because his grandmother had died and he wanted attend the funeral. From there he went to the Bob Hope Chrysler Classic, where his teacher, Wilson, watched him. Wilson says that Weir essentially put on a clinic of how to play golf in the last round. Weir hadn't had a practice round, but won the tournament anyway, and, after his win in the Nissan Open near Los Angeles, he was on top of the PGA Tour's money list. But it was more important that he had won again, that he had hit the right shots when he needed to hit them.

Weir had won with his mind as well as his swing. At the Hope, he and Jay Haas were tied for the lead starting the final hole, a par-five with water in front of the green. Haas had driven perfectly, and

would surely go for the green in two shots. Weir had also driven perfectly, a few yards behind Haas, so he would play first from the
fairway. But his ball had settled into a treacherous lie, sitting well
below his feet. It was risky to go for the green from there, so Weir laid
up short of the water.

Haas went for the green, and why not? He had an excellent lie,
and a four-iron in his hands. But he mis-hit the shot, and his ball
splashed into the water. Weir hit his third shot ten feet to the right
of and beyond the hole, smartly taking the water out of play. Haas,
playing his fourth shot after taking the required one-shot penalty,
came up outside Weir's third shot, putted first, and missed for par.
Weir had two putts to win, but made his first for a birdie. He had
birdied the last three holes and won again on the PGA Tour.

The next week Weir played the AT&T Pebble Beach National
Pro-Am, where his friend – and hockey superstar – Wayne Gretzky
was his partner in the team section of the event. Weir hit the ball on
a string, and tied for third. He had one of those ball-striking weeks
when a golfer seems able to command the flight of the ball. Terry
Wiens, a Canadian professional, once said that, when he played this
way, he felt, "I'm the pilot of the flying white moon." Weir has his
own way of describing the feeling of being in the zone.

"Whenever I'm feeling really good I try to hole it from wherever
I am," Weir says. "At Pebble, and also at the Hope, I was hitting it
exactly where I was aiming. I was looking at trees and drawing the
ball off them. That's the kind of golf I always envisaged I could play."

Two weeks after tying for third at Pebble Beach, Weir started the
last round of the Nissan Open seven shots out of the lead. He hadn't
been hitting the ball with nearly the precision he had during the
Hope and AT&T, but, as he says, "I was finding a way to hit the golf
shots I needed to hit to get the ball in the hole. Some weeks you can
thread the needle with the driver, and some weeks you're just off, so

you have to know your own abilities and capabilities. That's how Jack Nicklaus won so many tournaments. [Nicklaus won seventy-three PGA Tour events.] It's all about scoring. It's not about hitting it perfect every time."

Weir was looking for a solid round of golf on Sunday at the Nissan, a round to build on, a round from which he could continue to gain confidence. As it proceeded, he moved up the leader board, and shot five-under-par 66. His game had become supple, in that he could stretch it to fit the circumstances; its elasticity gave him room to play even when his ball-striking wasn't ideal. Weir's 66 got him in a playoff with Charles Howell III, one of a group of talented young power players who are expected eventually to challenge Tiger Woods – if indeed any golfer proves capable of challenging him.

Howell and Weir's sudden-death playoff started and ended on the 311-yard 10th hole. It's one of the game's most interesting short par-fours because of the player's options for his tee shot. Howell went for the green, but pushed his ball into a bunker about forty yards from the hole. Weir, who couldn't reach the green with his drive, laid up short of fairway bunkers in play. His attitude over his approach to the green, and the shot he played, indicated that he had done some excellent work on himself and his short game during the off-season.

"I had a seventy-four-yard shot there," Weir recalls. "I was telling Brennan that I wanted to land my ball seventy-one yards, just to the right of the pin, and have it spin just a little. I pulled it just a bit, but when you're that precise with your plan, you'll still hit a pretty good shot, even if you're off a little. It's really a matter of trusting not only the mechanics of your swing, but your feel, by really zeroing in on what you're trying to do and visualizing the shot."

Weir's second shot finished eight feet to the right of the hole. Howell hit a superb bunker shot, which came up ten feet to the left of the hole. Howell missed his putt, after which Weir made his to win. He went right over to Howell to shake his hand. Weir loves to win, but he knows what it is like to lose. He commiserated with Howell for a moment, and then moved on.

With the Nissan Open, Weir had won his second tournament of the season. He was back on form, and, because he was enjoying the game again, there was every reason to believe he was in for what golfers and observers often call a monster year. Might that mean a major? The Masters was seven weeks away. The Masters was on Weir's mind. Challenging himself to contend in a major was on his mind. Winning a major was on his mind.

•‿

It was five weeks before the Masters, at the Doral Golf Resort & Spa in Miami. Weir was there to play the Ford Championship, the first tournament on the PGA Tour's Florida swing, which golfers consider the run-up to the Masters. He was leading the PGA Tour's money list, so the media officials asked him to come to the press room for a Tuesday interview. Garry Smits of the *Florida Times-Union*, a Jacksonville newspaper, had a question for Weir.

"Mike, you're the marquee player here this week," Smits said, suggesting that Weir was in this position because other top players, such as Woods, Ernie Els, Phil Mickelson, and Vijay Singh, weren't entered. "How do you feel about that?" he added, laughing.

"Well, why are you laughing?" Weir responded, bristling. "I feel that, as well as I'm playing, maybe I am one of the favorites to win here this week."

The next day, following the pro-am, Weir sat down to chat. It was blistering hot and humid, but he situated himself on a chair under a lawn umbrella to engage in a wide-ranging discussion.

Asked about Smits's question, he responded in a way that showed where he thought he stood in golf.

"He was chuckling when he asked his question," Weir says, "but I don't view myself in the way he was suggesting. I view myself as one of the best players out here. The way he posed the question struck me as odd."

Weir went on to consider the evolution of his golf swing. He has been working with Mike Wilson for seven years, and knows that his swing has changed, and improved.

"I go back and look at old videos from when I started working with Mike, and I think, wow, that wasn't pretty," Weir said. "I couldn't hit a three-iron higher than this umbrella. My swing is more controlled now, but I still feel I need to work on it and get it better. But for the most part I strike the ball pretty well. My short game is a lot better this year, too. I think that the strength of my game is my distance control. I feel like I can control distances from wherever I am."

Considered as a whole, these developments add up to a golfer who has been doing exactly what he's wanted to do: getting better and better in the long run. Weir has learned so much about his swing, and also about himself and what he needs to do to get the most out of his game.

"In the past I felt like I had to be out on the range for a certain amount of time, and to play as many holes as I could in practice," he elaborates. "Now, when I feel fatigued or I feel that my swing isn't where it needs to be, I'll just get away from it because I know that I'm a little tired. So instead of standing out there and hitting balls, I'll just go away, maybe get some extra rest and have a workout, whatever I need to do."

Just the day before Weir had followed his own prescription when, feeling jet-lagged after the trip out east from Utah, he left the course after eleven holes of practice. He had planned to play a full round, but was losing swing speed and, generally, dragging. He knows the course, so he didn't need to finish the round to study the holes that remained. Weir went back to his room, had a nap, and then worked out. "I came out today and felt great," he said, and he had just come off the course after a five-hour pro-am in the heat.

He has also applied plenty of heat to other golfers this year, winning those two of five tournaments before starting this swing up to the Masters. On his way to winning the Hope and the Nissan he applied pressure to his direct competitors, Haas and Howell. He was in control of his game and his emotions, which isn't to say that he doesn't get nervous.

"I'm nervous sometimes," Weir said. "I'm always nervous when I go to the first tee; I'm a little anxious to get things going. But I know how to handle things now. I've worked on this with my sports psy-chologist Rich Gordin, and my experience is also a big factor. Definitely when I'm in those situations like at the Hope and Nissan, I feel more comfortable, even though I might be a bit nervous. I feel a comfort level because I do know how to deal with it. I've had success handling nervousness, and I can draw on some good memories."

Those good memories have helped Weir loosen up on the course, so that he can bring out the shots that he sees and feels – the shots he hit at the Hope and Nissan, for example.

"I'm really enjoying myself," he said, while television crews milled around under the hot sun and caddies ate their lunches at tables under other umbrellas in the area at Doral, in front of the clubhouse. "I'm having fun out there, trying to hit little fades and draws, using my mind and my creativity. I think that's when you really enjoy the game, when you see a shot and you pull it off. It's just like earlier today in the pro-am: I hit this nice little five-iron into 18, a low one into the wind, and even though it came up short, it was just a beautiful little shot in there. Sometimes these shots that you try turn out and sometimes they don't, but I'm enjoying the challenge of trying them. That's made the difference this year."

The subject of the Masters came up, and Weir got into it with gusto.

"Augusta is a little more complex than some people give it credit for," Weir said of the course. "A lot has been made that you can drive it anywhere out there, but they make changes every year so that this isn't the case. There's a little intermediate cut of rough which makes a big difference hitting your approach shots into the greens, and they've added some trees that overhang some of the fairways so that you don't want to be in some spots, depending on where the pin is. You really do have to think there.

"The one great thing about Augusta," Weir continued, warming to his subject while picturing the holes at Augusta National, "is that you really do have to shape it off the tee. There's a shot that I've worked on in particular, a right-to-left shot, that I have to use a lot." His hands gestured to show the flight of the ball. "Number 2, number 9, 10, 13, 14, a lot of shots are right to left for me. Then there's 18, a little left to right. You have to shape your shots and then the greens are small and undulating, so your distance control with your irons has to be pretty sharp. The course played very long last year because it was very wet, but still, there's always a premium on iron play.

"You also have to be sharp with your mental game. I've played the 12th hole dead into the wind sometimes, and gone to 13, which goes in the opposite direction, and that's been dead into the wind too. The wind can really swirl through those holes, and you have to be able to handle some adversity that you'll get. You may get a shot where you get a lucky break and the wind doesn't gust up on you, but sometimes at Augusta it seems like you get fooled by the wind and make a mistake. You have to be able to handle that.

"In the past, I've had some success in individual rounds at Augusta, but I haven't strung together a whole tournament there. My short game and putting hasn't always been as sharp as it needed to be, but that's what's improved this year. Hopefully I can bring it to Augusta. If I can combine the creativity and better short game with a little better ball-striking, I should be okay."

Discussion of Augusta National and the Masters led naturally into the four major championships, and Weir's desire to win a major. His eyes narrowed. His voice deepened. There was emotion there, strong emotion.

"I don't like to talk about it a lot, to tell the truth," Weir says. "But obviously it's very important to me for a number of reasons. First I wanted to get on the tour and establish myself as a decent player out here. Once I'd gotten to a certain level, I wanted to take the next step. No Canadian [male] has won a major before. It's not only that factor, but it's also for myself. I really want to challenge myself at that level and have that sense of accomplishment, to do that once in a lifetime or maybe more than once in a lifetime. Just to do it would make me feel fantastic. Just winning two tournaments this year has been satisfying. What goes into winning a tournament is more than what the public knows. And when I sit back in my hotel room, after winning those events, I feel a sense of relief because I'm tired, but I also know that it makes all the work worthwhile. I can't imagine how I'd feel to do it in a major championship."

•‿

Weir played Augusta National fifteen days ago so that he could have an early look at the course as Masters week approached. Contestants in the Masters are allowed to do so. He had originally planned to bring his father to play the course for the first time, but a player can bring a guest only if an Augusta National member is in the group. Unfortunately, George Roberts, the Augusta member who had invited Weir to bring his father, could not play on the appointed day.

Weir wanted to see any course changes that had been made since the 2002 Masters, but there weren't many. The most significant was that the complex of fairway bunkers down the left side of the par-four 5th hole had been moved some sixty yards forward, so that it would come into play for the golfers, who were now hitting the ball so much farther. The bunker was supposed to have been moved in 2001, when Augusta National made some radical changes to the course, repositioning bunkers and tees, lengthening some holes, and redoing the greens. But there wasn't time then to make the modification to the 5th. Weir examined the change.

"I walked down in there and it's ugly," Weir remarked after his visit. "You can get out, but I don't think you can get to the front of the green, about 150 yards, unless you get unbelievably lucky and get right in the middle of the bunker. I was right at the front of the bunker and I couldn't see anything. I guess it's seven or eight feet deep in there."

Weir got his practice round in, and felt good about it. He'd been working on hitting the ball right to left, a fade for him, a left-handed golfer. A fade isn't his natural shot but, as he had said at Doral a few weeks earlier, he would need it on a few holes at Augusta National. He'd been thinking about this shape of shot since his 2002 season ended in November.

It's not easy for a player to alter his natural ball flight, but complete players have to do that. When Nick Faldo overcame Greg Norman's six-shot lead heading into the final round of the 1996 Masters, he was able to hit draws and fades, low shots and high shots, whatever he needed. Faldo played impeccably. Only that type of golf wins majors. This is especially the case at Augusta National, where co-founder and thirteen-time major-championship winner Bobby Jones wanted to put a premium on shot-making skills. Augusta National is for the golfer who likes to move the ball around, and who isn't afraid to try different shots. Weir relishes such demands, and people who have been following him know this.

Bob Toski is one of golf's leading teachers and keenest observers. He was also an excellent player, and led the PGA Tour's money list in 1954. Toski follows modern golf, and certain players grab his attention because of their methods and styles. He's been following Weir for some time. Toski spoke about Weir a few weeks before the 2003 Masters. "Mike has every shot in the bag," Toski said. "It's just a question of him hitting them at the right time. Augusta to him ought to be a piece of cake. I see his creativity, and a lot of guys don't have that."

Weir's coach feels the same. Asked to assess Weir's chances at Augusta, Wilson said, "He can really become one of those historical-type players. He has the ability to hit the ball far, his short game is great, and he has a great putting stroke. We've had long-term goals all along, and we're reminding each other not to get sidetracked from those."

⋅➤

That's why Weir and Wilson are out on the range and the putting green in the rain today. The first round is scheduled for three days away, on Thursday, and they are looking in that direction while refining Weir's impressive form. His statistics are telling. His scoring average last year was 70.88, while this year he has brought it down to 68.9, nearly two shots a round or eight shots a tournament. He was 121st in putting last year, but is 10th coming into the Masters. He hit 66.2 per cent of the fairways in regulation in 2002, for 130th place on the PGA Tour, but has increased the frequency this season to 70.5 per cent, 28th on the tour.

"This is the most confident I've ever felt since I joined the tour," Weir is saying at Augusta this soggy Monday. "I don't really care who else is playing. I like my chances."

After his practice session, Weir plunks his TaylorMade golf bag – it's yellow and green, the color of the Masters flag – into the trunk of the Cadillac courtesy car with which players have been provided for this week, and drives the couple of miles to the hotel where he's staying. TaylorMade is an equipment company based in Carlsbad, California, and Weir is in the final year of a nearly three-year contract to play with its clubs. Wilson returns in his rental car to the house where the Weir contingent will gather during the week. Weir prefers to stay alone, to visit the house for some meals, to watch some of the National Hockey League playoffs which had just started, and to shoot some pool. But he also needs his time alone. Tom Kite, who didn't win a major until he took the 1992 U.S. Open, once called golf "the onliest game." It's only the player out there on the course. He hits the shots. He has to create the circumstances that are most likely to allow him to play his best golf. That takes practice. That takes will. Maybe it will stop raining by tomorrow. Maybe Weir will be able to have a day of thorough practice. That's what he likes, more than anything in the game, besides playing tournament golf. Weir played all of three rounds away from competitive golf last year, and one of those was his charity tournament at Huron Oaks. Otherwise, he's that "onliest" golfer of whom Kite spoke.

Many athletes like to be alone: Wayne Gretzky, as a youngster skating in the backyard rink that his father, Walter, made at the family home in Brantford, Ontario; a basketball player, a lone figure on the court, whirling toward the net; a tennis player, returning serves from the machine on the other side of the court under the lights at night; Weir, checking his posture in a mirror downstairs in his home, or hitting balls outside in the snow.

"I think that's true for any successful athlete," Weir says of the "onliness" factor. "A lot of the work goes on behind the scenes. It's the work you do on your own, when nobody's around. That's what people don't see and that really pays off."

When Weir left the course today to return to his hotel, the ground was getting more waterlogged by the moment. It's been a frustrating day for everybody: the grounds crew that has labored for so long to prepare the course; the players who wanted to get in a full day of practice; the spectators who have come from near and far to watch them practice. Jeff Sluman, the 1988 PGA Championship winner, hasn't seen such a day in the fourteen Masters he's played. "Everybody is itchy and wants to do something," he was saying. "You're ready to play. Everybody gets here early and is excited. You want to get that atmosphere going."

But the only atmosphere today has been a gloomy one, and nobody got in much practice. Weir is hoping to get in plenty of work tomorrow. It's Masters week, and he'd like to get started. The forecast isn't good, though, because the wedge has stalled over Augusta, so the forecasters are calling for a high on Tuesday that's only in the upper fifties, and a nearly 100-per-cent chance of rain. Still, golfers being golfers, they're hopeful for better conditions during which they can practice hitting wedges, not having their session felled by weather wedges. Tomorrow, please.

CHAPTER TWO

Brights Grove

It's all there, isn't it? If you're looking for a game in which past is present and all things coalesce, or fracture, golf's the one. What's past is present and not only prologue, because the golfer expresses his history in every shot, and most obviously in the critical shots. The golfer knows this, and people who follow the game closely – and are keen golfers themselves – know this. He is revealed as a golfer, yes, and no more. Not a bad person because he misses a shot. Not a good one because he makes a shot. But *this* shot will tell you plenty about him as a golfer. It will tell him too. Consider a golfer's background and you can appreciate him so much more, right now.

Some history and background, then. Mike Weir was eight years old when his father, Rich, took him to play the Holiday Inn Golf Club, a nine-hole, par-twenty-eight course that sits almost underneath the Bluewater Bridge that connects their hometown of Sarnia, Ontario, to Port Huron, Michigan. The youngster enjoyed himself on this 1,399-yard course located between a marina and the bridge across Lake Huron, and to this day remembers that he later made his first par and his first birdie there.

"I hacked it up around the green on one hole and chipped on from twenty-five feet and made the putt," Weir says of the first par he made in his life. He was playing with his brother Craig when he made his first birdie. "I hit a driver on a par-three and the ball ran through the green, but I chipped in for the birdie." He's smiling when he remembers these red-letter events. Today, a few items that Weir signed hang on the walls of the small cottage of a pro shop: a 2000 Masters cap, a photograph signed to Dan and Mike Nimmo, the sons of Gord and Michele Nimmo, who run the course now. They look out to the 142-yard 1st hole which is surrounded by trees on three sides and where the green is slightly raised, with a mound on the left and bunkers to the right. It's easy to see how a ball would bounce around the green here, and why a youngster would need a crafty short game to make a par or birdie. Kids registered in the Sarnia Minor Athletic Association's golf program show up here on Tuesdays and Thursdays to learn and play golf. Craig Weir brings his twelve-year-old son, Christopher, out occasionally.

Sarnia is an hour northeast of Detroit, and its most important industry is petrochemicals. Oil was discovered in Petrolia, twenty miles away, in the mid-1800s, and the area is full of refineries. Mike's dad, a chemist, worked in technical marketing management in the rubber industry, and two years after his youngest son took up golf, the family – Rich, Rosalie, ten-year-old Mike, seventeen-year-old Craig, and nineteen-year-old Jim – moved across the street from the Huron Oaks Golf Club in Brights Grove, a small town in southwest Ontario, seven miles from Sarnia, and close to the U.S. border. Brights Grove was incorporated into Sarnia in 1990, and remains a postal address. Mike, the youngest brother, played a variety of sports:

hockey, baseball, table tennis, basketball, volleyball, and golf. He was a fierce competitor, and he was small, not reaching five feet in height until after his fourteenth birthday. But what he lacked in size he made up in sizzle. Hockey's a contact sport, and he didn't mind making contact, laying out his opponents to take them out of the play. Once or twice, at his suggestion, his coach let him wear jerseys with different numbers from one game to the next, so that players on opposing teams wouldn't so readily be able to single him out for retaliation. But, he says, "It didn't really work, because they found out soon enough. Still, I definitely loved the physical part of hockey. I just liked that part of sports. My brothers were really physical with me. They told me to play like that. I needed to stick up for myself."

Weir believes that he was a better baseball player than hockey player. He pitched and also played first base and catcher. He even enjoyed blocking the ball when the pitcher threw it in the dirt; he scrambled to get after it. He had a good arm and could throw out runners who had the audacity to try to steal bases against him. In volleyball, he couldn't spike the ball over the net because he was too short. But he played center and dove around to dig the ball out of the ground, finding a way for his side to stay in the game. The youngster wore out his opponents, whatever sport he played. And he often played with fellows who were two or three years older than he was, so again, he had to be physical. Anybody who played against Weir in any sport learned that he wouldn't back down. He found a way. He competed.

He also did it all in sports. He swam in the pool at the Huron Oaks Recreation Centre. On the golf course, playing left-handed – he wrote right-handed, played hockey left-handed, and threw a ball right-handed – he liked the feel of a golf club in his hand, and the idea that he was in control of his own sporting fate. Golf provided a complement to team sports. Meanwhile, the golf course was so much more spacious than a hockey rink or a baseball diamond or a volleyball court or a swimming pool. Mike was soon spending hours on the course, alone much of the time, using an old half-set of golf clubs for which his father had paid fifty dollars. The course wasn't a plush, manicured lawn, nor was the club an exclusive, posh enclave. Huron Oaks was a working-class club in a working-class town – a place for everybody to hang out, to play sports, to lose oneself and to find oneself. For many kids, it was summer camp, and a place to discover that they were athletes.

Mike spent hours, then mornings, then days, then entire days and evenings in the summers there. The fluidity that he demonstrated in other sports revealed itself in golf. Skills and habits from other sports transferred: rhythm, timing, and a feel for the instrument in his hands. His golf swing had echoes of his slapshot in hockey. He lifted the club in a high arc and brought it down across the ball, covering it as he struck it, in the way he covered a hockey puck while shooting it. His downward arc flattened somewhat, as if he were swinging at a baseball. It was a hockey-baseball golf swing. The clubface closed through impact. The ball hooked, and flew low. But Mike was a natural athlete. He played with what he had and discovered ways of getting the ball around the course.

Mike was intrigued. There was more to golf than power, so he could be wily and clever. The cliché applied: it's not how, but how many. The score is what matters. There are ways to get the ball in the hole quickly besides hitting it a long way or reaching par-fives in two shots. It's fine if these things happen. But if they didn't, the kid knew that he wasn't out of the hole. He'd give it his best on each shot, each hole, and add up the numbers at the end. Low score won, not the prettiest or most classic swing. He'd pretend this ball was Lee Trevino's, that one was Jack Nicklaus's, and this one was his. Picture him, standing over a six-foot putt on the last hole at Huron Oaks as the sun sets, or maybe it has already set, and there's some light

from the clubhouse, or the moon. This putt for the Masters. Or the
U.S. Open. Read the putt. Settle in. Make the stroke. Do it again. And
again. And again. Get the reps in. Mom and Dad don't mind waiting.

Jack Nicklaus was playing an exhibition at Huron Oaks with the club
professional, Steve Bennett, who couldn't have been more pleased.
This was September 9, 1981, when Mike was eleven years old. "I was
a Nicklaus nut," Bennett recalls. "He was my idol." Mike already knew
about Nicklaus. He read golf magazines and was aware that Nicklaus
had won the U.S. Open and the PGA Championship the year before,
and that he had won seventeen professional majors. Mike couldn't
make it for the front nine, but followed Nicklaus for the back nine.
There was something about Nicklaus, the way he carried himself, the
manner in which he prepared for every shot, always using the same
routine. Nicklaus looked ahead of the ball at a spot on the grass,
using it as an aiming point and meaning to start his ball along that
line. Then he cocked his head behind the ball, which ignited his
swing: it was, and remains, the trigger for his swing. The kid
watching Nicklaus wasn't studying these mannerisms consciously,
but was absorbing images and information. His learning was instinc-
tual, not intellectual; osmotic, not memorized. He was absorbing
the rudiments of the game as practiced by Nicklaus. Later, much
later, his golf coach Karl Tucker at Brigham Young University would
advise him to spend his time with positive people, with winners.
Gary Player often says, "Don't go to dinner with poor putters."

   (Still later, in the spring of 2003, Weir would play a practice
round with Nicklaus for the Memorial Tournament at the Muirfield
Village Golf Club in Dublin, Ohio, a suburb of Nicklaus's hometown
of Columbus. Nicklaus invited Weir to play; they had never played
together, in practice or a tournament. Nicklaus and his son Gary, a
professional golfer, played a match against Weir and Alejandro

Larrazabal, the 2002 British Amateur champion. The Nicklaus father-and-son team was one hole up on Weir and Larrazabal on the sixteenth green, and Jack Nicklaus couldn't play any more holes because his presence was required elsewhere. His son had a fifteen-foot putt to win the match no matter what the other side did; Weir's ball was twelve feet from the hole and he was aching for the chance to have to make the putt. "Go ahead and bury these guys," Jack Nicklaus said to his son, but Gary missed the putt. "I really wanted to bury mine," Weir says now. "I did too." The match ended all square. "I loved the way Jack tried on every shot," Weir remembers from the first time he saw Nicklaus, at Huron Oaks in 1981. "That's the way I want to play.")

Mike Weir was learning how to approach the game and how to win. He learned that preparation is important, and to take every shot seriously. This putt for the Masters? He made the putt count at Huron Oaks. If he made it, he could add, incrementally, to his self-confidence. If he missed it and asked why, he could do the same. If he missed it and ignored the lesson, he would stay in place. But he wanted to move forward. Nicklaus has always played this way, taken every shot seriously and learned from it, then moved on. Mike was beginning to learn these things. He was watching Nicklaus at the course where he spent most of his recreational time and he intended to apply these lessons. Who knows where? Or when? But he would apply them. He was sure of it.

The Canadian Open was at the Glen Abbey Golf Club near Toronto, three hours away by car. Mike wanted to follow the tour pros. He had a new and improved set of clubs by then, Wilson Staffs, and was working at Huron Oaks as a range rat, picking up balls at the end of the day, pitching and chipping them toward a pile so that he could scoop them up there. Now twelve, he was also working in the bag

room, cleaning clubs, and in the pro shop. He was learning the game
under club pro Steve Bennett's guidance, and when he was thirteen
he would tell Bennett that he wanted to be a professional golfer, not
a club professional. He wanted to play the game, the game that
Nicklaus played. It beckoned.

He visited Glen Abbey with his brother Jim to watch the Canadian
Open. There, in the Royal Canadian Golf Association's headquarters,
in an old Jesuit retreat – the abbey itself – he discovered the Canadian
Golf Hall of Fame. He walked around the room, stopping to study the
Hall of Famers represented there: Gary Cowan, Stan Leonard, Nick
Weslock, among others. His brother wanted to leave so that they could
follow the golfers out on the course. But Mike wasn't ready to go. He
was transfixed.

On the course, he worked his way to the front of the gallery.
Johnny Miller, one of the game's top players, and a former Brigham
Young University student and golfer, was there. Miller had won the
1973 U.S. Open and the 1976 British Open. Miller was a shot-maker
who could make the ball dance, hit it left to right, right to left, high,
low. He had different swing speeds. Miller was a golfing artist who
knew the swing, but who also played by feel. He'd put the ball
forward in his stance to hit it high, allowing his weight to stay back
through impact. He'd put the ball back in his stance to hit it low,
ensuring that he would transfer his weight forward through impact.
Miller listened to himself, to the golfing voices that suggested he play
a certain way or hit a particular type of shot. He had heard one of
those voices just prior to teeing it up in the last round of the 1973 U.S.
Open, when he was six shots behind the leaders. The suggestion he
heard was to open up his stance dramatically so that he would
be almost facing his target at address. Miller hit only a few practice
shots that way, and then started his final round. He shot a U.S.

Open–record 63 at the Oakmont Country Club near Pittsburgh and won the championship.

At Glen Abbey, Mike followed Miller and was amazed when he chipped a ball from a corner of the 10th green over a bunker that cut into the green, and on toward the hole. He caught Miller's eye, and Miller winked at him and gave him a thumbs-up. The boy remembered the gesture. A tour pro, one of the best, had singled him out.

Andy Bean was also playing the Canadian Open. His physique was more that of a football player than a golfer. Bean was giving a clinic on the range at Glen Abbey, and Mike was watching. Bean finished his clinic, looked at the kids gathered around him, and invited them to scramble out to the range to retrieve as many balls as they could. He told them they could keep their harvest, so Mike tore out to the range, gleefully. A tour pro had just hit these balls, and he would hit them the next day. He filled his hands and pockets with golf balls, and then returned home with signatures from a few tour pros on a cap that he showed to his father.

At thirteen, Mike was now playing tournaments. He knew he could play. A writer for a local paper followed him at a tournament and noted that the youngster "proved that you don't have to be big and strong to play golf," adding that "Mike hits the shots right down the middle and putts like a demon."

He was playing in a junior tournament at the then-nine-hole Seaforth Golf and Country Club in southwestern Ontario, and shot 36 for the first nine holes of the eighteen-hole tournament – the golfers played the course twice to make up the full round – and then went in for lunch. The youngster was excited.

"My low score until then for nine holes had been 39 at Huron Oaks," he remembers, "and now I'd shot 36. My best score for eighteen holes was 79, so I kept thinking that I'd beat that if I shot 42 on the last nine. I shot 34 to shoot 70, and I holed everything. On the last green I had what looked to me, a thirteen-year-old, like an eighty-foot putt from the back left of the green, but it was about forty-five feet, and I made it." Mike was playing in the juvenile division of the tournament but won the overall event, beating golfers as much as five years older than he was.

Back home, he was attending St. Clair Secondary School. He had told Al Davidson, a teacher and the school's golf coach, that he'd like to try out for the team, and Davidson invited him to do so, although he thought that he was too small to make it. But Mike made a putt on the last hole of the qualifying tournament to win a spot. While in high school, he also took part in a co-op program as part of a course; in the program he worked at the Sarnia Golf and Curling Club under the guidance of superintendent Gord Nimmo, who along with his wife, Michele, was now running the Holiday Inn course where Mike had been introduced to golf years before.

Mike was fourteen when he shot 86 in a junior tournament in Sarnia, which got him into a four-way playoff for first place. Brennan Little, who lived in St. Thomas, Ontario, was in the playoff, as was Michael Dean, from Windsor, who won. Mike wasn't pleased with his score. He asked himself what went wrong. Mike Weir will always ask himself questions, when things go wrong and when they go right.

On the course, he started to realize that there was more to golf than the short game – there's the swing, and it should be made to work reliably. Mike's play was inconsistent. He thought things through and concluded that he might have to do something radical. Maybe he should play right-handed and not left-handed. Bob Charles was the only left-handed golfer to have won a major championship. If golfers who play right-handed win all the majors, he thought, perhaps he should learn to play that way. Mike figured that he might be able to make the change. He had some ambidexterity, after all. Besides, Nicklaus played right-handed. Miller too. Bean. Trevino. Ben Hogan before them. Those Hall of Famers at Glen Abbey whose photos and biographies Mike studied? All right-handed golfers.

It was time to seek advice from the best, so he wrote a letter to Nicklaus. Why not? The letter was brief and direct. "I want to be a professional golfer. I play left-handed. Do you think I should switch?" It was November 1984, the golf season in Brights Grove was over, and the fourteen-year-old's play had remained inconsistent. Maybe he could work indoors during the winter to change from left-handed to right-handed. He would do that if Nicklaus advised him to go ahead – but would Nicklaus write back?

He did, in a letter dated December 5, 1984. His answer was as simple as the question: "I have always believed that a left-handed player is better off sticking with his natural swing." There was his signature at the bottom of the letter: the high, flowing "J," the loopy "N," the long line representing the last letters of his surname. Mike Weir was thrilled, and decided then and there to stick with his natural swing. If it was good enough for Jack, it was good enough for the young fellow who wanted to be a tour pro, maybe to tee it up with Nicklaus someday. The subtext to Nicklaus's advice was "Be yourself." Nicklaus's right elbow flew during his backswing, contrary to conventional teaching, and he had done all right. He'd won those seventeen professional majors by the time he and Mike corresponded: five Masters, five PGA Championships, four U.S. Opens, and three British Opens.

The junior golfer practiced his left-handed swing during the winter in Brights Grove. He wore out the practice net in the family's unheated garage. When Lake Huron froze, he walked the block from his home to the shore. The lake for him now represented a vast driving range, a massive open space for a kid who liked to watch the flight of golf balls. He cleared a small space in the snow and hit balls out to the ice, a kid swinging freely, in winter. He turned fifteen in May, and his handicap was three. His advantage was his determination. A summer of competition loomed.

In early June 1985, Mike traveled to Ohio, where he finished eighth in a fifty-four-hole tournament, shooting 78-78-81. He finished second in July in the Ontario Junior championship, and in August represented the province in a team event in Quebec City. He won a couple of events during the summer and was never out of the top ten in fifteen tournaments. But he won only those two tournaments, which wasn't good enough for him. He continued to practice during the winter, and in April 1986 he continued to study Jack Nicklaus by watching him on television. Nicklaus won the Masters by playing seven-under-par golf the last ten holes. The teenager who wrote to Nicklaus was inspired by the performance. He had been writing to American colleges, because he hoped that they would consider him for a golf scholarship. Mike Holder, the golf coach at Oklahoma State University, responded. The school had a highly regarded golf program. Bob Tway, an alumnus, would win the 1986 PGA Championship that summer. Holder wrote Mike, "With your record you should have little difficulty getting a scholarship at a good school. Keep working hard and I will follow your progress." He enclosed a brochure for Weir to peruse.

That summer of 1986, Mike won four of the ten events he played on a popular junior series called the Tyson Tour, and led its Order of Merit. He won the Canadian Juvenile championship in Edmonton, shooting 298 on rounds of 75-76-74-73, while putting poorly during the first three rounds. He got up and down from greenside bunkers on the last five holes, doing what he needed to do. Brennan Little shot 313, tying for thirty-fourth. Mike was seventh in the overall Canadian Junior championship.

An Edmonton writer recognized an important factor in the developing golfer's approach to the game. "He kept his composure during the final rounds and won the juvenile championship," he wrote. "His hard work in the tournament is a good example to his peers about what can be accomplished with determination."

Ten American universities had now expressed interest in him. The list included not only Oklahoma State but Louisiana State, where former U.S. Amateur champion Buddy Alexander coached the celebrated program. "I want to become a pro," Mike said during one junior tournament, "but it's a lot harder than it sounds." He planned to attend college first, for sure. "You can turn pro whenever you like," he said. "But school's first for me."

He'd never played in the Ontario or Canadian Amateur championships, and wanted to test himself against more experienced players in these advanced competitions. Already he was a golfing philosopher and strategist of the play-one-shot-at-a-time school. He got frustrated, but he didn't throw clubs. A putter might hit the bottom of the bag with a thud, or he would grit his teeth. But he soon forgot what happened so that he could concentrate on the next shot, the next tournament, opportunities to learn, to improve, to succeed.

"I play shot to shot," said the youngster, who wore glasses because of declining vision that would get as bad as 20/450 in college, "and don't think holes ahead about parring this or getting a birdie on that one. I just follow my instincts." Steve Bennett at Huron Oaks was helping him trust these instincts. He advised Mike to play the shot he saw and felt.

Mike shot 71 at Huron Oaks to lead his high school to a win over twenty teams in the Western Ontario Secondary School tournament.

His handicap was down to one, and he knew where he was headed: to an American university. There was no doubt. The last sentence of his resumé noted that he "is in contact with several American universities where he is seeking a golf scholarship and has hopes of pursuing a career as a professional golfer." He compiled his statistics for the season: fairways hit, greens in regulation, par-threes hit, ups and downs from bunkers, putts taken, score. He regularly took thirty-two to thirty-six putts. There was room for improvement. His average score was 74.4, he hit 61 per cent of the fairways and 64 per cent of the greens. He had only one more year of high school.

Accolades off the course rolled in. In June 1987, he was named Sarnia's Sports Person of the Year, over four other nominees, though he didn't expect the award. He finished third and sixth in a couple of one-day amateur events during the summer, while also continuing to play junior golf, and tying for fourth in an American Junior Golf Association event, shooting 74-71-75. Phil Mickelson won, finishing four shots ahead of Mike; Mickelson, like Mike a left-handed golfer, was the number-one-ranked junior in the United States the previous year. A few weeks later, Mike and Brennan Little shot 143 in Grand Rapids, Michigan, to qualify for the U.S. Junior that would be held in Vail, Colorado, in August. Karl Tucker, the Brigham Young golf coach, traveled to Vail to watch Mike, who qualified for match play and got through his first two matches before losing his third. Tucker had coached Canadians Jim Nelford, Richard Zokol, and Brent Franklin, and they'd had success at the school. Zokol had told Tucker that Weir was a fine young man and a talented golfer. Tucker was impressed with Mike's feisty style and his get-it-done attitude.

"You never know what a kid is interested in," Tucker says now. "What sort of path are they looking for? Well, Mike and I hit it off right away. He said he had a lot to learn and that he wanted to go to a school with good golf and academic programs. I never watched anybody else at that Colorado tournament. We got to know each other and went out to dinner during the week."

Weir went on from the U.S. Junior to finish third in the Canadian Junior, shooting 76-76 the last two rounds. Tough game, golf. Mike visited Brigham Young University and surroundings. He liked the mountains, the golf program, and the fact that Canadians had succeeded there.

Back at his high school, Al Davidson advised Mike to consider a marketing program in college in case he became a club professional. Mike said that he didn't plan to be a club pro. He would be a tour pro. One day he played golf with his baseball coach, and didn't play very well. His coach told him that he should consider baseball and not golf for a career. But Mike was on the road to playing professional golf.

After visiting five universities that recruited him, Mike chose Brigham Young. BYU played in the Western Athletic Conference against schools such as Arizona State and the University of Southern California, which had excellent golf teams. He started with a half-scholarship, because Karl Tucker didn't offer full scholarships. Mike was playing during the same period in American college golf as Mickelson, David Duval, and Jim Furyk, which meant that he was competing against many of the best amateurs in the game. He studied recreation management, won a tournament in his freshman season soon after the winter break, and returned to Brights Grove following the academic year to stay at home and hit the road playing amateur tournaments.

He and Brennan Little were set to play in the Ontario Best-Ball tournament at the Oakdale Golf and Country Club in Toronto, but he showed up without his handicap card, and so Ontario Golf Association officials refused to let him start. Chris Goodwin, a London businessman, and John Drake, a criminal defense lawyer there, who were playing with Mike and Brennan, intervened and suggested that the officials allow Mike to have Steve Bennett fax confirmation of his handicap to the club. By the time Mike contacted Bennett, his tee time was past, but Brennan went out on his own anyway and parred the 1st hole. After the fax confirming Mike's handicap arrived, he joined Brennan on the 2nd hole, a par-three, where he chipped in for birdie. Brennan eagled the par-five last hole to get him and Mike into a playoff, and Mike holed a ten-footer on the first extra hole for a winning birdie. Goodwin and Drake would go on to join forces in business and to found the Redtail Golf Course near St. Thomas, Ontario, Brennan's hometown, and they would help Mike out in a variety of ways: financial support, a place to play and practice in solitude when he wanted, and simple friendship.

After his freshman year, Mike qualified for the Canadian Open at Glen Abbey and shot 80-71, missing the cut. He won the 1990 and 1992 Ontario Amateurs. He made a 9 during the last round of the 1991 Canadian Amateur when he ran into some tree trouble, and lost by a shot, and was leading the 1992 Canadian Amateur by two shots when his driver snapped on impact at the 13th tee. The shaft split and cut him on the right cheek and, while he was unsettled, he wasn't injured. Still, he double-bogeyed the hole and lost by a shot. Jim Nelford and Richard Zokol, his predecessors at Brigham Young University, had each won the Canadian Amateur, and Weir had hoped to join them as national champions, but it wasn't to be.

Back at BYU, Weir didn't win a tournament during his sophomore year, but played more consistent golf and won in an even more important area of life when he met Bricia Rodriguez at a party during this second year. They were living in the same dorm, but didn't know each other, although Bricia had noticed Mike and liked his looks. "I'd see him on campus and thought he was attractive," she says. "I liked his dark hair and his tanned look, and when I saw him at the party I thought, 'That's this guy I've seen.'" Even though Mike was at the party with somebody else, he and Bricia were clearly taken with each other.

Bricia, a Mexican-American, grew up in the Huntington Park area in South Central Los Angeles, a legendarily rough part of the city. Though it was well before her birth, the infamous Watts race riot had occurred nearby in 1965. In 1992, the Rodney King police beating and subsequent rioting scarred the barrio once more.

The home in which Bricia grew up with her parents, two brothers, and sister was often burgled. Interestingly, her dad, Jose, worked as a greenkeeper at a nearby course for a short time, and then as a serviceman on X-ray machines. Bricia's mother, who had been a teacher in Mexico, focused on homemaking. There was always enough food to go around, but things were tight, and when a carton of milk was half full, well, it was filled with water to last a little longer. During the Rodney King riots, Bricia's father was held up at gunpoint and had his truck stolen as he came off a freeway ramp. The nearly destroyed truck was recovered two weeks later, and, while cleaning out a corner of the truck afterwards, he uncovered a loaded machine gun, left there by the man who had held him up.

Despite the problems in the area in which she grew up, or perhaps because of them, Bricia concentrated on school, and did very well. She chose Brigham Young University, where she studied social work.

Bricia didn't know anything about golf when she met Mike, but, she says, "I just liked the person, I didn't care about the occupation he was going to choose." Mike told her that his goal was to reach golf's highest levels. Coach Tucker certainly believed he was on his way there.

"Mike always wanted to know if he was doing the right thing to keep getting better," he says. "After a while he didn't need me to tell him. He knew what he wanted to do. From day one he just wanted to find a better way, so we'd evaluate all aspects of his game."

Weir lost the Western Athletic Conference's individual title to Paul Stankowski in a playoff, and was named a second-team All-American in 1992, which was Coach Tucker's last year at BYU. Tucker remembers what he calls a defining moment when he thinks about the young man who was headed for a career as a professional golfer.

"We'd had quite a bit of success that year, and we were looking forward to playing the Fresno [California] Classic," Tucker says. "We loved it there, and we had a ten-shot lead with nine holes to play. I was horsing around, figuring we had the thing won. But then we hit shots out of bounds and missed short putts and suddenly we were tied for first with the University of Southern California. The last hole we were playing was a par-five around a corner. Mike had hit a good drive and his second to just short of the green and about twenty feet from the hole."

Weir was in the last group, and he thought that BYU had sewn up the tournament, so he wandered over to Tucker and asked, "Coach, how many are we winning by?" Tucker told him that the team needed him to birdie the hole for the win, after which Weir nearly chipped in for eagle. His birdie gave the team the win and Weir a tie for the low individual score.

"Put the ball in Mike's court and he knows what to do with it," Tucker says, of then as much as now. "Some people can handle it, and others can't."

His college career over, Weir hoped to represent Canada in the World Amateur Team Championships in the fall of 1992 in Vancouver, but was considered a professional once he sent in his entry for the PGA Tour's qualifying school later that year. Every fall, golfers who hope to make it to the PGA Tour enter the qualifying school. The school isn't truly a school, except in that it tests every aspect of a player's game and makeup. Weir was required to start at the first stage of the school, or tournament. Players who got through the first stage, known as local qualifying, made it to the second stage, called regional qualifying. The players who got through that stage made it to the final, six-round, tournament, where the low thirty-five golfers and ties would win the right to play the 1993 PGA Tour. Weir made it through the first stage of qualifying school, but struggled in the second stage and didn't advance. He decided to try to qualify in May 1993 for that summer's Canadian Tour – a couple of rungs below the PGA Tour, but an excellent training ground – and then to try again in the fall for the PGA Tour.

When Weir came to Toronto in the spring of 1993 to accept the Score award from the Canadian golf magazine of the same name as the best Canadian male amateur of 1992, he was asked whether he could see himself winning on the PGA Tour.

"It's tough seeing myself there real soon," he says. "I'd just like to put myself in position to do that. I just need experience, to get in the heat of the battle. I feel like I have a lot of talent."

Bricia also felt that way, and believed him. "He just knew that he would be on the PGA Tour. He just knew. He never had a doubt."

CHAPTER THREE

The Pro Road Begins

Every player who makes it to the PGA Tour is obviously talented, but he's still likely to have a teacher. Jack Nicklaus was ten years old and a junior member at the Scioto Golf Club in Columbus when the professional there, Jack Grout, started working with him. Butch Harmon has been Tiger Woods's primary instructor. David Leadbetter works with Nick Price and Ernie Els, while Rick Smith works with Lee Janzen and Phil Mickelson. It can take a player some time before he makes the commitment to work with a teacher, and before he finds the right one. Mike Weir found Mike Wilson in December 1995, and they've been working together since. Weir believes that Wilson is a genius of the swing and of communicating its nuances. Wilson has been part of what can be called Team Weir since that first meeting.

Wilson wasn't Weir's first teacher, though. Steve Bennett worked with him at Huron Oaks when Weir was a youngster. They didn't work much on his swing, but rather on learning to get the ball in the hole – scoring, that is. Weir played with his natural athletic talents then. He saw the golf ball at his feet, he looked at his target, and he swung away without thinking much about technique. It was golf of the hit-it-and-find-it variety, which isn't the worst way for a kid to play his early golf. He didn't really know how to control the flight of the ball, but that didn't matter too much when he was a junior golfer whacking it around courses in southwestern Ontario. Bennett encouraged him to work on his short game, and that's what Weir loved to do anyway. He spent most of his practice time around the putting green, which is the opposite of what most kids do. Most youngsters in their early days enjoy hitting the ball miles, and so spend their time on the range when they're not playing. Weir liked to play, but he also enjoyed chipping and putting the night away. That's how a kid learns to save pars and make birdie putts when he has his chances.

After Weir turned pro, however, he began to realize that he needed to understand what made a golf swing tick. He had to understand his own swing first, particularly his tendencies, which came from the other sports that he had played prior to taking up golf. Weir shot a puck and hit a baseball with a fast, hands-oriented swing; he reacted to the object coming at him and swung hard with his hands. He didn't think of how his body moved, or whether he should reduce his hand action. He didn't consider arcane matters such as how to grip a hockey stick or tennis racket, or how to stand at the plate while facing a pitcher. Thought wasn't what mattered. Action mattered.

His swing in sports other than golf was a blur, and his golf swing was also fast, for it was only natural that he bring to golf the same tempo that he had at the other sports. One problem was that his hands outraced his body, and that, primarily because of hockey, he still tended to close the face of the club as soon as he started his backswing, and maintained this face angle through the ball. These weren't the only problems. Sometimes Weir's body turned too fast, getting ahead of his hands. No wonder he was inconsistent. His golf shots took off like his slapshot in hockey, low and hooking. The result was that he never knew when he would hit a shot so far off line that it would cause him problems. He couldn't rely on his golf swing to hit the ball where he needed to hit it, which is no way to live as a pro golfer. He had his ball on "wide spray," as an errant ball flight is sometimes called. As Johnny Miller said about his own game when he lost control: "It's as if the ball is coming out of a popcorn popper. It could go anywhere."

Although Weir wasn't much of a student of the swing when he turned professional, he had enough natural talent to – usually – neutralize his flaws and get around the course. He won the Tournament Players Championship on the Canadian Tour in July 1993, battling Richard Zokol down the stretch. His shot-making talent and creativity were obvious, as was his inconsistency. Having eagled the par-five 14th, Weir drove into a water hazard on the next hole. He took his penalty drop, then, as he would say later, "three-quartered" a three-wood to twelve feet from the hole. He already knew the power of imagery, for, when he got over the putt, he said to himself, "You're on the practice green at Huron Oaks. It's just a putt." He made the par putt, and then hit a six-iron to two feet on the next hole, made his birdie, and went on to win the tournament. He finished eighth on the money list for the season, and was named the 1993 Canadian Tour rookie of the year.

But the next year Weir missed three of ten cuts on the Canadian Tour, and fell to fifteenth on the money list. He shot 76 in the last round of the Canadian Professional Golfers' Association Championship to lose to Steve Stricker. He held a four-shot lead in the Manitoba Open on the back nine, but got it into his head to try to win by ten shots, and lost. During the year he felt his motivation wane, and still didn't work on his short game. Meanwhile, he continued to play all over the world, and one bright spot was an eleventh-place finish in the Australian Open. He was on the road, a road that is still vivid in his mind.

That road is full of storage units, where Weir and Bricia left their belongings while he played tournaments in Australia and Asia and Canada and Europe – wherever he could get experience. Their home was in Salt Lake City, but they didn't have the money to pay rent for an apartment while on the road. A storage unit rented for fifty dollars a month, so they could save some money that they could use to lease another apartment when they returned. In Australia they holed up for three weeks in a small apartment because they didn't have the money to fly home and then return to Indonesia for the next tournament. Half the time their main meal was baked potatoes and ground beef. In this apartment one night, Weir found a tarantula the size of his hand in the bathroom. "I went back to the bedroom to tell Bricia that she has to see this," Weir remembers, "but when I told her what was there she wouldn't go. She was screaming. I crawled around in the bathroom until I finally got it on a big piece of paper."

Bricia didn't always travel with Weir, because she would stay back in Utah to work, but she heard from him regularly, from distant places where he played tournaments. He registered for a hotel room in Auckland during one tournament, and learned it would cost two hundred dollars a night – "way outside my price range," he says. A courtesy driver was taking him to the course, and mentioned that the tournament life must be expensive for a young guy. "Yeah, it is, as a matter of fact." She invited him to stay with her and her husband, which he did. He would play in New Zealand two more times and stay at the same house.

Perth, Australia. Weir had his playing card for the Australian
Tour, which gave him the right to try to qualify on Mondays for tournaments. He arrived at one tournament in Perth to qualify, but the
clubhouse was closed. It was 113 degrees Fahrenheit, "smoking hot,"
he recalls, and there were no caddies. "I was one of the last groups,
so all the pull carts were gone. I had my tour bag, and had to stuff my
running shoes in the side of the bag and put my golf shoes on. I
carried my clubs and qualified." He qualified five times in a row on
Mondays. He missed five cuts in a row.

Jakarta, Indonesia. Weir was playing the Indonesian Open, and
the course was an hour from his hotel. Two buses took players to the
course at two different times. Given the schedule, if he took one bus,
he would have been at the course three hours before his starting
time, and too late if he took the next one. He hailed a cab. The driver
didn't speak any English, but somebody in the hotel said he knew the
way to the course. Weir had taken the bus there, and knew in a
general sense where it was. But the driver took back roads.

This was far from the world of courtesy cars and gourmet food
to which PGA Tour players such as Phil Mickelson and David Duval
were becoming accustomed and which Weir still believed was his
ultimate destination. A smelly, unclean river running through
Jakarta was overflowing into people's houses because of heavy rains.
Weir felt as if he were being driven through a river, not a road.
Inevitably, the taxi broke down. Weir had no idea where he was. The
taxi driver asked him to help push the car, but he declined the invitation, removed his clubs from the cab, put his heavy tour bag on his
shoulders, and tramped back to a main road five hundred yards
away. He was also carrying his two-iron as a weapon in case anybody
tried to go after this strange character wearing golf clothes and
lugging a big golf bag. Weir flagged another cab down when he

reached the road, and, luckily, the driver knew the route to the course and Weir made his starting time.

Weir did have some help in those early days, so soon after he'd turned professional. Steve Bennett at Huron Oaks organized a dinner there on August 31, 1992 that raised $10,500 to help Weir and Bricia with expenses. Bennett, who is from Seaforth, Ontario, told the 150 people there that Weir, who, with Bricia, attended the dinner, was going to be the best Canadian golfer yet.

Weir needed the money, and any support he could get, to subsidize his tournament play around the world. He struck an agreement with the financial-services company Midland Walwyn, because of a connection he had through golf with Kelly Roberts. Roberts, long one of Ontario's top amateurs, was working for the company in London, Ontario, when he and Weir discussed a possible sponsorship arrangement. The company decided to support Weir for $10,000 in the first year and $20,000 in the next, with a bonus based on his performance. He was also required to conduct a clinic for Midland Walwyn employees in every city on the Canadian Tour that had a company office. Roberts chatted with Weir when they were putting the deal together.

"I asked him what his plans were," Roberts says. "I figured we'd talk for a couple of minutes. He took me aside and laid out his plans for the next ten years, including that he would probably need to make some swing changes in two or three years. Then he said, 'I think I'll be ready to win a major in ten years.' He's the most mentally focused player I've ever seen."

During these early days of Weir's professional career, he became affiliated with the International Management Group in Toronto. IMG is the largest company in the world involved in athlete representation;

its clients include Arnold Palmer and Wayne Gretzky, to name two, and now Tiger Woods as well. Richard Zokol had told IMG representatives that he thought Weir had great promise. IMG did its due diligence and soon signed him as a client, a relationship that continues.

Meanwhile, Jim Bazuik, the owner of a Toyota dealership in Timmins in northern Ontario, provided Mike and Bricia with a car to use on the Canadian Tour that first season of 1993. Anybody who met Weir was impressed with his commitment to reaching the PGA Tour. Chris Goodwin had taken notice when Weir first played his Redtail Golf Course. Weir showed up there for the first time during the summer of 1993 with Bricia. Goodwin had played that morning, still had his clubs on a cart, and asked Weir if he'd like to see the course. They rode around, and when they reached the 9th hole, a downhill par-three over a pond, Weir liked the look of the hole so much that he got the itch to hit a shot. He asked Goodwin what club he had used in his morning round. Goodwin told him he'd hit a nine-iron, so Weir asked if he could use his eight-iron – a right-handed club. Weir took the club and hit a shot, right-handed, within eight feet of the hole. "I thought, 'This guy is good,'" Goodwin says. He continued to follow Weir's development. In April 1994, Goodwin was present when Weir's friends held a stag for him at Redtail prior to his marriage to Bricia. Brennan Little was also there. Weir had proposed to Bricia at her favorite Mexican restaurant in Provo, Utah. They were married in Brights Grove on April 30, 1994. They didn't have a true honeymoon, because Weir played the Canadian Tour that summer. His new bride was his caddie. He finished fifteenth on the Canadian Tour's money list, winning $18,441, not a banner season after being eighth in 1993 when he was the rookie of the year. Still, he was learning what he needed to do to succeed as a tour golfer, so his year was a mixture of progression and regression. Weir still had his eyes on the PGA Tour, even if he didn't make it through qualifying school again in the fall. "I never thought of giving up," Weir says. "I always knew I'd find a way."

Bricia, having caddied for Weir on the Canadian and Australian Tours for two years after he turned pro, was keenly aware of her husband's focus. She saw how organized and methodical he was, and that he would never express any doubt about what he considered his destiny as a golfer. Bricia also had to learn what every golfer's spouse, and even every golfer, has to learn.

"It's such a high degree of tension out there," Bricia says of tour life. "I had to learn not to take it personally when Mike hit a bad shot, that it wasn't my problem."

By late 1995, Weir had hit a golfing wall. Although he had had a decent season in Australia and Asia – he finished tenth in the Australian Open and in the top twenty-five in tournaments in Indonesia and New Zealand – he again failed to get through qualifying school and onto the PGA Tour. He couldn't attribute it to a lack of commitment or motivation, on or off the course. In the previous four years, he had missed only two days of a daily forty-minute stretching session, which was part of a workout program designed to keep him fit, was as determined as ever to make it to the PGA Tour, and believed he would get there. During the summer he had told a reporter in Vancouver, "I just know it's going to come. I don't think my expectations were unrealistic. Any good player wants to get out there quickly. It's just that you see players [on the PGA Tour] and you say, 'I used to kick their butts in college.' But I know it's going to come."

What came was his realization that he needed to change his swing, having stalled once too often in his bid to reach the PGA Tour. It was time to become a scientist of swing mechanics.

Weir realized that he had a few things in common with Ben Hogan, the ball-striker of ball-strikers. He felt Hogan was a perfect model for him, because he was of similar height, weight, and build – about five-foot-nine, wiry, and in the 150-pound range. Hogan, when he struggled in his early days as a professional, played with what Weir called a "substandard" grip that encouraged a hook, and Weir had similar tendencies. Hogan's swing was long and loose, and so was Weir's. Hogan experimented with his grip to try to make it more neutral, but found it difficult to make the change. Weir knew he would have to follow a similar path if he were to improve over the long term. Hogan tried to get away from his tendency to hook the ball by fanning his club open during the beginning of his backswing. This was something Weir would also try.

Weir's self-study course gave him a rudimentary technical understanding of the swing, an intellectual appreciation of its science. He read Ben Hogan's book *Five Lessons: The Modern Fundamentals of Golf*, David Leadbetter's *Faults and Fixes*, and Nick Faldo's *A Swing for Life*. Faldo had gone to Leadbetter at the end of 1984 and told him that he wanted to become a world-class player and that he would completely revamp his swing if necessary. Some observers thought that Faldo was crazy, because he had already won tournaments on the European Tour. Faldo, however, knew that he had little understanding of the swing, and – more important – of his own swing and inclinations. But Leadbetter worked with him, and Faldo won the 1987 British Open and went on to win five more majors. Weir was also aware of the work that Leadbetter had done with Nick Price, who had altered his swing under his guidance. While Weir was playing professional golf in his early years, 1993 and

1994, Price was becoming the number-one player in the world. Weir studied Price closely.

Weir also went beyond studying books and examining great swings. Richard Zokol encouraged Weir to see his teacher, Clay Edwards, in Houston. Weir was playing some tournaments in Texas, so took the opportunity to see Edwards, and he also made the long drive from Salt Lake City a couple of times to work with him.

"I saw a lot of talent and fire in him," Edwards says. "His swing was a little loose, but the mission to be a great player was there. I could tell he was going to be a permanent player. There was more than just his foundation as a golfer. It was also the quality of the person. He had all the components to make it on tour."

Weir and Edwards worked together for a while, and Weir made progress in managing his game and understanding his swing. Edwards, Weir says, helped elevate his ball-striking to a higher level than it was at when he was in college. But Houston was far from Salt Lake City, and Weir realized that he needed to find somebody closer to home.

Earlier in that critical 1995 season, Weir had played in the Canadian Open at the Glen Abbey Golf Club, where he hit balls on the range beside Price. "I really didn't want to hit balls beside Nick," Weir remembers. "I was intimidated by the way he hit the ball, but the only spot open was beside him. I started warming up, but I couldn't hit the ball worth a darn then. I knew how to score but not how to play, and Nick was hitting these shots that were so crisp. I couldn't believe how someone could have that much control. I could shoot 80 one day and 70 the next. I had no security in my game at all, but he knew that he'd hit the ball well every day and that he'd score low if he made a few putts. That's what I wanted."

Weir watched Price, whose shots erupted off the clubface and tore through the air with hardly any curvature, while his own shots were going all over the place. Price's ball flight was penetrating, while his shots were high and appeared to flutter. That was when Weir concluded that he needed to make major changes to his swing if he hoped to compete with a golfer such as Price; after all, Price was one of the golfers he would have to beat if he meant to get to the top.

Weir's opportunity to revamp his swing came in December 1995, when he accompanied Brennan Little to Palm Springs. Mike Wilson was an instructor at the Indian Ridge Country Club there, and Little had scheduled a lesson with him. Weir watched Wilson give Little a lesson, and liked what he saw. He and Wilson chatted, and began to work together.

"Brennan told me about Mike and what a good player he was," Wilson says. "He asked if I'd take a look at him. I could see the athleticism in his swing right away. What struck me was the way his body worked through the swing. He kept his angles and his midsection and hips working well, which is hard to teach. He'd ingrained these good habits in other sports, I guess. His short game was amazing, and his putting was exceptional."

But there were problems, notwithstanding Weir's athleticism. "He hit the ball too low," Wilson says, "especially his long irons. He didn't have the control he wanted. Mike didn't consider himself a real good ball-striker, because he couldn't hit some shots that other guys could hit. He had a big forward press at address, and then his arms would roll away. He'd shut the face going back, then roll and lift the club. I also noticed that he had the face wide open at address with his irons, and that he closed the face with his woods. He'd compensated as a kid and learned to play with what he had, but he decided that wasn't enough any more."

Weir told Wilson that he wanted to become a world-class player, and would take as long as necessary to improve his technique. He didn't care if he hit poor shots during tournaments, as long as he could see steady progress. "Our goal was for him to improve a little every year," Wilson says. "Mike had a long-term view, and he still does."

The two men felt they were kindred spirits. "I liked Mike's approach," Weir says of Wilson. "I could tell the guy really wants to teach. He's not doing it for the money. He does it for the love of golf. You can see it when he's teaching twenty-handicappers. He gets a bigger kick out of watching my brother Jim hit it straight than when I hit a shot we're working on." His point is clear. Weir wanted somebody who would take the same journey as he chose: the one that would never be complete.

"You can play good golf to a point with a swing that doesn't have good fundamentals," Weir adds, "because your short game keeps you in there. But it's going to wear you out. It's hard under the gun to be able to trust your swing when you know in the back of your mind that it's not mechanically sound. When things are sound, you never expect anything to go wrong."

Wilson, the man who had made such an impression on Weir, was born in Albuquerque, New Mexico. He was a more-than-adequate golfer who enjoyed studying the game as much as, if not more than, playing it. What made golf swings work? Why did some swings look good, but not perform well? He attended the University of Arizona, and worked at golf courses in the area while studying for a degree in business and communication. After graduating in 1989, Wilson turned pro in 1991 and taught at the El Paso Country Club in Texas. J.P. Hayes, who had attended the University of Texas at El Paso, turned pro in 1989 and played at the same club, where he met Wilson. They started working together, and continue to do so. Hayes has been a steady player on the PGA Tour the last six years, and had won twice through the 2002 season. Wilson also worked with Paul Stankowski, who had beaten Weir in that playoff for the championship of the Western Athletic Conference while they were in university, and had begun to establish himself on the PGA Tour.

Wilson was a David Leadbetter disciple by the time Weir met him. Weir liked Leadbetter's ideas, which emphasize the use of the big muscles of the torso, shoulders, and back rather than the smaller muscles in the hands, so he and Wilson were compatible on this score.

Rob Roxborough, the head professional at the Magna Golf Club in Aurora, north of Toronto, watched the first lesson Wilson gave Weir. He remembers that they worked right away on getting the club-face into the proper position at the start of the backswing. This was the origin of the Weir rehearsal waggle, as Weir began to try to set the clubface on the correct angle going back. He and Wilson checked its position during the backswing, there on the range at Indian Ridge and in the video room. From the start, Weir believed in what Wilson was saying, and Wilson believed that Weir could, and would, make whatever changes were required for him to elevate his game.

They worked on the fundamentals. Weir's posture was rounded, so he tried to stand up more to the ball. He used an interlocking, strong grip that promoted a hook, so he began to make the difficult switch to the more conventional overlapping grip. He also took the club back too far inside and around his body. But Wilson saw right away that Weir made a powerful move through the ball. He could make compensations to hit the ball solidly, and accurately, most of the time. But most of the time isn't good enough to win on the PGA Tour.

Weir went from glasses to contact lenses in 1996, believing this could only improve his vision and comfort. Concerning his swing, he learned from Wilson and Wilson learned from him. Teacher and student: they were works-in-progress, and their work progressed. So did Weir's game. His most impressive performance came in the 1996 Greater Vancouver Open, a PGA Tour event in which Weir came to the last hole needing a birdie to have a chance to get into a playoff with Guy Boros. He drove the ball perfectly and made a confident swing with a six-iron to attack the hole that was cut on the front of the green, just beyond a lake. But his ball came up short and in the water. Weir double-bogeyed the hole to drop into a tie for fifth place. He was disappointed but unfazed, because his swing had held up throughout the tournament. He had also demonstrated that he didn't play golf for the money, during a period when he was making only expenses. Weir went for a chance to win on the last hole rather than taking an extra club and playing beyond the hole, thereby taking the water out of play.

Still, he didn't get through qualifying school again that year. His swing was improving, but it was back to the road for him, the road to the PGA Tour, if not the PGA Tour road itself yet. He longed for his apprenticeship in golf's minor leagues to end. Weir had finished twenty-second on the Canadian Tour's money list in 1996, with $20,715 (Canadian), and had made two of five cuts on the PGA Tour in tournaments in which he had made the field. But it was back to further seasoning, primarily on the 1997 Canadian Tour.

CHAPTER FOUR

Tuesday

April 8, 2003

To the rest of the world, Augusta is a one-week-a-year city. When the Masters is on, it's *the* place in the golf world. Motel rooms quadruple in price along the strip-malled Washington Road, the main thoroughfare that runs in front of the treed and high-fenced club. The course itself is an enclave within an enclave, inaccessible to most Augustans unless they work there. Atlanta, where club co-founder Bobby Jones was born, practiced law, and lived, is 150 miles to the west, while Columbia, the capital of South Carolina, is sixty miles to the northeast. Some visitors commute from Columbia or points farther east and west, because rooms in Augusta aren't easy to find during the Masters, and even small homes rent for $7,500 a week. The house that Weir has rented for his friends and family is a twenty-minute walk from the course.

Augusta is a city that the golfers and the spectators don't know or care very much about. In truth, it's a poky kind of place: conservative, not particularly prosperous, and racially divided. There are pleasant tree-filled neighborhoods with tidy homes – ranging from modest to fairly grand – where the prevailing decorative motif runs to whimsical bunnies, a strangely recurrent variant of Southern kitsch. (Ersatz rabbits seem to breed in Augusta, be they lawn ornaments, on wallpaper, or on teapots.) Augusta's downtown has pretty much run to seed. It includes James Brown Boulevard (yes, *that* James Brown, a native Augusta son, raised in poverty in the hardscrabble segregated South). Sadly, many of the houses and businesses lining it are in depressing states of disrepair.

The golfers and their avid followers arrive during the second week in April not to visit or become familiar with the city, but to compete in or attend the Masters. Exploration for visitors to the Masters starts and stops at the golf club, a few restaurants, and events that golf companies hold during the week in the private homes they rent. When asked about the city, golfers go blank, as do most visitors. Asked about the course and the Masters, however, golfers become animated. They genuflect. This is just the way things are.

Truth be told, Augusta National doesn't feel in any way like part of the city. Jones chose the town because of the property he and Clifford Roberts found, and also for climatic reasons, thinking that Augusta would be an ideal place for a club in use only from early October through late May. The weather is mild enough for golf during the winter and early spring months – milder than Atlanta, which is one thousand feet above sea level, while Augusta is only about 150 feet above sea level. Augusta does become too hot for most golfers in the summer, but most of its members live outside Augusta and belong to clubs in their home areas; Augusta is a retreat for them during non-summer months. Jones and Roberts, a New York stockbroker and man-about-investments, found the property for the course in 1931, and loved it immediately; the site of the former

Fruitland Nursery, the first commercial nursery in the South, its rolling landscape was ideal for the golf course that Jones envisaged.

But in many ways the course could have been anywhere in this part of the South, had Jones found an equally alluring property and not focused on Augusta. The high fences that separate the club from the city outside its gates define its relationship to it. They declare, "This is a private enclave, and you will not enter." Augusta National has never tried to be anything else but what it is, an intensely private club that opens its gates to the public for one week a year, during the Masters.

Thus, even players who have been coming to the Masters for decades know or care to learn very little about the city. This approach is understandable, in a way. A golfer's week is regimented on the PGA Tour, and it's even more buttoned-down during a major. Weir likes to get to a regular PGA Tour event on Monday night or Tuesday, which leaves him a couple of days for practice before the usual Thursday start. His week consists of practice, often a pro-am prior to the start of the tournament proper, workouts in his hotel or rental house, and, maybe, just maybe, meals at restaurants or even a movie. Such are the boundaries of his life: he's a tour golfer, not a tourist.

Majors are even more demanding than the regular PGA Tour events, in ways both physical and mental. The courses are more challenging, and because there's no pro-am, every player has more time on his hands. Players usually arrive on Monday, and can get three days of preparation in if they choose. Many come in earlier, and some play the course well in advance of tournament week. Jack Nicklaus, a six-time Masters winner, has been here three times in recent weeks. His objective was to see if he could handle the long course. At sixty-three, Nicklaus doesn't hit the ball nearly as far as younger players, but he was the game's longest hitter in his prime. When Nicklaus won the Masters in 1965, with a then-record score of seventeen-under-par 271, he didn't hit a club longer than an eight-iron into any green during the last round. Contemporary players, especially long hitters such as Tiger Woods, Ernie Els, Phil Mickelson, and Davis Love III, are said to have a big advantage now at Augusta National, because it has been lengthened considerably in recent years. They hit the ball high and it carries a long way, which allows them to take advantage of the slopes in the fairways that send the ball further. The player who can carry his ball close to three hundred yards on the par-five 2nd hole, for example, knows that it will bounce off the sharp downhill slope there and run down the fairway. When this happens, he can hit a middle- and sometimes even a short-iron second shot into the hole.

Golfers who drive the ball shorter distances must hit woods into the green, or lay up short. The course is so wet for this Masters, however, that even the longest hitters won't get as much advantage as in recent years, because their shots won't roll much. The course will play dead, no matter how much wind and sunshine may arrive, and right now wind and sunshine seem distant prospects. Meanwhile, Nicklaus and shorter hitters will be hitting even longer clubs into the greens because of these conditions. Els was here last week to check out the course, when it played fast. But he may as well not have visited, because the course he'll play this week will differ so much from the one he encountered.

Still, Nicklaus decided to play. He loves the Masters, and the tournament wouldn't be the same without him, but it's obvious that his chances of scoring decently would be enhanced if the course were playing fast and dry. That's the way Jones and the designer Alister MacKenzie always viewed it. Jones admired the Old Course in St. Andrews, Scotland, and wanted to introduce its design principles into Augusta National: generous fairways that allow a golfer to take a mighty whack at the ball, but which still demand accuracy

to find the best angle into the heavily bunkered and intensely contoured greens. Those greens also run off down knobs and bumps in
the ground, so that the player who makes a mistake coming in, or
misses the green, will find himself with an awkward chip or pitch to
get near the hole. Strategy matters at Augusta National. It's a long-
ball hitter's course nowadays, but the wily player can still get around
the course with a good score.

The course is certainly fit for a major championship, because it
demands that a player think. This isn't a course where a player can
simply fire shots at the hole as if he were playing darts, even when
the turf is as full of moisture as a steam bath. There are places a
golfer just doesn't want to be, and to go for the hole sometimes
leaves little or no margin for error. When the hole is cut toward the
front left at the 3rd hole, to cite one of many possible examples,
the astute golfer will play to the right of it and beyond. The player
who tries to get near the hole with his second shot – even the short
second shot that he faces on this par-four that's only 350 yards – will
often see his ball spin off the front of the green and back down a hill
toward him. If he misses to the left, he'll have little or no room to
play his third shot as he tries to save par.

As the first of the four annual major championships, the Masters
attracts global attention. This is in part because of its well-known
course, which is indeed exceedingly private, but also, somehow,
public during the tournament. Golfers around the world are familiar with its holes, because they've seen them, especially the back nine,
on television. The Masters is the only major that's played on the same
course every year. The U.S. Open in June, the British Open in July,
and the PGA Championship in August, move around, so that people
rarely become as steeped in their lore and as aware of their holes as

they do with the Augusta National. The golfers themselves have a sense of competing against legends and ghosts during the Masters.

Olympia Fields, site of this year's U.S. Open, hasn't hosted the championship since 1928, when Bobby Jones lost a thirty-six-hole playoff to Johnny Farrell by one shot. Greg Norman won his second British Open when it was held in 1993 at Royal St. George's Golf Club, this year's venue. The PGA Championship is at Oak Hill in Rochester, New York, which last held the event in 1980, when Nicklaus won; Oak Hill also hosted the 1989 U.S. Open.

These majors are not PGA Tour events. It's an anomaly of professional golf that the PGA Tour does not conduct the three major championships held in the United States. Similarly, the PGA European Tour does not conduct the British Open, or, as it's more properly called, the Open Championship. Both tours conduct their own championships. The PGA Tour conducts the Players Championship each March at its Tournament Players Club in Ponte Vedra Beach, Florida, near Jacksonville. The PGA European Tour conducts its most significant event, the Volvo Masters, each November at the Valderrama Golf Club in Sotogrande, Spain.

Every year there's a debate about whether the Players Championship constitutes, or should constitute, golf's fifth major. As the argument goes, it has the deepest field of top golfers in the game, and it's played on a difficult course for a gigantic purse. These points advance the argument for the Players being the fifth major, but they don't seal it. It takes time and history and something ineffable for a tournament to be considered a major. There are four majors and four majors only. When the Players was held this past spring, Tiger Woods was asked whether, in his opinion, the Players Championship will ever be considered a major. His words echo those of his fellow players.

"No, I don't think so," said Woods, who won the 2001 Players. "I think it's probably the highest tournament in the world next to the majors. I don't think it ranks up there in the majors' category now."

Woods has won eight major championships since turning professional in the late summer of 1996. Nicklaus won eighteen between the 1962 U.S. Open, a year after he turned professional, and 1986, when, at forty-six, he became the oldest player to win the Masters. He's won more majors than any player, but Woods may surpass him in time. Woods was eleven years old, when, as Tim Rosaforte wrote in his biography of him, he made up a chart that listed in the left-hand column the major championships. Having cut out a photograph of Nicklaus, he put it on top of another column and wrote the age at which Nicklaus had won a major for the first time. Above a third column he put his own name. Woods knew that, if majors matter most, then Nicklaus was clearly the greatest golfer yet. And he wanted to win each major at a younger age than Nicklaus had.

"Let's look at this subject of majors," David Abell, Nick Price's business manager, says as a discussion turns in this direction under the massive oak tree on the Augusta National lawn, with its octopus-like limbs stretching and twisting in all directions. Price has won two PGA Championships and the British Open. He remains one of the best players in the game, and believes that, at forty-six, he can win another major. "I was talking to Nick," Abell says, "and he felt that he'd rather have won his three majors and fifteen PGA Tour events than one major and, say, twenty tournaments. He says that the majors are what count in the end. Nobody knows how many tournaments on the PGA Tour that he's won, but people know that he's won three majors. People know that Nicklaus won a lot of tournaments, but very few can come up with the exact number. But they know that he's won eighteen majors. Meanwhile, they don't know how many tournaments Greg Norman won around the world, but they know that he won two British Opens. They also know that he should have won more, because he's so talented."

In Norman's case, then, golf watchers think of how many majors he hasn't won – as much or more than the two he has won. They speak far more often about Phil Mickelson being the best player not to have won a major, a dubious honor, than they do about the twenty-one PGA Tour events this gifted left-hander has won. They remember the thirty-inch putt that Doug Sanders missed on the last green at the Old Course in St. Andrews, which would have won him the 1970 British Open; Nicklaus won in a playoff over Sanders, who never did win a major. Then there's Scott Hoch, who missed a two-foot putt on the 10th hole in a playoff against Nick Faldo that would have given him the 1989 Masters. He's known more for that missed putt than for the eleven PGA Tour events he's won. Ed Sneed missed three short putts in a row on the 16th, 17th, and 18th holes, any one of which would have given him the 1979 Masters. Hubert Green missed a five-foot putt on the last green in the 1978 Masters that would have put him in a playoff against Gary Player. Later that Sunday evening, Green returned to the green to try the same putt, over and over. Green had already won a major, the 1977 U.S. Open, but people remember him more for the Masters that he lost.

Missing a putt on the last hole of a major championship, or making one, can define a player's career. A golfer is sometimes remembered for what he did, or didn't do, there. Mark O'Meara made a twenty-five-foot birdie putt on the last green to win the 1998 Masters, his first major championship. Anybody who watched that putt glide down toward the hole, and then drop, remembers it.

Weir knows the crucial role of the majors in defining a golfer's career. He plays for the championships, and not for the accolades, the money, the appearances on television shows, or the articles in national magazines or headlines in newspapers. He wants to win majors.

WHTB, a local radio station that bills itself as "Gospel Alive," is dreaming this morning. The host of the early-morning drive show says, "Remember, this is a beautiful Masters Tuesday, even if it is raining. We are going to bring you inspirational music." She predicts a high of sixty-eight degrees Fahrenheit for today, while every other station in Augusta is calling for fifty-two or fifty-four degrees. The wedge remains locked in over Augusta, and the forecast is for rain, on and off, all day. The lack of sun, cold air from the north, and the damp conditions are making for a day that is less than an inspiration. Still, optimism is helpful, even when it does not seem warranted. Why not conflate faith with a weather forecast? There's also another conflation in Augusta this week. This one somehow associates Martha Burk, chair of the National Council of Women's Organizations, with the war in Iraq, and manages to turn the discussion about whether Augusta National should admit a female member into one about freedom. "Free Iraq and Hootie too," pleads a message written in chalk on the back window of a white Cadillac Escalade SUV.

Burk herself had made an unfortunate association between the war and Augusta's men-only membership policy, pointing out, before the Masters, that American women are participating in the war in Iraq, but they can't belong to Augusta National. She called on CBS not to telecast the tournament for this reason. Burk trivialized both her own cause, which is essentially about opening doors for women, and that of the war effort, by linking the two events. They have nothing to do with one another in any obvious or even subtle way. She had also hurt her cause right from the start when, after learning that Augusta National held the world's most popular tournament but did not have any female members, she said that the Masters should be held elsewhere. Burk couldn't be faulted for knowing nothing about golf or the tournament, but she should have done her research before issuing her proclamation. The Masters is never played anywhere else. It wouldn't be the Masters if it were held anywhere but Augusta National.

Still, the issue of membership at Augusta National became popular in the press and in general conversation. Private clubs by law are allowed freedom of association, though it's understandable that Burk, whose role is to lobby on behalf of women's issues, would take on Augusta National's exclusionary membership policy. She concluded that Augusta National was more than a private club, that it was a corridor of power, and, moreover, a for-profit corporation that made millions from the Masters. Burk argued that the club effectively became a public institution during the Masters, and that it therefore was obliged to have female members. The club's chairman, William "Hootie" Johnson, on the other hand, consistently maintained that the club was private, and the fact that it hosted the Masters didn't change that. Johnson was roundly criticized in mainstream publications, especially the *New York Times*, which published many columns, articles, and editorials decrying Augusta's membership policy. The club didn't admit its first black member until 1990, and, as David Owen wrote in his book *The Making of the Masters*, it "was certainly a part of the culture that for decades made golf virtually unapproachable for black players."

Johnson, a pugnacious sort, never wavered from his position after Burk's letter, which only inflamed her more. She promised action during the Masters, and by the week of the tournament it was clear that the National Council of Women's Organizations would protest in Augusta. The question was how many people would attend, and whether the protests would influence the tournament. As the rhetoric heated up, it obscured an important debate that might have ensued about whether there's a place in modern golf and society for men-only clubs, or women-only clubs, for that matter.

•⁓

Inside Augusta National's gates, everything seems normal, except for heightened security. Security is always tight at Augusta, but this year it's even more evident. Journalists are required to open their kits upon entry, and spectators are checked for anything they might be bringing in. Once inside the gates, however, it's the same club as always: a place where traditions matter. Golfers and spectators know that they won't see electronic scoreboards; changes are made manually by people perched behind the boards. They know that they won't see corporate logos all over the place; there's not a hint of advertising on the course, while soft drinks and beers are poured into green Masters paper cups, which many people take away as souvenirs. They can get the same spongy pimiento-cheese sand-wiches that an outside vendor has been making for years, although one wouldn't want to analyze their composition for nutritional value. They'll pay the low prices for food that will make them feel that they're in the 1960s, and maybe that's the idea: a dollar-twenty-five for a pimiento-cheese sandwich, chips and candy for seventy-five cents, ice cream for a dollar, water for a dollar-twenty-five, a soft drink for a buck, and a beer for a dollar-seventy-five.

Tradition, tradition. The badge-holders enjoy having their pictures taken while standing in front of the huge scoreboard a couple of hundred yards or so inside the club's front entrance, from which they can look behind them to the gleaming white clubhouse and the dazzling green course, whose contoured hills sweep away from there. They can linger outside the clubhouse near the front of the pro shop and study the Masters trophy that's on display, and stare at the folks lucky enough to get inside the ropes and onto the lawn. If they have the appropriate badges they can saunter into the clubhouse and see the same old photos of the same old players, and they're likely even to see the same old players themselves. Sam Snead and Gene Sarazen were regulars at the Masters until their deaths in recent years. Why, there's Byron Nelson. There's Arnold Palmer, and he's playing. He's played in every Masters since 1955, and he's won four green jackets.

It's easy to consider these traditions fustiness, and the whole place as stodgy and anachronistic. But they provide Augusta National's and the Masters' unique charms. They're why golfers and spectators crave an invitation.

Once a player has won the Masters, he's invited to play the tournament every year. This is why Byron Nelson, for one, receives his annual invitation, which falls under category number one for qualification: Masters Tournament Champions (lifetime). Nelson hasn't played since 1966, but his biography and statistics still appear in the players' guide that the club issues every year. The grim reaper alone disqualifies a player from the guide.

Palmer, meanwhile, is very much alive. He's playing his forty-ninth Masters, although he said last year that he would compete in no more. Of course he hasn't truly *competed* in the Masters since 1983, the last time he made the halfway cut. But Palmer belongs at the Masters, if not as a player, then as a permanent invitee to the tournament.

Palmer shot 89-85 last year. He said after his first round, "Tomorrow will be it." He was also aware of a letter that Hootie

Johnson had sent to some past champions, such as Gay Brewer, Doug Ford, and Billy Casper. Johnson asked these players, none of whom is still competitive, not to enter the Masters. They were welcome to attend, to play in the Par 3 Contest that took place every Wednesday of tournament week on the property's short course, and to enjoy the week. All tournament participants, honorary invitees, and non-competing past champions are eligible, but not required, to play. But Johnson believed that players such as Brewer, Ford, and Casper were compromising the competitive nature of the event. He felt that Bobby Jones's intention had been that only those players who think they can make the cut should play. The letter he sent decreed that former champions aged sixty-five and over would no longer be eligible to enter the Masters, as of 2004. Players did not receive this letter kindly. Palmer and Nicklaus felt that former champions should be allowed to make up their own minds about when it was their time not to enter, and told Johnson so.

Younger players, for the most part, feel that the presence of the older golfers enhances the atmosphere at the Masters. Nobody thinks that Tom Watson, who won the 1977 and 1981 Masters, will win another this year. But Weir is drawn with Watson for the first two rounds, and is looking forward to playing with him. As for Palmer, Fred Couples, the 1992 Masters winner, said last year, "His score is irrelevant. I'm sure he's not bothering anyone out there. Even if he hits one good shot and shoots a high score, that's okay." But Palmer said after last year's Masters, "I think it's time."

A year later, Palmer is back, playing in the tournament. He'll play with Ryan Moore, the current United States Public Links champion. Palmer is seventy-three and Moore is twenty. Palmer is here because, shortly before this year's Masters, Johnson rescinded the letter that he wrote last year, having realized that he had made a grave error. Palmer could have played this year, even if Johnson's letter applied, because it wasn't to take effect until 2004. But now, by playing this year and next, he will have racked up fifty consecutive Masters. Nobody has done this.

Palmer is on the grounds today, working on his game. So is Doug Ford, the 1957 Masters winner. He withdrew after the first round of the 1998, 1999, and 2000 Masters, having shot, respectively, 86, 88, and 94. He withdrew in 2001 after one hole, and didn't play last year. Some people feel that Johnson's objective, in part, was to ensure that Ford didn't enter, because he wasn't even bothering to play a full thirty-six holes before missing the cut. He's here now, but he won't play the tournament.

Billy Casper, a Masters and U.S. Open champion, is here. He has lost eighty pounds, and is hardly recognizable as he sits in the upper grillroom having lunch with some friends. Casper was famous years ago for going on a diet that included buffalo meat, but over the years he gained a tremendous amount of weight. He's looking healthy now, but has decided not to play in the Masters. He's here for the Par 3 Contest and for some socializing.

This upper room in the clubhouse is just the place for socializing. Members and visitors who can get into this private preserve might first enter the clubhouse through the front door at the end of Magnolia Lane – the three-hundred-yard-long path from Washington Road that is lined with magnolia trees on either side and ends at a circular drive with a grassy oval where the U.S. and Augusta National flags are raised.

Walking in during the Masters, one finds a receptionist who seems to be doing everything: taking packages for delivery to players and other folks; presenting cigars from a portable humidor, for a price, to people who request them; dispensing directions to this and that area of the antebellum manor clubhouse that always feel more home than house. A table across from her holds the day's papers: the

New York Times, the *Wall Street Journal*, the *Augusta Chronicle*, the *Atlanta Journal-Constitution*, *USA Today*. To reach the upper dining area, one walks up a winding staircase. A locker room reserved for Masters champions is to the left, while the small dining room is to the right. A guard protects the champions' locker room from anybody else who might want to have a look. The dining room itself includes bookshelves and a few tables on either side of a path through a door to the outside balcony overlooking the lawn and golf course. The balcony is full of diners during the Masters, although they do more stargazing and newspaper-reading than eating. It's a fine thing to sit here for an hour or so, whiling away a Masters morning. Or afternoon. Or early evening.

The color photograph on this year's breakfast and lunch menu is of the par-five 2nd hole, called Pink Dogwood, and there's also an inset photograph of the clubhouse. Breakfast items include creamed chipped beef on toast, grits, corned-beef hash with a poached egg, and Southern buttermilk biscuits. Lunch offerings include Augusta National seafood chowder, hickory-smoked ham and cheese and junior club sandwiches, various salads, and mandatory desserts such as peach cobbler and chilled white nectar peaches.

The bookshelves and walls tell what really matters here, and who rules, or whose spirits rule. There's a portrait of Clifford Roberts wearing a red tie, white shirt, and glasses, his close-cropped hair and receding hairline suggesting a severe man. There's a black-and-white photo of Bobby Jones, in a tie and a V-neck sweater and white plus-fours. One shelf includes books by and about Jones, including a recent one called *Secrets of the Masters*, by Sidney Matthews, a trial lawyer with an abiding interest in all things Jones, all things Augusta National, and all things Masters. Matthews has even caddied in the Masters, and produced a documentary film about Jones.

While Casper has his breakfast, surrounded by a history of which he is a part – he won the 1970 Masters – Doug Ford walks into the dining area. Larry Mize, the 1987 Masters champion, comes in, as does two-time Masters winner Seve Ballesteros. They're all holding court at one table or another. Their presence adds to the Masters all right.

Weir appreciates that Casper and other older players contribute to the atmosphere at the Masters, but he won't pretend that those who play make the tournament more competitive. He is not one to dance around a subject when asked about it. In his opinion, while the Masters includes all the current top players in the game, it isn't as deep in talent as the other major championships. The British Open is his favorite tournament, he says, because it's played on a links, which often demands that a golfer cope with rugged weather, especially wind. He also likes the fact that a player is required to hit the ball along the ground as well as in the air; it's not just a matter of getting the yardage and flying the ball to the hole and watching it stop right there, as if it's landed in a green the consistency of peanut butter. When the wind blows as hard as it can during a British Open, a player often has to hit low shots that run and bound and scamper along the ground – and that are subject to its vicissitudes. The clever player also learns how to use the ground by playing his ball into areas that will deflect it toward his target.

The British Open also has more players from around the world than does the Masters, the U.S. Open, and the PGA Championship. It's *the* world golf event, *the* international championship.

•

At the same time, Weir took to Augusta and the Masters the moment he walked on the grounds for the first time. That was on a Monday in the second week of March 2000, when he and Brennan Little visited the course a few days before he was to play the Honda Classic in Ft. Lauderdale on the PGA Tour. He hoped by doing so he would learn something about the course that he would play a few weeks later during his first Masters, and that he would get any awestruck rookie's feelings out of the way.

Weir was surprised by a couple of things that he saw during his first trip to Augusta National. He told *Globe and Mail* reporter Michael Grange then that Magnolia Lane was shorter than he'd thought it was, and that more people were playing the course than he'd envisioned. Weir was learning something important about Augusta National. It's a member's course first and foremost, despite hosting the Masters, and the members don't necessarily make way for the professionals. Weir had to start on the back nine during his first visit, and found play more than a little slow.

But he learned a few other things, too, because a Masters participant has to use one of the club's caddies, except during the tournament. Although Brennan walked around with him, Weir used one of the local caddies, "a real veteran," he said. The fellow provided Weir with an education about the greens, while Brennan worked out the yardages on the course from one place to another. Weir, in taking the trouble to get an early look at Augusta National, was only emphasizing what those people close to him know: majors are important to him. He'd already had a taste of contending in one, the 1999 PGA Championship, where he was tied with Woods heading into the final round before shooting 80 and tying for tenth place. That was Weir's third major. This 2003 Masters will be his sixteenth, but he has finished no higher in a major than he did at that PGA Championship.

"There's definitely a different feel during major weeks," Weir said prior to his first Masters, in 2000. "It doesn't feel like a golf tournament, it feels like a championship, and I'm sure the Masters will be the same way and probably even more because it's the first major of the year." He added, "Do I think I can win? No question. I'm ready to win this year. I feel very ready. I've never been afraid to win, and if I get in contention I'm not going to settle for a high finish. I think I have the mental capacity to get in there and do it."

Weir's results in his three Masters have been encouraging, although he has yet to finish in the top twenty. He tied for twenty-eighth in 2000, for twenty-seventh in 2001, and for twenty-fourth last year. His scoring average at Augusta National is 72.5, although he has had more rounds under par – five – than over par – four. He has also come to believe that the course suits him, because he has proven to himself that he has the short game to handle the shots required around the greens, and he's usually such a fine putter that, as Greg Norman said when Weir and he were teammates in the 2000 Presidents Cup (a biennial competition between teams of twelve professionals, one side drawn from the United States and another from international players born outside Europe), "He can put the ball in a thimble on the greens."

Weir had quite an introduction to that first Masters in 2000. Bricia had given birth to their second daughter, Lili, on the Monday of Masters week. Weir hoped to play the Masters, but was prepared to forgo the tournament if Bricia hadn't given birth yet. He stayed home until the birth, and arrived in Augusta late that night to learn that his clubs had been lost in transit. He didn't get any practice in until late Tuesday afternoon, but shot 75-70-70, and was in fifth place after three rounds, six shots behind the leader, Vijay Singh. He shot 78 in the last round, as Singh went on to win with a score of ten-under-par 278.

One could think that Weir might have felt disoriented during that first Masters, since his wife had just given birth and he was so quickly on the road. He did find it difficult to stay focused at first, but, he says, "On the other hand I was happy that Bricia and Lili were healthy, so it helped with my perspective and made the week better. I knew that once the Masters was over I'd be home with our new little wonder."

Looking back at that Masters, Weir believes it was a good start for what he hoped would be an annual visit to the tournament. "I had an outside chance to win starting the last round," he recalls. "But my first three rounds were done with smoke and mirrors. I wasn't playing all that well. I was relying on my short game and it caught up with me on Sunday. My ball-striking was the same as it was before, but my short game wasn't there. But it was still a great experience to be in that situation."

Weir's play in the second and third rounds in particular demonstrated that he had the short game to do well at Augusta National. He was swinging poorly, but kept saving pars and made birdies when he had his few rare opportunities. He got up and down for par from sand on the 4th during the second round; Jonathan Yarwood was following U.S. Amateur champion David Gossett, whom he teaches and with whom Weir was playing, and said of Weir, "He's a sensational bunker player." He added, "I like everything about him, the way he dresses, smart and snappy, the way he conducts himself. He oozes professionalism."

Later, on the 12th, Weir pulled his tee shot, yet it landed near the hole on the par-three. But he wasn't aiming at the pin, because of Rae's Creek that comes close to the green there. He pulled the shot ten yards, but he got away with it and holed the putt for birdie. He made a fifteen-foot par putt on the 14th, and birdied the last hole from six feet. "It was just mental toughness," he says of his second round. Then he went to the range to try to figure out what was going wrong with his swing.

But on Saturday, his swing still wasn't right, and the weather turned foul. By the time Weir reached the back nine it was cold, with winds constantly in the range of twenty to twenty-five miles an hour, and gusts up to forty. Weir said he'd never played in a more difficult wind. Still, as temperatures dropped to fifty degrees Fahrenheit, he seemed to steel himself. He got up and down seven of the eight times that he missed greens on the back nine, hitting a series of inventive little shots. The wind was screaming from behind him as he stood in the fairway on the 17th, with the hole cut toward the front left of the green. Downwind, or downgale, it was impossible for him to hold the green. Weir accepted this, so he wasn't surprised when his ball rode the wind and ran through the green. The green from there moved away from him, and it was as hard as a diamond. But he played a finely judged pitch-and-run that finished near the hole, so he saved par. Weir shot even-par 36 that back nine, which, after his front-nine 34, gave him a two-under-par 70 for the day, "a heck of a score in those conditions," he says now. "It was a case of getting it up and down and being creative."

Weir had played his back nine in conditions that Jack Nicklaus described as the toughest he had seen at the Masters. Nicklaus shot 44 on his way to an 81, the first time he hadn't broken 80 at the Masters. "I'm not a great wind player," Nicklaus said, "but you couldn't stand up." Somehow, Weir did. But he wasn't able to keep saving par after par on Sunday, and so shot that 78, which pushed him back to a tie for twenty-eighth place.

A year later, Weir was drawn to play the first two rounds of the 2001 Masters with Tiger Woods, who was going after his fourth consecutive major-championship win – the Tiger Slam as it was being called: wins in four consecutive majors, although not during the same year, which would have made it an authentic Grand Slam. Weir looked forward to the experience, and vowed that he wouldn't let himself be distracted by the mayhem that can swirl around Woods. Certainly he wouldn't hit a shot until he was ready, unlike his experience in the 1999 PGA Championship when he played the last round with Woods. At Augusta, he hit the ball well the first round, but took thirty-six putts on his way to shooting 74; he came back with 69 the second round, and shot 72-72 on the weekend. He was witness to history while it was being made, as Woods won that Masters and became the first golfer to win four professional majors in a row. But Weir had come to Augusta to try to make his own history – a win in the Masters.

Last year, 2002, Weir tried something new at Augusta. He decided to treat it more like a regular PGA Tour event, figuring he was taking the majors too seriously. Normally, his family and friends aren't with him on the PGA Tour. Bricia hadn't been with him in his first Masters, in 2000, when she was home with Elle and their newborn daughter, Lily, but some of his family had been down. In 2001 she and their two small daughters were in Augusta, along with other family and friends. In 2002, he decided to go it alone at the Masters, in the sense that he was by himself in a hotel room and his family stayed home. He was also continuing without his unusual waggle, although he thought its absence might have accounted for some poor Sunday rounds when he was in contention during the winter PGA Tour events. But Weir really didn't have the opportunity to learn if his new strategies would work on Sunday, because he didn't get into contention after shooting 72-71-71. He was in twelfth place, nine shots behind Woods after three rounds.

Weir also had more to worry about after his third round than how many shots he was behind Woods. He was about to play his approach shot to the 9th hole during the third round when he suddenly lost focus and couldn't see. Dropping nearly to the ground, Weir rubbed his eyes, put a towel over his head, and felt terribly frightened. He was provided with some headache medication, but couldn't see the clubhead behind the ball for four or five shots, nor could he see the ball when he set the clubhead down. By the 13th hole, he was able to see clearly again, and after speaking briefly with reporters following his round he was examined by two eye doctors and a neurologist at the Medical College of Georgia, and given a CAT scan. A tumor was ruled out, and he was told he had suffered from a classic "aura of a migraine," something he had never had before.

Weir shot 76 the last round, to tie for twenty-fourth place. He decided to take three weeks off, and was comforted when the visual problems he had in the Masters didn't return. The difficulties aside, Weir had again played a Masters in which he came close to finishing up in the field. But he had taken 122 putts, forty-first in the field. It's too much to ask of a golfer to win a Masters averaging more than thirty putts a round, and Weir knew that.

·⤳

After playing the front nine alone in this, his first practice round of the 2003 Masters, Weir has joined Jeff Maggert for the back nine. Steve Bennett is here. He's seen Weir hit every shot at the Masters since he played his first. "I think he has a good chance," Steve says. "The biggest improvement he's made this year is that his putting and driving stats are so much better than they were last year. He's making more birdies. Ever since he was a kid, he's always made a lot of birdies." Weir made twenty birdies during the Players Championship a few weeks ago, but finished even-par for the tournament. It's not always the raw number of birdies a player makes, then, but the number of offsetting bogeys he makes that matter. Except for the Players, Weir has been making many more birdies than he has bogeys, which is why he has won twice and had two other top-ten finishes this year.

Over the years, Weir has become a bogey-hating golfer. He's not alone. Probably more than any golfer, Tiger Woods hates making bogeys. He has said that it feels better to save par when it looks like he's about to make a bogey than it does to make a birdie; that sort of par keeps a round going, while a bogey can often derail it. Glen Hnatiuk, a Canadian on the PGA Tour, who has been trying to find within himself the fight that Weir has, wishes he were more of a bogey-hater. He played with Weir on the weekend at the Players Championship in March, and said that he didn't realize until then how much Weir hated missing a putt. Weir gets a mean look on his face when he misses a putt, especially one that would have saved par.

Steve Bennett knows that Weir, like every golfer in the Masters, will face holes where he'll have to save par by getting up and down, and rarely from easy spots around the greens. There aren't many easy shots from around these greens. Since he played in his first Masters in 2000, Weir has become wiser in the ways of how to play Augusta National. "You learn a lot playing around here: where to hit the ball, where to put it on the greens," he said after that Masters. "That's the neat thing about playing here, the experience factor."

Weir also knows plenty about posting a low score when he has the chance to do so. He's not afraid to go deep. It helped that Weir learned his golf at Huron Oaks, a fairly short course that was accessible to low scores. Bennett points out that Weir wasn't afraid to keep making birdies when he reached three- or four-under-par during his round. Many golfers actually are afraid to make birdie after birdie after birdie, as if they don't deserve to do so. Every golfer seems to find his own comfort zone, and it's not always easy to move beyond it. Jack Nicklaus has said that, for some reason, he always felt most comfortable when he had to make two pars and a birdie over the last three holes to win a major championship, and added that other golfers fall into a variety of comfort zones: there's the golfer who never makes it beyond lesser professional tours; the golfer who makes the PGA Tour but can't get into the top 125 money-winners; the player who sabotages his score every time he gets into a position to finish in the top ten; the player who won't let himself win. (Bobby Wadkins played 712 PGA Tour events between 1975 and 1998, and, while he made a good living, he never won. His older brother Lanny played for twenty-nine years on the PGA Tour and won twenty-one tournaments, including the 1977 PGA Championship, a major. They had different comfort zones.)

Weir always expected to break through from one zone to another. "Now," Bennett says, "he's not scared when he gets to six-under. He's not afraid to go to seven."

People in Weir's camp think he's ready to win his first major. They feel it in his demeanor. "He's pretty quiet about the majors," Jim Weir says. "It burns him. He really wants to win a major. I can sense it going into the majors. He's never said anything to me about which one he would want to win more than the others, but majors are where you leave your legacy."

Jim has been acutely conscious of how much his brother wants to win a major since the 2000 British Open at the Old Course in St. Andrews. Jim, middle brother, Craig, Rich, the boys' father, and Weir's friend Adam Oates, who plays for the Anaheim Mighty Ducks hockey team, were having dinner one evening at the house in St. Andrews where they were staying. Weir was staying there too, and was at the table with them. He had shot 76 that day in the first round.

"Mike was quiet and excused himself and went to his room," Jim remembers. "He'd brought everybody over and felt bad that he hadn't done better."

Weir thought things over in his room. He likes to visualize how he plans to play a round, but golf being golf and humans being humans, things don't always work out as planned. This doesn't negate the value of a plan. Weir shot 69 the next day to easily make the cut.

Jim has watched Mike develop into a fighting athlete who has framed his game around trying to be the best he can be, no matter how long it takes. Weir has done so well that he's Canada's most popular golfer, and one of the country's best-known athletes. In March 2001, Jim took a two-year leave of absence from his work at a rubber plant, and has just taken a one-year extension. He runs <mikeweir.com>, and has also been helping develop Weir Golf Accessories. He and Weir will be in Toronto the Monday after the Masters to launch a line of golf products for Sears Canada. The line will include umbrellas, hats, travel bags, chipping nets, and other items, about twenty in all. They also plan to get into framed photographs and memorabilia, since Weir has been providing many happy memories for his enthusiastic supporters across Canada.

·ᐧ

In Augusta, the wind has switched around from directly out of the north to the northeast by mid-afternoon, but it's still cold and damp; the rain starts, continues, stops, and then the cycle repeats. The pattern isn't going anywhere, since the wedge remains, well, wedged over Augusta. Weir is in the middle of the back nine this Tuesday afternoon, hitting a few pitch shots from just left and short of the 14th green, while his instructor, Mike Wilson, watches from the right

Holding the
Nissan Trophy

Commentary: Mike Wilson with Matthew Rudy; Photographs: Stephen Szurlej

A balanced, athletic setup. Ball position and left-hand placement are great.

Mike turns his chin slightly to let his shoulders pass.

Flexible, coiled, and well behind the ball. Very nice.

More upright at address than he used to be. More arm extension.

He does a much better job maintaining his spine angle throughout.

Most players lose control this far past parallel. Mike doesn't.

Swinging in
perfect balance

A modest fist
pump, now a
Weir trademark

The young golfer,
swinging freely.

Mike always
knew how to putt.

Mike and his first coach, Huron Oaks pro, Steve Bennett

Mike wins the 1986 Canadian Juvenile Championship.

Mike could play hockey, too.

Brothers Jim, Mike, and Craig

A practice
round with Jack
Nicklaus during
the Memorial
Tournament

Matt Flick/ Courtesy MikeWeir.com

Courtesy Golf Digest

Much taller than before.
So conventional you almost
forget he's a left-hander.

Here, you can
see how powerful
his legs are.

Awesome plane, and look
how fast he's fired his
hips from the last frame.

I really like this frame –
he's fully released against
that firm right side.

Nice, controlled finish.
Spine angle is still retained.

With Bricia, Lili (left), and Elle

side. The hole is cut on the front right, and the ground between Weir and the hole is tilted, with the high side behind the hole. He throws the ball up in the air so that it lands thirty-five feet left of the hole and ten feet behind it. The ball takes the slope and rolls to the right, curves back toward him, nearly reversing direction, then stops eighteen inches from the hole. Some imagination.

On the par-five 15th hole, Weir hits a good drive down the left side, then a smooth five-wood to the back fringe of the green. Steve Bennett lights up another stogie. Asked how many he smokes while watching Weir, he says, "That depends on how he's playing. If he's playing bad, I'm chewing. I grind through them." No need to grind today, but then it's only a practice round. Weir makes his birdie on the 15th – not that it matters, except for building confidence, and that does matter. Then he and Jeff Maggert have a little fun on the par-three 16th hole in what has become a Masters tradition. They skip their shots across the water, as if they're skipping stones. Weir's ball flies low and slams against the water, skipping and then jumping onto the green, where it scoots forward on a direct line to the hole. The ball turns left as it catches a slope and finishes forty-five feet from the hole. Maggert's shot also skips across the water to the green. High-handicap golfers might be able to hit this shot, but they'd probably do so by accident.

Weir is smiling as he walks up to the green. He's had some fun, hitting an unconventional shot. "I'm a golfer," he likes to say. "That's all I am. A golfer." He enjoys trying a variety of shots, spending late nights on the golf course alone, moving the ball around at will. In this way he's still the boy at Huron Oaks, and Steve is still his tutor, reveling in the shots he can play.

Once, Weir and brother Jim visited the Sand Hills club in Mullen, Nebraska. This is one of those remote courses that appeal to many golfers: Royal County Down in Newcastle, Northern Ireland; Royal

Dornoch in the Scottish Highlands; Machrihanish on the small island of Argyll in western Scotland; the Highlands Links on Cape Breton Island in Nova Scotia; Bandon Dunes and Pacific Dunes in Bend, Oregon. There is a variety of ways to reach Sand Hills, which was designed by Bill Coore and two-time Masters champion Ben Crenshaw, an aficionado of course architecture. None is easy. The nearest airport is in North Platte, and it's eighty miles away. Course-architecture writer Brad Klein says that Sand Hills therefore has the longest entrance of any club in the world, and he could be right. Golfers who visit Sand Hills report feeling as if they're on another planet. That's how the Weir brothers felt.

"It was so windy," Jim recalls while watching his brother finish his practice round today. "There was no way to get the ball up in the air." Crenshaw and Coore believe golf should be played on the ground as well in the air, and they knew that the wind would blow hard and often at Sand Hills. So Weir did what was asked of him: he hit the ball low and used the ground.

"It was a neat experience," Weir recalls, "playing through the sand dunes with the wind howling. You'd hit low, little shots. It was a fun course to play. If you missed the fairway, you'd be hitting your next shot over these sand dunes that were fifteen feet high."

"Mike loved it," Jim says. "He had a big smile on his face. I think that's why he loves Augusta so much. You can use your imagination."

Weir wasn't using his imagination much in 2002, when he let himself be tied up by the mechanics of the game. He was trying too hard to perfect the imperfectible. Perfection is unattainable in golf except for brief intervals, and the attempt to find it can stifle the pleasure that the game can afford. Weir knew he had to return to having fun at golf. He had to return to playing Sand Hills golf.

He had done that for a brief time during the 2002 British Open at the Muirfield Golf Club in Gullane, Scotland. Weir and friends

and family were staying at a hotel overlooking the North Berwick ·
Golf Club down the road, and he decided one evening to head out
on his own, after everybody else had settled down for the night. Weir
carried a five-wood, five-iron, wedge, and putter under his arm, as
golfers here did in the 1800s before the golf bag came along. He
took three balls with him, as he had when he was a kid, pretending
one belonged to Jack Nicklaus, one to Lee Trevino, and one to him.
He played from the second hole behind the hotel until darkness,
which comes late to the northern sky, made it impossible for him to
see the ball. He lost his last ball there and came in.

"I was having a heyday out there," Weir says. "I loved it, just
loved it."

It's scrum time. Weir meets with the Canadian media after every
practice and tournament round these days. They're asking him
about his chances this week, since everybody is saying that the course
is so long that only long-hitters will be able to win. Weir isn't a short
hitter, but he ranked only number one hundred in driving distance
on the 2002 PGA Tour. Still, he won't buy the idea that only long-ball
hitters can win the Masters. What sort of chance would he have if he
did believe this notion? Why bother showing up, then? He'd be one
of those golfers Jack Nicklaus used to speak of at major championships. Nicklaus would listen to players complain about the course
difficulty, or the weather, or the high rough, and mentally cross
them off one at a time – "This guy can't win. This guy can't win" –
until he figured he had to beat maybe a half-dozen or so players.

"I think that a medium-length hitter still has a chance to win,"
Weir tells his interrogators. "Everything has to fall into place. You'll
have to hit it well."

The scrum over, Weir moves along. It's pouring again. The
spectators have gone into the cavernous golf shop to spend their

money on Masters caps, shirts, key chains, ball markers, drinking glasses, and memorabilia, while a few are perusing a display of Masters history across the way in an area set up specifically for the purpose. There's a segment on caddies at Augusta National. The display indicates that William "Cemetery" Poteet caddied for President Dwight D. Eisenhower when he played the course. Thor "Stovepipe" Nordwell caddied for Gene Sarazen during the Masters, Nathaniel "Ironman" Avery for Arnold Palmer, and Willie "Pappy" Stokes for Ben Hogan. This week Brennan "Butchie" Little is caddying for his friend Mike Weir. Little has no idea why, when, or where he was given the nickname.

There's also a panel commemorating Tiger Woods's win in the 2002 Masters, which includes his four scorecards. The Saturday card reads 34-32, but it's added up as 68; a player isn't responsible for adding up his score, only for verifying the score on the individual holes, which Woods did; he shot 66, the score that went into the books. Woods won the green jacket the next day. Hootie Johnson told him, "I think we're going to wear this jacket out putting it on you before your career is over." Woods had won his third Masters, and his second in a row. Nobody has won three in a row, which Woods is hoping to do this week, so it's only natural that his attempt to do so has been a big subject leading up to this year's tournament. He won his Tiger Slam of four majors in a row – the 2000 U.S. Open, the British Open, and the PGA Championship, and then the 2001 Masters. Why shouldn't he be able to win three consecutive Masters?

"When I've competed, even when I was a little boy," Woods is saying today during his pre-tournament press conference, "I was always intense. I've always had that. My biggest thing as a kid was to learn how to relax on the golf course. I used to get too into it. I used to get tired by the time I got to 13, or 14, because I was so focused on what I was doing. I've learned how to be more relaxed on a golf course. You can't be focused for five straight hours. You can't do it. I've learned to break it up. So I've always had that ability."

Weir is also learning how to relax on a course, and in majors. The more he talks about Augusta National, the more evident it becomes that, for him, relaxation has everything to do with grasping the essence of the course and with accepting and relishing its multi-faceted challenges.

"I enjoy the place," Weir says. "You look at the fairways and you think they're pretty generous. But if you don't leave yourself the best angle into the pin, it can still be difficult. Tradition would say that you don't have to drive it that well here, but I feel like you do. It's even more important since they've added a first cut of rough, almost a fringe, around the course. If you miss the fairway, it's more difficult to control your shots into the greens. Some people say that this means they've tricked up the course, but I don't see it that way. It's just another little element. If you miss the greens because of the rough, you have these little bump-and-run shots to play, or maybe you have to flop a shot. That's what appeals to me about Augusta National, all the varieties of shots you can play around the greens."

Weir speaks as a golfer who appreciates the nuances of an endlessly stimulating course. He speaks as a golfer who is ready to play another Masters, and to contend.

CHAPTER FIVE

Wednesday

April 9, 2003

What do you know? The rain has stopped, although it's still cold, and the ground remains squishy. Still, the forecast is for more rain, which neither the course nor the players and spectators want. But, for now anyway, there's golf, practice-round golf. Players are trying to get in their last inspections of the course and their own games before this afternoon's Par 3 Contest.

On the 1st tee, jittery players are much in evidence. The two most likely places for a golfer to feel skittish are on the 1st tee at the Old Course in St. Andrews and here. More deep breaths have surely been taken on the 1st tees at these courses than anywhere else. Jack Nicklaus himself was so wound up when he started the 1987 Masters as defending champion that he hit a low pull-hook through the trees on the left side of the hole and almost to the other side of the 9th fairway. He laughed later when recalling the state of his nervous system there – this was Jack Nicklaus, who had won six Masters, but still he felt fluttery. Nicklaus composed himself and drilled a long iron back through the trees and up to the front of the first green. He got his par.

The 1st tee at Augusta National sits on a high point of the course just beyond the clubhouse and the immense, usually populated lawn, with the famous oak tree standing sentinel in its midst. It's just a few feet from the practice green and only a few steps from the 9th and 18th greens, so things are normally congested around it during the Masters. As with many classic older courses, the 1st tee here is well integrated with the clubhouse and pro shop, which is but a short walk away. Augusta National is very much a walking course; players practice at the range on the other side of the clubhouse, walk over to the putting green after saying a few hellos on the way through or past the clubhouse – at least during practice rounds – and then amble over to the 1st tee. It's as easy as that.

This morning Nicklaus happens to be on the 1st tee at Augusta National, playing a practice round with three-time Masters champion Gary Player and Alejandro Larrazabal, the twenty-three-year-old Spanish amateur who was invited to the Masters as the current British Amateur champion. The Masters has always invited some of the top amateurs in the world. Bobby Jones played all his competitive golf as an amateur and, in the space of eight years, from 1923 to 1930, he won five United States Amateurs, four U.S. Opens, three British Opens, and one British Amateur. He won each of these events in one year, 1930, and retired from competition at the age of twenty-eight, following this exceptional feat that was once considered the Grand Slam. The Grand Slam changed in composition over the years, as professional golf assumed ascendancy over the amateur variety, so that it now comprises the four majors. No golfer has won the Grand Slam in one year, however it's been constituted, since Jones did so in 1930. He was golf's consummate amateur.

Jones is also Augusta National's President in Perpetuity, and is so designated at the top of the club's letterhead. Anybody who has studied the history of the club and the Masters is aware that, although he died in 1971, he remains a presence here, a strong presence. Herbert Warren Wind, the celebrated *New Yorker* essayist, wrote many wonderful passages about Jones, but perhaps his observation in a 1992 piece best sums up his feeling for the man: "Of the people I have met in sports – or out – Jones came the closest to being what we call a great man," he wrote. "Like Winston Churchill, he had the quality of being at the same time much larger than life and exceedingly human." Jones not only had a law degree, but also a science degree in mechanical engineering, and another degree in English literature. "There was very little he couldn't do if he set his mind to it," Wind declared.

Jones's influence is one main reason that, despite pressure over the years to reduce the number of amateur participants, Augusta National has held to his original intention to include them, at least for the most part. The list of amateurs invited this year includes the current U.S. Amateur champion (Ricky Barnes) and the runner-up (Hunter Mahan); the current British Amateur champion (Larrazabal); the current U.S. Amateur Public Links champion (Ryan Moore); and the current U.S. Mid-Amateur champion (George Zahringer). This is a much-reduced group from the 1935 Masters, when the first official eligibility criteria were issued. Past and present U.S. and British Amateur champions as well as members of the U.S. and U.K. Walker Cup teams were invited. Still, the Masters is the only major championship that, by its criteria for invitations, proclaims that amateur golf is an important part of the game. The U.S. Amateur champion and the runner-up are exempt from qualifying for the U.S. Open, but any other amateurs hoping to get into that championship must qualify by other means.

Amateurs often say that the first thought that passes through their minds when they qualify is that they're in the Masters. From that moment on, they find it difficult to avoid feeling anxious about their appearance on the 1st tee. The U.S. Amateur champion also has the honor of playing with the defending champion, which means that Barnes will tee it up in the first two rounds with Tiger Woods. He's been saying that his primary concern is his opening tee shot.

Larrazabal has golfing blood. He, his younger brother Pablo, and their mother, Elena, once represented Spain in the same international tournament. Pablo tried to qualify for last year's British Amateur, and when he didn't do so, he decided to caddie for his brother. Their father, Gustavo, has played for Venezuela in the World Amateur Team Championship, an important competition. Larrazabal's win in the British Amateur marked the third time a Spaniard had won that championship. José Maria Olazabal won it in 1984; he turned professional in 1985 and won the 1994 and 1999 Masters. Sergio Garcia won the 1998 British Amateur and, while he has yet to win his first major, is considered one of the game's finest young players. He's only twenty-three, yet he's playing his fifth Masters. Meanwhile, Seve Ballesteros, Masters champion in 1980 and 1983, must still be considered the finest Spanish golfer ever, notwithstanding a bewildering fall-off in recent years. He has not made the cut here since 1996. Ballesteros had a pianist's touch around the greens; it was said of him that he had *manos de plata* – hands of silver.

As sound a golfing pedigree as Larrazabal has, it's daunting for him to stand on the 1st tee with Nicklaus and Player. A huge crowd has gathered around the tee, and people from farther away have fixed their sights on the area through their binoculars. The spectators give Larrazabal a sustained and warm round of applause, but he's obviously nervous and hits a poor drive. He tries again, but this time he hits a pop fly. This is as clear a sign of 1st-tee jitters as golf offers; a pop-up shot indicates that a golfer's legs have turned to spaghetti. They don't work through the shot, so he flails at the ball with his arms. It's all too understandable, so nobody in the crowd snickers. After the three golfers have hit, they move off the 1st tee. Larrazabal can breathe again.

Not far away, on the other side of the clubhouse, Mike Weir is signing a few Masters flags on his way to the practice range. The flag shows the Masters logo – a flagstick with a yellow background depicting the shape of the United States, with a red flag marking Augusta's location in the country. No other place is indicated, as if to say, this is the only game in the U.S. this week. In fact, it's the only golf event that matters this week, anywhere.

Weir signs a few more autographs as he makes his way to the range, then gets to work. He'll pay no attention, nor need he pay any attention, to what is about to transpire a hundred yards away in the press center. There, at eleven, Hootie Johnson will conduct the club chairman's annual Wednesday press conference. This is probably the most anticipated such affair in Masters history, because of the escalating controversy about the club's men-only membership. The room was packed twenty minutes prior to the start of the conference. Augusta National members in their green jackets stream in; never have so many members attended the chairman's press conference. They wear the green jackets on the property so that outsiders can ask their help should they require it. They're here today – and they do stand out in their Masters green – to show solidarity with their club chairman and, implicitly, with Augusta National's stance on the membership issue.

The wall of green jackets around the interview room makes it look like the outfield fences at a ballpark, full of advertisements for products. One's eye can't help but be drawn to the jackets, which are so symbolic of the club. And the *club* rules here. Even the city's minor-league baseball team is called the Augusta Green Jackets. Writers sometimes refer to members by that term too, "those green jackets over at Augusta National." Television crews are at the ready to record Johnson's comments, while journalists have pens and paper at hand; not that they need them, because a company called ASAP Sports is here to record the conference. The company provides transcripts of each press conference for the media, which means that writers can quote participants accurately even if they don't attend. Still, there's more to language than words – there's body language, for one, and this press conference will likely be as much about tone and manner as about words. It's a circus. It's a sellout. It's Hootie Johnson versus Martha Burk, except that she's not here.

Johnson sits down on the small, elevated podium. He's between Will Nicholson, chairman of the Masters competition committee, on his right and William Payne, chairman of the media committee, on his left. "Welcome once again," Payne says to the media, and introduces Johnson, who reads a statement prior to taking questions.

"Over the last ten months everything that could possibly be said on the subject of Augusta National and its membership, everything that could be said, has been said. We are a . . . the fact is that we are a private club. A group getting together periodically for camaraderie, just as thousands of clubs and organizations do all over America. Just because we host a golf tournament, because some of our members are well known, should not cause us to be viewed differently. I have also stated that there may well come a time when we include women as members of our club, and that remains true. However, I want to emphasize that we have no timetable and our membership is very comfortable with our present status."

Johnson adds that he will now take questions about the Masters, and that he will have nothing more to add about the club's membership or related issues. That said, he then answers questions, more or less, about these matters for the rest of the press conference, without adding anything substantial to his statement. His position is clear. "Our private club does not discriminate," he says. "Single gender is an important fabric on the American scene." Men like to get together with men occasionally and women like to get together with women occasionally. There the matter rests, as far as he's concerned.

Most players in the Masters have danced around this issue. Tiger Woods has said that he'd like the club to invite women to join Augusta National, but that he's only one voice and he's not a club member and that he can't do anything about the matter except to state his opinion. Asked about Woods's view, Johnson's eyes flash: "I won't tell Tiger how to play golf if he doesn't tell us how to run our private club."

Weir, for his part, supports the idea of female members at Augusta National; it's not a big deal with him, and he addresses the subject publicly only when asked about his position. He also supports the right of a private club to invite whomever it wants as members. The Irish player Padraig Harrington, who will join Weir and Tom Watson in the first two rounds, has pointed out that, since the right of association is enshrined in U.S. law, perhaps the subject of memberships at private clubs should be addressed at the constitutional level. But Weir, like all players, isn't about to let the issue bother him this week. "It's not that stressful," he says when asked if the situation is affecting him. "This is a private club. It's their decision. It's between the two parties."

He's here to play the Masters. Over at the range, he's concerned with what he *can* control, or what he's working to control: the flight of his golf ball. It's the day before the Masters is supposed to start, and that's where his focus lies: on the tournament, not club or gender issues.

While Weir works on the range, a well-known figure stands near the 1st tee. He's carrying a briefcase, and he's willing to chat with anybody who approaches him. This is Doug Sanders, who missed the thirty-inch putt on the 72nd hole of the 1970 British Open at the Old Course that would have given him the championship. A native Georgian, Sanders has a special feeling for the Masters. He played in eleven between 1957 and 1973, making the cut ten times. His best Masters was in 1966, when he finished fourth. Asked how often he thinks about that missed putt at the British Open on golf's most famous last green, his stock answer is, "Every day."

Sanders is seventy. He won eighteen tournaments on the PGA Tour, his first being the 1956 Canadian Open, when he was still an amateur. He was always known for the flamboyant clothes he wore – orange or mauve shoes to go with matching slacks. But he also had plenty of game, notwithstanding one of the shortest backswings of any top-class player; his follow-through wasn't much longer than his backswing, so that it was said that he could swing in a telephone booth. Sanders attributed the brevity of his swing to the narrow fairways at the course in his birthplace of Cedartown, Georgia, where he learned the game, and to the fact that golf balls were in short supply then. Something in him suggested that a shorter swing had less margin of error.

Sanders has something to say about what it takes to win a major. He came so close so often. He lost the PGA Championship by a shot, the U.S. Open by a shot, and two British Opens by a shot.

"The difference between playing in a major and in a regular tour event is the difference between going to an Academy Award–winning movie or to an average movie," Sanders says. "There's such a buildup. There's more people, more press, and the tournament is always played on a championship course. If you come in playing well, then your good play should show. But you won't find your game at a major. You can know on the 1st tee if you're fighting something. You can't get away with errors at a major. Your flaws will show. That's so true here. If you're putting is off just a little, you're in trouble, just to take one part of the game. The greens are so fast that you drop a coin and it slides three feet before you can pick it up."

Sanders concludes with this observation: "A winner makes a commitment. A loser makes a promise." The comment applies to Weir. He committed himself long ago to becoming the best golfer he could, and has let nothing stand in his way. The long-term view he's taken has brought him to the Masters this week as one of the elite players in the world. Sure, he'd like to hang out with his family and friends, but his commitment requires giving himself every chance of playing well. This isn't a week for socializing. It's a week for trying to win the Masters.

Weir works for a while longer on the range, and then gets out on the course for nine holes. This morning was hardly pleasant, but at least the skies weren't leaden, though they're getting that way, and rain can't be far away. Still, golf isn't played under a dome, so Weir might as well practice as much as he can – or decides is necessary. He'll play the Par 3 Contest this afternoon, which will provide him with some short-game practice. But the event is more entertainment for the spectators and fun for the players than it is serious stuff. The club takes this jovial event seriously enough that it posts a tentative listing of groups. According to this, Weir will play at 3:36 with Arnold Palmer and Vijay Singh. Palmer has those four Masters green jackets, while Singh has one, for winning the 2000 Masters.

David Owen makes clear in *The Making of the Masters* that Clifford Roberts in particular wanted a short course to supplement the main course, so designer Alister MacKenzie drew up plans for what he termed an "approach and putt" nine-hole course. Bobby Jones walked the proposed site in 1932, but wasn't enthusiastic about the idea. The club also didn't have the money to pay for the little course; in fact, Augusta National, which opened in 1933, had trouble attracting members in its early days. MacKenzie maintained his interest in a short course, however, and came up with plans for an eighteen-hole, 2,460-yard version. But it too failed to be built, and there the matter rested until twenty-five years later. That was when the architect George W. Cobb's design for a Par 3 course was implemented, along with input from Roberts. Roberts referred to the Par 3 course as "my pet project."

Tom Fazio, the architect who has worked closely with Augusta National on modifications to the main course for some twenty years, added two holes to the Par 3 course. This project was required to create more room, so that spectators could use the original 1st and 2nd holes as viewing stations during the Par 3 Contest; the two new holes became the current 8th and 9th holes.

The contest is a popular event. A party atmosphere prevails, because of the condensed space in which the holes are situated and their sheer beauty. The nine holes add up to 1,060 yards, and the landscape is a garden, really, meandering around two ponds. Roars leap across the hills and ponds regularly as players hit shots that spin on the small greens, and it's a rare Wednesday afternoon when the golfers don't make a few holes-in-one. Fifty have been made since the Par 3 Contest started in 1960, and a record five were made last year. Sam Snead won the first Par 3 Contest with a four-under-par 27. He didn't win the Masters that year; nobody who has won the Par 3 Contest has gone on to win the Masters the same year, so the idea of a jinx has developed. Players in contention to win the Par 3 Contest sometimes intentionally hit their shots into the water on the last hole so that they won't have to deal with the mental burden of the jinx. Snead had won the 1949, 1952, and 1954 Masters already, so by 1960 he already had a good supply of green jackets. Jack Nicklaus never did win the Par 3 Contest. This did not trouble him.

As for Roberts, his objective was to separate the Masters from any other tournament, and the course from any other course. He was always coming up with ideas to accomplish these goals, and the Par 3 Contest was an ideal way to help meet them. The contest, he wrote in 1959, the year before the first one was held, "can be quite a feather in the cap of the Masters Tournament. I say this because no other club holding a tournament could duplicate what I am proposing we do at Augusta. So far as I know, no other club has a Par 3 layout and, even if they do, I am sure they don't have anything to compare with ours."

But today the Par 3 course doesn't have its usual festive atmosphere, because it's too soggy underfoot and too gray above. Another outburst of rain has arrived. Players have no chance of keeping dry, no matter how resistant to the elements their rain gear is. Weir's wearing a jacket that doesn't provide the waterproofing he could get from one that's thicker, but then he wouldn't be able to swing as freely as he likes. The trade-off is elementary: choose the lighter material and stay under the umbrella as much as possible. Weir's brother Jim is caddying for him during the Par 3 Contest, and they're both trying hard to have a good time. Where's Palmer? Weir is playing with Singh, but not with Palmer. The list did say that the groups were "tentative." Jeff Maggert is the third member of this group. It's the second time Weir has played with Maggert this week.

Weir hits a shot across one of the ponds and onto the 4th green, and it finishes eight feet from the hole. He makes the putt for birdie. A few holes later he has a twenty-footer for another birdie. Jim hands him his putter, but Weir says, "What am I supposed to do with this?" Water has pooled between his ball and the hole. He chips the ball through the water, and holes that. Skip, skip, and in. Enough. This is a contest, not the tournament, so the threesome decides it's time to come in and get dry.

In a moment Weir is talking about a few tournament-related matters. The potential impact of the constant rain on the course concerns him the most. If it keeps raining so hard – and there's every indication that there's more to come – Weir wonders if the tournament committee will elect to play what's called "lift, clean, and place." Under this policy a player who hits his ball in the fairway can pick it up, clean it, and replace it. Golf balls will accumulate mud in these gooey conditions. It's not easy to predict how a ball will fly when that's happened.

"They haven't been able to get the mowers on the course," Weir says, referring to the wet conditions. The grass is growing longer than the Masters people want it, which means that the ball won't sit down on top of the fairway but will, instead, settle into the turf. Weir mentions the possibility that golfers will face flier lies, which happen when the ball snuggles into the grass rather than rests on top of it. Blades of grass intervene between the clubface and the ball at impact, so not as many grooves on the clubface contact the ball, which spins less and flies farther. Again, players lose control. There's all this to contend with, and mud too.

It would be shocking, though, if Augusta National were to allow the players to lift, clean, and place. Nicklaus calls this "lift, clean, and cheat." The Masters is a major, and nobody can recall when lift, clean, and place was used in a major. But conditions are getting ugly. Weir and every golfer will have to deal with whatever they face.

"I feel good," Weir says, however. "I got some good work in today. I wasn't clicking so well yesterday, but was better today."

The course is playing exceptionally long because of the rain. It's 7,290 yards on the scorecard, but playing more like 8,000 yards, because golf balls aren't rolling forward when they hit ground. They might as well be landing in vats of molasses as on fairways, even those as manicured and shaved as Augusta National's. The 465-yard 18th hole is playing particularly long. Here the golfer is asked to hit his drive down a narrow chute between stands of tall pines. Weir hit a perfect drive during his practice session today, but still had 225 yards uphill to the green and into the wind. The shot played 250 yards. Weir said to Brennan, "I love it." His objective for the week? Find a way to get the job done.

Weir's attitude is right where it should be. He seems at ease, perhaps because he's already won twice this year. He's a little surprised that the U.S. and international media aren't giving him more attention this week, given that he's ranked tenth in the world and is third on the PGA Tour's money list. The media committee hasn't scheduled him for a pre-tournament press conference, and the Las Vegas bookmakers have him at 40-1.

Not that Weir minds. He's likely to use these minor slights as motivation. That's the way he is. Other people can see it, too. The golf world knows his stature in the game, even if the bookmakers and some golf media don't.

"How about Weirsy?" Joe Moses, the senior director of global marketing for the equipment company TaylorMade Golf, asks in the grillroom. He's using the name by which many of Weir's friends know him, although his family never calls him Weirsy. "Good for

Canada. I talked to him today. He's really focused. If he gets that flat stick going, watch out," Moses adds.

Weir has endorsed TaylorMade since the summer of 2001, although he didn't put their irons into play until later in the year. The company produced three versions of irons before he felt confident enough to use in competition. It's not as if TaylorMade had clubs ready to go for him. It had never made a set of irons from scratch for a left-handed golfer, and Weir worked closely with the designers so that they would come up with what he felt he needed. He listened to their experts and they listened to him. Each set of irons cost about fifty thousand dollars to make, but the company didn't want him using them until he was 100-per-cent satisfied. Weir marked up the works-in-progress as if he were an engineer, or a draftsman, or a violin maker. His clubs are his tools, and he needs to feel sure that they'll respond properly. Having worked so assiduously to improve and refine his swing, he wants equally reliable clubs. His upcoming new line of golf accessories doesn't include clubs, but he's been enjoying learning about equipment, and works as hard at understanding them as he does his swing.

Anybody who examined his clubs in various stages of development would see just how precision-oriented Weir is. The folks at TaylorMade in Carlsbad, California, just north of San Diego, keep some examples in the shop. There's a five-iron clubhead that Weir marked in red, with lines, and one word, "radius." He wants the radius of the sole of the club increased; he has also marked the date, 10/26/01. On a six-iron he has written "create edge" on the hosel, the point where the shaft meets the head. On a three-iron he has drawn a circle at the hosel, and written one simple word, "meat." He wants a little more thickness there. On an eight-iron he has instructed the designers to bring the sole in one millimeter, and to add bounce.

Weir's level of interest in how his clubs are designed isn't unusual among tour pros, but he's not yet in the Nick Price or Arnold Palmer category. Price has a workshop in his home where he likes to change shafts and grips, grind away at his irons, take a little bounce off one club here, or add some there. Arnold Palmer is even more of a club maven. He has twelve thousand clubs in his workshop at the Latrobe Country Club in Latrobe, Pennsylvania, the club where he grew up and where his father, Deacon, was the super-intendent; Palmer owns the club now. He'll sometimes walk off the tee during a casual round, take an X-Acto knife out of his pocket, and remove the grip of a golf club. He enjoys working with clubs. Weir doesn't work on his own clubs, but he involves himself in their design and is learning more about them. It's a long way from the first set of Kroydon irons his father bought him for fifty dollars.

Weir's done for the day, and heads for the locker room. Starting times have been pushed back a half-hour tomorrow to allow the grounds crew to have as much time as possible to work on the course. Weir will now play at 10:41 with Watson, who won the 1977 and 1981 Masters, and Padraig Harrington, who has won five European Tour events. He's played three Masters, the same as Weir. Harrington's best finish was last year, when he tied for fifth, six shots behind Tiger Woods.

While Weir is drying off in the locker room, Rich Gordin, his mental coach, waits for him. There's no questioning the importance of the mental side of golf at any level, but especially with tour pro-fessionals. Any golfer who reaches the PGA Tour has the skills to hit quality golf shots most of the time, but what frequently separates winners from losers is that proverbial six-inch space from one ear to the other: their minds. The literature on the psychology of golf goes back centuries. Bobby Jones wrote, "The most important part of preparing for a tournament is to condition oneself mentally and physically so that it will be possible to get the most out of what game one possesses." It's revealing that Jones placed the word "mentally" before "physically." Weir works with Gordin to fulfill Jones's dictum. He means to get the most out of the game he possesses.

Gordin, fifty-two, tall and slender, was born in Columbus, Ohio, and got his Ph.D. in Education in 1981 from the University of Utah, specializing in physical education and sport psychology. A professor of physical education and an adjunct professor of psychology at Utah State University in Salt Lake City, he has written publications and papers that include: "How to Manage Stress and Avoid Burnout," in *American Fencing*; "Concentration Skills for Race Walkers," in the *USA Track & Field Newsletter*; "Psychological Skill Development Leading to Peak Performance," in *Track & Field Quarterly*; and "The Shaping of the Athlete: From Selection to Competition," presented in 1991 at the First World Congress on Mental Training, in Sweden.

Gordin arrived in Augusta last night and is staying with his parents. His father, who was a university golf coach, is an authority on Bobby Jones, having written his doctoral dissertation on him. Gordin's parents have been coming to the Masters since 1966, and Gordin came to his first Masters in 1990. He was working with some golfers by then, but not with anybody in the tournament.

Gordin's first sport was football, which he played in college. He knew that football was a physical game, but believed it also had a mental dimension. He decided to pursue the psychology of sport and performance through further studies, eventually acquiring his doctoral degree. Gordin studies the psychological response of athletes to competition and the use of altered states of consciousness to facilitate improvement in performance. He's been working with Weir since January 1997, when Weir sought him out because of his difficulties in getting through qualifying school. He had tried five times and failed every year to make it through to the PGA Tour. Weir had already been tightening up his swing under Mike Wilson's guidance for more than a year, and was making progress, so, in the interest of taking a comprehensive approach to his development, he decided to see whether he could learn something from Gordin.

Weir had heard about Gordin from BYU's golf coach, Karl Tucker. Tucker and Gordin's father were colleagues, and Weir was aware that Gordin had worked with Olympic athletes in track and field, fencing, gymnastics, and skiing. When they met in Gordin's office and chatted about golf, Weir was struck immediately by Gordin's calmness, and how well he understood the demands of tournament golf. "He really knew the mentality of a tournament player," Weir says. "That's what hit me the first time we met. He just really understood the game so well." It also didn't hurt that Gordin had some golf memorabilia in his office.

It wasn't long before Weir saw the benefits of working with both Wilson and Gordin. He led the Payless Open in Victoria, British Columbia, on the Canadian Tour in May 1997 after three rounds, but shot 73 to tie for eighth place. He then shot a six-under-par 65 to open the BC TEL Pacific Open in Vancouver in early June to take the lead. "I don't think the public understands how difficult it is to win," Weir, who hadn't won since the Canadian Tour's 1993 Tournament Players Championship, said at the Mayfair Lakes course there. "It's tough to deal with sometimes."

Weir continued to play well at Mayfair Lakes, and came to the par-five, 523-yard last hole tied for the lead with U.S. player Ken Duke. He hit a huge drive and had 189 yards to the green, all over water. He also had two or three minutes to consider the shot while the group ahead finished. He couldn't forget the shot that he put into the water on the last hole at the Greater Vancouver Open the previous summer, but that was okay. He wasn't afraid of his thoughts, nor was he, thanks to Gordin, anxious about the shot. His swing had improved, so he could trust it in this situation, and he had also learned, with Gordin's help, to make a putt just a putt, a shot just a shot. It wasn't by accident that he looked forward to the shot he was about to play, with the tournament on the line. Gordin had helped him with breathing exercises to calm himself down. He had learned not to hit a shot until he was absolutely ready to hit it, which meant until he saw the shot clearly in his mind's eye. Sometimes he would not take his hand off the clubhead as it sat in his bag until he saw the shot vividly, until he had the right picture.

"This is what it's all about," Weir told his caddie there on the final fairway at Mayfair Lakes. "This is why I practice and work as hard as I do."

His seven-iron shot came off perfectly, and finished thirty feet from the hole. Duke had pushed his tee shot, and couldn't go for the green, so laid up short of the water. His third shot finished fifteen feet from the hole on the back fringe of the green. Weir putted up close to the hole, after which Duke missed his birdie putt. Weir tapped in for the win, and later won the Canadian Masters at the Heron Point club in Hamilton, Ontario, by eight shots. Wilson was with him that week. "I had one swing thought all week, to wind and unwind my upper body," Weir said there. "Other than that, I thought only of my target, and never varied in my game plan from the first hole through the last."

"It's amazing how much longer I'm hitting the ball now, twenty-five to thirty yards longer," Weir said while he played that summer of 1997. "But my swing seems easier. It's a lot tighter. There's a big difference from when I started working on my swing."

Weir played in the German Open two weeks after his Canadian Tour win in Vancouver, thanks to an invitation that IMG secured for him. "Mike wanted to be a world player, and so we tried to get him into tournaments around the world," IMG Canada's senior vice-president and managing director, Kevin Albrecht, remembers. Weir shot 65 to tie for the first-round lead, and finished twentieth. In August he tried to qualify for the Buick Open, a PGA Tour event in Grand Blanc, Michigan, an hour across the border from Brights Grove. He shot 68 to miss a playoff to get into the tournament by a shot, and then decided to play that week in the Canadian Professional Golfers' Association Championship at the Mandarin Golf and Country Club just northeast of Toronto. Stan Leonard, Al Balding, George Knudson, and Moe Norman had all won this tournament, and Weir wanted to add his name to the trophy for the national championship. His priority was getting to the PGA Tour, but that didn't mean he lacked enthusiasm when he drove to the Mandarin course after not qualifying for the Buick.

As things turned out, Weir found himself in a playoff for the title with American golfer Guy Hill. He pulled his second shot on the par-five last hole into a hazard, and up against a pipe just to the right of the green and down a hill. He didn't get relief from the pipe, because his ball was in the hazard, and he could play a shot only by turning the head of his club and hitting the ball right-handed. He moved the ball only a few feet, chipped up to within six feet of the hole, but missed the par putt. Hill parred the hole and won the championship. Still, Weir had capped off a strong season on the Canadian Tour. He led the money list with $80,696, nearly twice as much as Ray Freeman in second place. He also won another $25,000 for leading the Tour's Order of Merit, a goal of his since the start of the season.

Weir soon played in the Bell Canadian Open, in early September at the Royal Montreal Golf Club, where he shot 75-79 to miss the cut.

He was in good company, for this was where Tiger Woods missed his first cut as a professional, but that didn't make Weir feel any better, because he thought he would play well at Royal Montreal's Blue course, a difficult, tree-lined layout with small, well-protected greens. Nevertheless, he looked back at what he had accomplished during 1997 so that he could look forward to what he hoped to accomplish in the PGA Tour's qualifying school. That's where he was headed, for the sixth time.

Weir went to the school in the fall of 1997 with more confidence than he had felt in any of the five times he'd played the grueling competition. He tied for first in the opening stage and was second in the next stage. He then went to Kiawah Island in South Carolina with Rick Gibson, a talented Canadian professional who was living in Manila. There they played in the World Cup, a competition for teams of two professionals from countries around the world. It had started as the Canada Cup in 1953, when Canadian industrialist John Jay Hopkins had the idea for a tournament that, he hoped, would promote international goodwill through golf. Weir and Gibson hit the ball well in the tournament but didn't make enough birdie putts to contend, and tied for eleventh place. "I don't think I've played with a better Canadian player the last three years," Gibson said. "Mike is ready for the PGA Tour."

Weir proved Gibson right at the final, six-round stage of qualifying school in December 1997 at the Grenelefe Golf and Tennis Club in Haines City, Florida. Ill with the flu prior to the opening round, he bogeyed the first three holes, but steadied himself to shoot one-under-par 71, and then shot 68-69-72-71 to put himself in good shape with one round to play. The low thirty-five golfers and those tied for thirty-fifth place would qualify for the 1998 PGA Tour. Weir's friend Dan Keogh, who had played the Canadian Tour and roomed there with Brennan Little, was caddying for him. Bricia was at home in Draper, Utah, waiting to give birth to their first child, Elle. The baby was due on New Year's Eve.

"We had been holding off on having a child," Bricia says, "but after the fifth time at qualifying school I told Mike, 'Honey, I know it's going to happen for you, but I'm not going to put my life on hold. Let's go for it.'"

Things didn't start in a promising manner in the final round of qualifying school, when Weir three-putted twice on the early holes. But he kept making a putt just a putt, a shot just a shot, and holed an important par-saver from twelve feet on the 11th hole. He missed putts for birdies on the next two holes, and then made a forty-footer for birdie on the 14th hole. His putter became his friend at that point, and he holed from twelve feet on the 15th to save par again. At the 16th, a 204-yard par-three, the hole was cut on the left side of the green near a bunker. Weir's tee shot carried the bunker, landed on the edge of the green, and rolled within a couple of inches of the hole. "How many guys could do that?" Keogh asks now. A golfer couldn't hit a more timely shot, and the tap-in birdie put him in position to qualify. It was a shot that he will always remember, for its timeliness and because the birdie allowed him to play the last two holes conservatively. He parred both, and was so locked into what he was doing that he wasn't sure whether he had qualified. He hadn't looked at a leaderboard all day, or all week for that matter. Weir had, with Gordin's wise counsel, forged a competitive attitude that allowed him to get the most out of the game he possessed – the prescription for success that Bobby Jones had described.

The Golf Channel carried the final round of that 1997 qualifying school, and Donna Caponi, one of its analysts, was behind the 18th green to interview Weir after he shot 71 and signed his scorecard. Weir knew he had finally qualified for the PGA Tour when he saw her approach him. All day he had tried to minimize the pressure, but it was there nonetheless. He couldn't ignore the fact that the direction his whole 1998 season would take depended on how he performed.

Weir was in tears as he spoke with Caponi; she was also choked up. "I held it together," he told her. "It means a great deal to qualify. I really improved this year and I just tried to stay within myself today, and to play the game I knew that I could play." Weir went on to say hello to Bricia and to his friends and family in Canada.

At home in Utah, Bricia had been watching. When the phone rang there, she picked it up with excitement, thinking it was her husband. A reporter was on the line. "It's awesome," she said. "I'm glad that Mike's wanting it so badly didn't get in his way."

Later that evening, Weir spoke from his car after leaving Grenelefe. He was heading – finally – for the PGA Tour. More than anything, he felt relief.

"It was just a gut check all day," he said. "I can't even imagine a major championship being tougher than this. It's so hard to explain. I didn't think it would be like this. At least when you're playing a major or any normal tournament, you have the next week. Here it's your whole year on the line."

Weir went to the PGA Tour's headquarters in Ponte Vedra Beach, Florida, where he attended an information session for rookies. The tour's commissioner, Tim Finchem, met him for the first time and had a brief conversation with him. "I thought, 'This guy belongs on the PGA Tour,'" Finchem recalled later.

Bricia gave birth to Elle on December 19. Weir didn't want to leave the house, he was so happy to be with his wife and new daughter. "I feel that it was lucky for us that I got pregnant," Bricia says, "because it was then that Mike got through qualifying school."

So much had changed for Weir on the inside and the outside. Gordin had helped him see that, if a shot was just a shot, well, a round was just a round and a tournament was just a tournament. Weir had kept playing through the five times he hadn't made the PGA Tour at qualifying school, and he needed to understand that there was more to his identity than just being a golfer. The fact that he was going to be a father eased his mind during qualifying school this time, and somehow he began to appreciate that the way he thought about himself didn't have to depend on how he played. Too often he took a good day on the course to mean that he was a decent fellow. Just as frequently, he concluded after a bad day that he was all but useless. Looking back while at home with his wife and daughter, he saw how much his quest for improvement had consumed him. It was, perhaps, easier to see this now that he would be playing on the PGA Tour, but his new feeling was no less real for that. Meanwhile, his first season as a card-carrying PGA Tour member would begin in late January 1998. He'd be teeing it up in the storied AT&T National Pro-Am in Pebble Beach, California.

Now, at Augusta National, the day before the Masters is to begin, Gordin remembers the young man who walked into his office. "I think that Mike felt that he wanted to investigate the mental side of the game and invest some effort in it. We struck it off famously. It's hard to put your finger on it, but Mike had it. I listened to him a lot, and I guess he liked what I had to say. I come from an educational model where we solve problems. It's not a problem model. It's a solution model. The important thing was that I could tell that Mike was a disciplined athlete. I can teach what I know to people, but it doesn't work unless they take it with them."

Gordin and Weir like to review Weir's rounds so that they can learn from them and make necessary changes. They examine what makes him feel good and what bothers him. He strives for, and often achieves, the calmness that he felt upon first meeting Gordin, while their comfort with one another is apparent as they leave the club now for the day and return to Weir's hotel. They'll review things during the drive, and, should they find any problems, they'll come up with solutions.

The rain continues to saturate Augusta National. In the press center, Nicklaus is asked about Tiger Woods, and says, "I think he's focusing on how he wants to be the best that there ever was. I want to be the first one there to shake his hand when he breaks my record. Hopefully I'll live that long. And I'll do that."

The course is getting longer and longer the more rain it receives. Tomorrow's forecast for the first round of the tournament calls for showers with a garnish of isolated thunderstorms; the chance of rain is nearly 100 per cent, and the high will be in the low fifties. Augusta in April is not supposed to be like this. What's with this persistent weather wedge?

CHAPTER SIX

Thursday

April 10, 2003

A golf tournament is one of sport's longest events, even when the weather cooperates. It takes place over four days, Thursday through Sunday. This week seems longer, since there won't be any golf today. The announcement comes at 10:50 that the first round has been washed out, since it's still raining, it's still cold, and the course is unplayable in spots. For warmth, look north. It's sixty-eight degrees in Fargo, North Dakota, and it's reached that mark in Winnipeg this week; meanwhile, the forecast high today in Augusta is forty-eight degrees, and it's the first time since 1983 that a tournament round has been postponed. "That's astounding," says a marshal working the spectator stand behind the practice range. "There's obviously more water out there than I think." Somebody says that lightning is predicted. The Masters, a high-pressure tournament, could use some high pressure in its forecast. So far it's been nothing but low-pressure systems; one cleared out yesterday, but it was followed by another band that moved in from the south with heavy rain. Perversely, some light appears in the sky every so often. There's broken cloud over Augusta, but the miserable weather hasn't broken.

Still, the stands behind the range are full. Players are gathering in small groups as they get the bad news. Nobody, least of all the golfers, wants to wait another day before the tournament starts; they've been here for three days already, and some longer. Since Weir got in on Sunday, he has played only one full round and another nine holes, and then those few holes in the Par 3 Contest. Otherwise, it's been a waiting game. On his way to the course, he learns that play has been called off, but continues to the club so that he can, perhaps, hit some balls and work on his short game.

Rules official Mark Russell is chatting on the range with PGA Tour players Brad Faxon and Fred Couples, and teachers Butch Harmon and Jim McLean, while Stuart Appleby, the fine Australian player, is talking with Ben Crenshaw, the 1984 and 1995 Masters champion. Somebody says to nobody in particular, while players absent-mindedly hit balls, dazed by what they've just learned, "This is all the golf you'll see today." Many people are disappointed because this is the only day they can attend the Masters. John Dempsey, the dean at Sandhills Community College four hours away in Pinehurst, North Carolina, drove in this morning with a friend. They'll turn right around and drive back. Long drive. Long day.

On a day like this the media swarm quickly around players, needing comments to fill their stories and broadcasts. Rocco Mediate is in one scrum in front of the clubhouse. He's surprised that tournament officials decided not to play today. "I can't believe it. It must be horrible out there." The subject of lift, clean, and place comes up. Are things so bad out there that the policy will be in force when play does begin? He's sure it won't.

"It's a major," Mediate says. "At other tournaments we'd play lift, clean, and place. But this is a major. You've gotta play it down. If there's mud, you have to play it like that. If we played lift, clean, and place here, there would always be an asterisk after the winner's name."

It's one of golf's charms – sort of – that players have to handle inclement weather and less-than-ideal conditions. The fundamental rule is that golfers should play the ball as it lies and the course as they find it. This notion goes back centuries, to when golfers slapped a ball around a field toward a target, and on courses that were little more than farmland. In a back-to-the-past sort of movement, there's a development nowadays called "pasture golf," in which some people, in reaction to the increasing manipulation of the ground to create unblemished surfaces, are playing in undisturbed environments. Pasture courses are developing more of a following than some people might imagine. Augusta National is at the opposite end of the spectrum. It's not pasture golf, it's perfect golf. It's perfect, as in manicured and maintained as if were a Rolls-Royce. This is the Masters. It's not the Pasture Golf Championship. The club's maintenance policies are sophisticated, too. A company called Sub Air, Inc., based nearby, just across the state line in Aiken, South Carolina, has provided Augusta National with a system underneath every green that sucks out moisture. As drenched as the greens are, this system can dry them out in four hours. The Sub-Air system is also being used this year to draw water away from the 1st, 8th, 9th, and 11th fairways. But even Augusta National, with these moisture-sucking ventilation systems, is at the mercy of the severe conditions, and the weather is winning so far this week.

No technological marvel can gulp mud off a ball when it bites into a soft fairway. This being the case, and this being the Masters, players will have to deal with mudballs. An aerodynamics of mudball golf applies. The ball will hook if the mud is on the right of the ball. It will slice if the mud is on the left. Ernie Els, the 1994 and 1997 U.S. Open champion, points out that the influence mud has on the way a ball flies increases as the club a golfer is using gets longer, and that no matter how much mud a ball picks up, it's hard to trust oneself. The tendency is to play a very conservative shot, well away from trouble. He hit a shot at the flag once on the 10th hole here, but the mud on the ball made it dive left into a bush. He'll be laying up on the par-five 13th and 15th holes short of the creek and pond if there's mud on his ball.

"It will be a slugfest out there tomorrow," Els says as he sits beside his locker. "A sloppyfest. It's also going to be the ultimate test in endurance. It will all happen out there tomorrow. This is one of the most demanding courses we walk all year. It's a test of endurance and stamina. It will be a battle of concentration and staying in the moment. You want to be under thirty-five years old." Els is thirty-three.

It's also going to be an endurance test tomorrow because tournament officials plan to have the golfers out at eight in the morning, and then have them play all day and as near to darkness as possible. Not all the players will finish both the first and second rounds tomorrow, but they should get enough golf in so that, come Saturday night, the tournament will be on schedule. That will leave a conventional eighteen-hole Sunday.

Tour golfers are used to these weather-related delays. The smart ones accept them without complaint. It helps to be fit, too. "Guys in sketchy shape will have trouble," Jerry Kelly says as he contemplates what he will do for the rest of today. "But not many guys out here are in sketchy shape." The days of hanging around bars are long gone from the tour; the golfers take part in workout regimens, not drinking sessions. The ruling players on both the men's and women's tours put themselves through strenuous workouts, and players either follow or fall back. Tiger Woods is super-strong. Annika Sorenstam, the top player in women's golf, began a workout program in November 2000 that was so intense one would have thought she was training for a triathlon, not for golf. Sorenstam hired a fellow who holds a fourth-degree black belt in karate. She was soon punching and kicking, and also swimming, doing yoga, cycling, weightlifting, throwing a medicine ball, and doing, oh, a thousand stomach crunches a day. Sorenstam had won five LPGA Tour events in 2000 before starting her high-intensity workouts. She shot 59 early in the 2001 season, won three consecutive tournaments, and eight all told that year, and then won eleven LPGA Tour events in 2002. Lorie Kane, Canada's top LPGA Tour player, and a good friend of Sorenstam's, was in position after three rounds to contend in the Nabisco Championship in March 2001, but shot 77 the last day as Sorenstam won. She decided then to put herself on a workout program.

"As prepared as I thought I was," Kane said then, "I got tired, and when we've played a lot of golf, my legs tend to go. I've never trained for golf, but I'm going to get on a fitness program. We all want to be number one, but the bar is being raised. Annika is a finely tuned machine."

Weir works out every day when he's not playing in a tournament, and even then he does some stretching and core strength work. He carries an exercise ball with him on the road, likes to run to keep his legs in shape, and works strenuously on his core, or stomach, muscles, which are major sources of strength and stability. The golf swing involves a lot of turning and torquing around the spine, so players have to maintain their flexibility.

Weir's cardiovascular work promotes endurance, and he also incorporates light weights in his workouts. At his home gym he likes to kid his brother Jim when he visits. "You think you're in shape?

Come on down here and I'll show you what a tough workout is."
Weir has always worked out, which for him means that he's simply
covering all the bases, as he says. His fitness consultant now is Janet
Alexander, who works with an organization called Paul Chek
Seminars, in Encinitas, California. The "Chek" works as a handy
near-acronym for Corrective High Performance Exercise Physiology.
Weir started working with Alexander after his instructor, Mike
Wilson, went to a seminar where she spoke. He liked what she had
to say and introduced Weir to her. Wilson also took the golf-
certification program that the organization offers.

"She's a biomechanics expert and she knows how to assess a
person's physical limitations," Weir says. "She knows how the body
moves, and she's also a flexibility and strength coach. We started first
with flexibility. I was very tight in my back and my hips and had to
get those opened up. She's really helped my posture and helped
me get stronger and achieve the positions in the swing that I wanted
to get to. I wanted a more stable and more powerful swing, which is
what you need today. It's the way the game is headed."

When Weir started on the PGA Tour in 1998, he was already well
aware of the need to get stronger. He was trying to build a swing that
had the fewest possible moving parts, while creating the most
control and speed. He had suffered some back problems in college,
which forced him to sit out one semester's golf. He practiced some
stretches that helped him overcome these problems, and later he
decided to focus on more golf-specific exercises. The path he was on
eventually took him to Janet Alexander, and he's gotten stronger
and stronger, which is one reason his swing has been getting more
efficient and powerful.

In the month between qualifying school and the beginning of Weir's 1998 PGA Tour rookie season, he had played only one round of golf. He wasn't too concerned about that, since he'd won three college tournaments after his winter break. Weir was used to taking time off after the golf season; that's what Canadians who aren't retired and living in Palm Springs or Florida do. Meanwhile, he didn't play eighteen holes during his first round at the AT&T National Pro-Am, because it was called off when bad weather set in. Weir started the tournament at the difficult Spyglass Hill Golf Club, and shot even-par 36. His PGA Tour career was under way. "I have a whole year to look forward to," he said then, "and am looking at the time it took me to get here as a blessing in disguise." This attitude was typical of Weir, always taking a positive view of what has transpired.

As the end of the 1998 season approached, he was still able to maintain that positive attitude, although he had missed the cut in fourteen of the twenty-six tournaments he had played coming into the final event, the Walt Disney World Classic in Orlando. His best finish had been a tie for fifth in the Greater Vancouver Open, where he bogeyed two of the last three holes and made $65,000. The next week he planned to play in the Greater Milwaukee Open, but withdrew to attend the funeral of his father-in-law. He missed the cut in the Bell Canadian Open, and then sunk a six-iron on the last hole of the B.C. Open in Endicott, New York, to shoot 31 on the last nine and tie for seventh, which made him another $48,375. By the time he came to the last tournament, he was in 126th place on the money list.

Weir bogeyed three of his last four holes at the Disney, shot 40 on the back nine, and dropped to 131st place on the money list. The top 125 money-winners keep their PGA Tour cards for the following season, but Weir would have to return to qualifying school. He wasn't bothered, though, because players who finish 126th to 150th will get into fifteen to twenty tournaments the following season. He was also eligible to go directly to the final stage of qualifying school because of his 131st-place finish. This last stage took place in Palm Springs, and Weir, after shooting 75 the first day, while using a new putter, reverted to a putter he'd used most of the time before, and he went on to win the tournament, shooting twenty-seven-under-par for the last ninety holes. This qualifying school was easy for him after what he'd been through in previous years. And now that he knew where to stay on the PGA Tour, now that he knew the courses, now that he had a year of experience, he was readier than ever to show how much game he had, and his commitment to excellence. This didn't mean just making it to the PGA Tour, or winning qualifying school. It meant contending in – and winning – tournaments, and confirming the belief he had in himself.

An important development in Weir's career was about to take place, because Brennan Little was taking over as his caddie. Dan Keogh, like Little, a close friend of Weir's, and an experienced Canadian Tour professional, had seen Weir through the 1997 PGA Tour's qualifying school, and had been at his side during the 1998 season. Keogh was sure that his friend would succeed, having seen first-hand how driven and determined he was. But Keogh was getting married and wanted to start a business and live in Toronto, and so he relinquished Weir's bag.

While Keogh and Weir were on tour in 1998, Little had been playing the Canadian Tour. He'd turned pro in 1993, but hadn't made much headway. He had plenty of talent, but wasn't able to bring it to the course often enough during tournaments. Little was one of those many players whose experiences raise the old question: What is it exactly that allows one player who doesn't hit the ball all that differently from another on the range to make a living as a pro, while others tread water?

Little had won the Ontario Bantam Championship when he was thirteen, and also the 1987 Ontario Junior, where he finished eleven shots ahead of Weir. Herb Page, a Canadian and the long-time golf coach at Kent State University in Kent, Ohio, ranked Little ahead of Weir in his assessment of promising Canadian juniors. Little had been part of the acclaimed junior program at the National Golf Club of Canada in Woodbridge, Ontario, which was led by Ben Kern. Kern had attended New Mexico State University in Albuquerque, played the PGA Tour with only modest success for a few years, and then assumed his role at the National. He had worked with George Knudson, and his program at the National was based on Knudson's teachings, which Kern integrated into his own impressive teaching ideas.

"Ben was great to me," Little says. "We were out on the course practicing in the morning, and then I'd caddie also and fill divots in the afternoon and play afterwards. Later, Ben also helped me get into New Mexico State."

Little graduated from New Mexico State, and decided, like Weir, to play professional golf. Despite limited success, he persisted, and played fairly well early in the 1998 season on the Canadian Tour. He came to the last tournament, at Huron Oaks in Brights Grove, needing only to make the cut to keep his playing card for the 1999 season. Weir's brother Jim caddied for Little there. They came to the last hole, a short par-five, where Little needed a birdie to retain his playing privileges for the following season. Little hit his typically massive drive, and had only a short iron left into the hole. He pulled his shot into the back bunker and up near its lip, from where he could make only par. Little missed keeping his playing card by one spot and, he recalls, by about ten dollars.

"Jimmy mis-clubbed me," he says, laughing now, so many years later. "I hit nine and should have hit wedge." A few years later Little ran into the golfer who had beaten him out of the last spot for the

1999 Canadian Tour. "I'm the guy who passed you for that last spot," the fellow said. "I'm just here to tell you that it's the best thing that ever happened to you." Little said, "You know what? You're probably right."

Weir called Little at his home in St. Thomas, Ontario, after the 1998 season. Little probably wouldn't have continued playing the Canadian Tour even if he had kept his card for 1999. "I wasn't really enjoying playing any more," Little says. "I just didn't trust myself enough. I was the kind of guy who thought too much on the course. I never had a routine to get me past that, and I never had a game plan. The way I see it, a lot better players than me haven't made it."

Little, an all-around athlete who had played not only golf against Weir, but also junior hockey, was looking for other work when he heard from Weir, who asked if he would be interested in taking over from Keogh. "I said, 'Sure, let's give it a try,'" Little recalls. The decision would prove rewarding both financially and, in terms of a deeper satisfaction, in seeing a friend win tournaments and develop into one of the world's best players.

Weir confirmed the promise of his 1998 rookie season when he got into contention during the first quarter of 1999. He was tied for the lead in Tucson in early March after he birdied the first two holes of the last round, but then he fell back to a tie for thirteenth. The next week at the Doral tournament in Miami he wasn't able to make a putt over a couple of feet when he was in contention in the final round. A few weeks later he was tied for the lead starting the last round of the BellSouth Classic in Atlanta, but shot 72, hitting the ball well without making putts, to finish fifth. Not only was he becoming a factor in tournaments, but he was feeling comfortable on the PGA Tour. He no longer stood beside Nick Price on a practice range and felt that he didn't belong in his company. His ball flight was improving, because his swing mechanics were advancing.

By early summer 1999, in the middle of his first year with Little at his side, Weir had made it through the two-stage qualifying procedure to get into the U.S. Open, to be held in June at the Pinehurst No. 2 course in North Carolina. He would be playing in his first major championship. Canadians were getting as excited about his play and his potential as he was. He missed the cut at the U.S. Open, but gained confidence by qualifying for it and by learning about major-championship golf.

"I was definitely nervous there," Weir says of his first major. "There was a buzz about the tournament, and I loved that part of it. I loved it right away, and I guess there's a tendency in that situation to want to work harder than you do at a normal tournament. I over-analyzed the situation at Pinehurst."

Canadians had been calling Weir Canada's best young golfer for some time, and they still were. He didn't mind the tag, much as he had to keep reminding himself that he wasn't playing for a country. Golf was an individual game and, if he played well, then Canadians would feel good about that. But when he heard people in his galleries say, "Go Canada," or, "Hi from Manitoba," he felt a complicated mixture of pleasure and burden. He'd have to learn to live with the attention, because it wouldn't go away. Maybe he would even learn to use the interest in him as motivation.

Of course there were benefits to being Canada's main man in professional golf. His managers at the IMG agency were able to help him get into the Bay Hill Invitational, which Arnold Palmer hosted in Orlando. They also conducted the Export "A" Skins Game, and had invited Weir in 1998, in Prince Edward Island, and again in 1999, when the go-for-broke competition – in which the player who posts the lowest score on a hole wins a "skin" for a predetermined amount of money – took place in Mont Tremblant, Quebec, in late June.

There, Weir played against Fred Couples, David Duval, and John Daly, and came into the event having won $313,000 on the PGA Tour, more than he had won during the entire 1998 season. Weir won ten skins, as well as the entire event, picking up $210,000 and a booster-shot of confidence. There was no doubt in his mind now: he could compete with the best golfers. Moreover, the skins format, in which a golfer gambles for birdies and eagles, and where total score over the round doesn't matter, further emphasized to Weir the value of narrowly focusing on each shot. He made nine birdies in the round and didn't try to hole a five-footer for birdie on the 13th hole because Duval and Daly had already tied the hole with birdies. Had Weir made that putt, he'd have shot 60. Leaving Mont Tremblant, Weir said he'd like to go that low when he did have to count his total for the round, on the PGA Tour.

Couples, Daly, and Duval were impressed with Weir. "He'll be on the PGA Tour forever," Couples said. Daly added that Weir deserved to win, because he played better than the other golfers in every part of the game, and observed, "It's probably the first time that I've played in a skins game where the best player won." According to Duval, "He just wore us out." Weir said, assessing his own performance, "I'm really comfortable with my swing, and when you hit a lot of good shots, you're feeling good and you narrow your focus. Instead of aiming at the green, you start aiming at the hole, and then you start aiming really close." He aimed, and he hit his marks. Now it was time to move on to the next PGA Tour event, which would start two days later near Chicago.

There, at the Western Open, Weir started the last round in second place, four shots behind Tiger Woods, with whom he played in the final group. Weir had made four straight birdies in each of Friday's and Saturday's rounds – a benefit of the Skins event in which he had learned the value of that narrow focus. "It's so easy to put the last hole behind you," he said of his experience there. "That's what I've been trying to do this week." But how might Weir react to playing with Woods in the final round?

"It's my first time chasing him," Weir said. "Obviously, he's a great front-runner and he's a great player when he's in the lead. I can't go out there tomorrow and just expect the thing to be handed over to me." He didn't speak of fearing Woods, though, nor did his tone suggest any anxiety. His self-confidence was borne out on Sunday, when Weir wasn't intimidated; never mind that he was in seventieth place on the money list and Woods was second, and clearly on his way to being the best player in the world. Weir played a solid last round, shooting 70 to Woods's 71, and winning $270,000. Again, he wasn't thinking of the money, but of winning. Tournament by tournament, Weir was impressing people and whittling away on his own game, taking the small steps toward long-term success.

"This young man has a lot of moxie," ABC Television's Steve Melnyk said, while Weir was playing the back nine. "Here he is thrown into the deep end with who should be or could be the number-one player in the world, and he's not bothered by it at all." It might have surprised others that he wasn't bothered, but it didn't surprise Weir. What bothered him was not playing well. What bothered him was not coming through with the golf he had in him. What bothered him was not committing himself totally to fulfilling his potential.

To continue giving himself every chance of doing so, he headed off to the British Open at Carnoustie in Scotland in July 1999. Weir wasn't exempt for the championship, so he had to qualify. He had never played links golf, and looked forward to the experience.

The thirty-six-hole qualifying event would take place on the Sunday and Monday before the British Open started the following Thursday. Weir arrived in Scotland on Wednesday night, and the next day walked the Monifieth links near Carnoustie, where his qualifier was to be played. He studied the holes and the lay of the land with Brennan Little. They took notes, and then Weir played practice rounds on Friday and Saturday when the course was closed to anybody but the golfers entered in the qualifier. But practicing over a links and hitting shots along the ground and allowing for the ball to roll fifty yards is one thing when score doesn't matter, and entirely another when it does. Links golf was different from anything Weir had played, but he wanted to put himself through the trial by competition. After shooting 71 the first round, he would have to go low on the Monday to get into the championship.

Weir came to the last couple of holes knowing he had to finish with no worse than a couple of pars to have a chance to qualify. He drove into the high fescue rough on the 17th hole, pitched out, and got up and down for par, making an eight-foot putt. On the last hole he carefully studied a three-foot putt before holing it. He had shot 66, and qualified with the exact score required. He was in the British Open.

Carnoustie is probably the most punishing course on the British Open rota, and it's almost impossible to shoot a decent score when the wind blows and the rough is knee-high. Some fairways were as narrow as twelve yards in landing areas, and rough was thigh-high, not knee-high. The course was looking and playing mean – so mean that scores were ridiculously high in the first round. Somebody asked a club member whom he thought would win. "Nobody," he answered. Another said of the course, "It's giving the fellows a right rattling in their brains." Justin Rose, a gifted young English player, found himself in deep rough on one hole and moved his ball ten feet from there. He said it was his best shot all day. Greg Norman whiffed a shot.

Weir shot 83, the same score as defending champion Mark O'Meara. Understandably upset by his first round in a British Open, he wanted to go directly to the practice range, so he chose not to speak to reporters. He had finished with a double-bogey, which only compounded his frustration. These were the days when he was trying to prove something to himself, when a bad round sent him reeling for longer than was necessary. His instructor Mike Wilson wasn't at Carnoustie, but David Leadbetter was with Weir that evening on the range, helping him sort out his ball position. The next day Weir came to the last hole with an eight-foot par putt that he knew he would have to make to get past the cut. He'd worked hard all day and had birdied two of the previous four holes. Now his trip overseas came down to this one putt.

Weir backed off the putt once, and then again. He settled in over it the third time, flooded his mind with images of putts he'd made in the past, and then holed the putt. He was the golfer back at Huron Oaks, making putts on the practice green on a summer's night. Once again he was the golfer who'd holed a big putt to win over two hundred thousand dollars' worth of skins the month before. "I wasn't ready to hit the putt, so I backed off," he said of his putt at Carnoustie. "I don't know. I just didn't have the right thoughts." Weir's 72 got him into the weekend; he'd made the cut right on the number. He went on to tie for thirty-seventh in the championship after a weekend of solid golf, a promising performance in his first British Open. Next up in the world of majors was the PGA Championship in August, at the Medinah Country Club, back in Chicago.

At Medinah, Weir played beautifully, shooting 68-68 to lie one shot off the lead halfway through the tournament. Steve Bennett, who

had in 1993 moved on from Huron Oaks to become the golf professional at the nearby Sarnia Golf and Curling Club, had been at
Medinah, and had told him a few things. Weir was still working on
his grip – he'd been working on it since meeting Mike Wilson – and
Bennett told him that it was looking good. Along with Bennett,
Weir's parents, who were living in the area at the time because his
father was working there, were at Medinah. He showed them
his good stuff. Weir made a seven-foot par putt on the last hole to
shoot 69 in the third round and was tied with Woods for the lead
going into the last round. A few fans serenaded him with
"O Canada" during his third round.

Tied for the lead after three rounds of a major, Weir would play
with Woods in the final group. This was only Weir's third major
championship. "I really wanted that putt on the last hole, and what
I did," he said after the third round, "was just convince myself that I
could make it." He added, "If you had told me at the beginning of the
year that I'd be here, I'd probably have said, 'No way.' But I've been
playing a lot better and gaining more confidence and momentum.
I'm definitely the underdog. Tiger is the best player in the world,
and I lost my card last year. I don't have anything to lose tomorrow.
It will be great experience for me." He wanted to win the championship, but he was also looking at the final round as another step in his
career, whatever might happen.

Things didn't work out well right from the start, when his
perfect opening drive settled into a divot and forced him to play
away from the hole. But he got his par anyway, and hit the green on
the par-three 2nd hole. There he missed a four-foot putt for par, the
length of putt he would miss all day. It wasn't long before he tumbled
out of contention, as he just couldn't get the feel of the putter. In fact,
he had lost the feel the night before while practicing his putting.
Where did it go? Was it nerves? Who could know? Weir wasn't

getting any feedback during his putting session Saturday night. The problem continued on Sunday.

Weir's experience that Sunday was not pleasant. The crowds would surge forward after Woods putted out, and sometimes Weir got caught behind people on his way to the next tee. He didn't have his own security people, and he needed them. Many spectators were taunting him, too. "Come on, Weir, you can do it," a beer-swilling spectator yelled when Weir was well behind Woods with no chance of catching him, and somebody else screamed mockingly, "Kick his butt, Mike!" People had been loud at the Western Open when Weir was in the last group with Woods, but they were merely loud, not obnoxious. His putting matched the environment – also foul. He spun putts out of the hole on the fifth and sixth holes, and lipped out half a dozen times during the round, all the while having to listen to lip. Woods couldn't help but hear the rowdy crowd either. He heard somebody call Weir a "choking dog," and refused to comment later on what else he heard, except to say that things weren't right out on the course. Meanwhile, Weir kept trying to play each shot properly. He did hit one eighteen-inch putt in haste and frustration, missed it, and said he wasn't proud of that. Lost in what he later described as "la-la land," Weir also kept his eyes on Woods, who was in a fight for the championship with Sergio Garcia. Woods had to make an eight-foot par putt on the 17th hole to take a one-shot lead into the last hole, and Weir, on his way to shooting 80 and tying for tenth, observed him closely as he got ready, and as he made the stroke and holed the putt. Woods went on to win.

"Sure, it's disappointing," Weir said after his round, scooping up his daughter, Elle, in his arms. Bricia was at his side, and Rich Gordin was nearby, as were his parents. "I gave it my best and I didn't give up. Eighty is the best score I could have shot, because I tried on every shot. I can be satisfied with myself, because I gave it my all and I never gave up. I'll be back again." To hear the strength of his voice was to know that the last round had only toughened him. Weir left the PGA Championship that night determined to learn what he could from it, and then to put it behind him. Bricia and Elle were in the car with him as he drove away. So was Gordin. He and Weir had a few things to discuss.

That night Wayne Gretzky called Weir not so much to console him as to encourage him. Gretzky knew what it was like to be the top athlete in the country in one's sport, and in his case he was the best hockey player in the game. But he had known failure, and reminded Weir of the 1983 Stanley Cup final. Gretzky was playing for the Edmonton Oilers then, and was in his first Stanley Cup final, against the New York Islanders. The Islanders swept the Oilers in four games, but Gretzky considered the experience to be part of his education, and went on to play on four Stanley Cup–winning teams.

Weir went on from the 1999 PGA Championship to play in the International at the Castle Pines course just outside Denver. Walking off the practice tee one day, Nick Price spotted Weir and told him not to worry about what had happened in the PGA Championship. He, too, said Weir should consider it another learning experience. Price knew this from his own years as a professional. He had led the 1982 British Open at Royal Troon in Scotland by three shots with six holes to play. Price made some mistakes coming in and lost the championship to Tom Watson. Like Weir, Price was a golfer who had to change his swing dramatically to compete. He said that the swing he had when he turned pro would have barely made him a living – if it made him a living at all. He slowly developed perhaps the most efficient swing in the game, but it took him a long time to win tournaments regularly. Price wrote three words in his diary at the start of every season: "Persistence, persistence, persistence."

His persistence paid off when, in 1993, he won his first major championship. Price knew that it takes some players years to find their form, the form that they have in them somewhere. Weir heeded Price's advice, because it was coming from somebody who had been down a road he was taking, a road he was determined would lead to major championships.

Weir played in the Air Canada Championship – formerly the Greater Vancouver Open – at the Northview Golf and Country Club, near Vancouver, three weeks after the PGA Championship. He liked Northview's Ridge Course, the venue for the tournament, unlike the Glen Abbey Golf Club in Oakville, Ontario, where he would play the Bell Canadian Open the next week, and where he hadn't made the cut in eight appearances. But Northview had been good to him, given his top-five finishes in 1996 and 1998. Mike Wilson was at Northview until Wednesday afternoon, and then Rich Gordin came in until Saturday. It was Weir's week. He shot 68-70-64 and was tied for fourth behind leader Fred Funk with one round to go; he would play that in the next-to-last group. He bogeyed the first hole, but then made four birdies to shoot three-under par 33 on the front nine. He then birdied the 10th and 12th holes, and was in the hunt for the title with Funk and Carlos Franco, the Paraguayan golfer who has one of golf's sweetest swings – positively Sam Snead–like in its metronomic, slow rhythm.

After bogeying the 13th hole, when he missed a short putt, Weir drove perfectly down the left side of the 14th fairway. Water protects the green to the right there, and the pin was on the middle-left portion of the green. Weir had 159 yards to the hole, and, after watching him nearly hole some shots through the week, Little, his caddie, said: "You know, you haven't holed one yet." Weir's eight-iron shot landed twenty feet short of the hole – "kind of a British Open

shot," he said – and rolled in like a putt for an eagle. Weir instinc-
tively threw his club in the air and raised his arms in excitement. It
was too early to celebrate anything, since he had four holes to play,
but the tournament had suddenly turned his way. He made a twenty-
five-foot birdie putt on the 16th to take a three-shot lead over Funk.
Weir had trouble composing himself as he walked to the 17th tee, and
was getting choked up. But he and Little talked a little sports, Weir
calmed down, and he parred the 17th hole. Meanwhile, Funk had
birdied a couple of holes behind him, so when Weir played the last
hole, he held a one-shot lead. Franco had fallen behind and was no
longer a factor.

Weir's drive on the last hole was ideal, but he had that lake in
front of him. He wouldn't let it come into play now, because there was
no need to try to get near the pin at the front of the green. He had
chosen to do that in 1996 because he wanted to make a birdie and
have a chance to win the tournament. He didn't need a birdie to win
now, so he took the water out of play by hitting a five-iron well
beyond the hole. He was left with a very fast, sixty-foot downhill
putt, but that was okay. He hit the most beautiful putt there, trusting
his instincts for a putt of that length. The ball rolled within inches of
the hole, and he tapped in for his par. "That might be the best putt
I've ever hit," he said of his first putt, "considering the circumstances.
Sixty feet, down over a slope, breaking away from me, and just not
wanting to leave myself a second putt."

Behind Weir on the last hole, Funk had been forced to hit his
second short of the water from heavy rough to the right; he had no
chance to get across the water to the green. Funk didn't hole his third
shot, so Weir had won his first PGA Tour event. He had learned from
the PGA Championship three weeks before. He had learned
from everything that had happened to him over the years. Soon he

was with his daughter, Elle, and Bricia, who was pregnant with Lili. Bricia hadn't been feeling very well, but Weir wanted her to come up to the tournament. "I really think you should be here with me," he told her. He felt something good was going to happen.

"It's hard to describe the emotion," Weir said after winning. He didn't need to find the words. Others would find them. Richard Zokol, who had been in contention at the Air Canada Championship after two rounds, said, "People were thinking that Mike had been in contention that one time," referring to the PGA Championship. "They don't realize the climb he's taken, that he's been in the final group and nearly won before. I think if Mike hadn't had that final round at the PGA Championship that he wouldn't have won here."

Weir arrived in Oakville, Ontario, the next week to play the Canadian Open, where he was besieged. "I just want to keep getting my golf swing better," he said one afternoon at Glen Abbey before the tournament began. "That's the one goal I set for myself. You have to be honest with yourself, and I try to do that. What's the quality of my ball flight? That's what I look at."

Weir missed the cut at the Canadian Open, which was hardly surprising given how tired he was after his win and his lack of enthusiasm for Glen Abbey. But that hardly mattered. He went on to play well the rest of the year, finishing twenty-third on the money list. He had laser eye surgery in late November, done by the doctor who had performed the same procedure on Tiger Woods. After his season ended, he said that he was still too inconsistent, in that he had missed ten cuts. In looking at his statistics, he figured that he needed to hit more fairways: he'd hit some 67 per cent of the fairways during the 1999 season, and wanted to get this up to 70 per cent in 2000. He was getting where he wanted, in his mind, in his swing, and on the course.

"It's very exciting for me to think about next year," Weir said as 1999 ended. "Next year I want to make the Presidents Cup team. I'd be the first Canadian on the team. I also can't wait to get to Palm Springs to work with Mike [Wilson] on my grip. It still needs work." He had a lot to look forward to in 2000, especially the birth of his and Bricia's second daughter. She was expected right around the time of the Masters.

At the 2003 Masters, Weir is trying to look after all parts of his game: the mental, emotional, and physical. It's already been a tiring week, considering the conditions, and he wants to feel as strong as possible for the long days ahead, Friday and Saturday. Yet, to the outsider, and even to most participants, golf doesn't seem all that physical a sport. This is especially true nowadays, when so many golfers ride in carts. But tour pros walk every round, and then there's the stress of contending in tournaments. Weir doesn't have a lot of weight to lose, but the pounds do come off when he's on the road. This 2003 season, as he's won twice and contended in other tournaments, he's noticed how easy it is for him to lose weight. That's why he took two weeks off after playing the Ford Championship at Doral in March. He had been playing hard, and had lost eight pounds. At Doral he was in contention heading into the last round, although he hadn't been hitting the ball that well. He felt fatigued, but was still only two shots behind co-leaders Scott Hoch and Bob Tway after three rounds. He bogeyed the second and third holes and double-bogeyed the par-five 8th on his way to a two-over-par 74 for the last round. He tied for fourteenth place. Weir is such a finely tuned athlete that he knows what's wrong. He was tired, that's all, and it affected his posture and, consequently, his swing. It was time to get some rest, recover his lost weight, and return to his strenuous home-workout routine, away from the stress of competition.

Players could easily feel more stress this week at the Masters, because it's taking so long to get to the first round. Then again, Els, for one, says that this might help him, because he's been struggling a little lately. Weir thinks that the wait could help him as well, given that he missed the cut last week at the BellSouth Classic and wasn't hitting the ball as well as he would like earlier this week. But he has improved every day.

"I feel that I've done a good job getting ready," Weir says when he arrives at the course after learning there won't be any play today. "There's frustration in waiting, sure. It seems like a much longer week now. But I felt a lot more comfortable with my swing yesterday than earlier. Maybe today I'll just fine-tune it a bit more. The wait could be good for me. You do all the conditioning and try to get yourself ready for something like this. If the physical fitness isn't there, then it's easier to get tired mentally."

But the physical fitness is there for Weir, thanks to his efforts to strengthen himself. "It's a different discipline when you're getting ready to play thirty-six holes," Weir was saying earlier today at the club. "You have to mentally challenge yourself to get up for it, to make it work for you. I try to make that an advantage for me."

The best players do this. "I do like playing in tough conditions," says Tiger Woods. "It doesn't mean you always play well" – he shot 81 in dreadful conditions last year in the third round of the British Open – "but I enjoy that challenge. I don't get bummed out when the conditions are tough. You've got to go out there and suck it up and play the best you can and sometimes the conditions are brutal and you have to deal with them."

Weir considers himself a good bad-weather player, so he's anticipating tomorrow rather than worrying about what the day may
bring. What does it matter if the course will play closer to eight
thousand yards because of how wet it is? Weir is realistic and knows
that he won't get any roll on the fairways. He'll be in the middle of
the pack when it comes to how far he hits the ball. If he has to rely
on his wedge play on the par-fives to make birdies, he'll do that. If he
has to rely on his short game to save pars when he misses greens
because of the longer irons he'll be hitting onto the greens, he'll do
that. Everybody is predicting, at this year's Masters, perhaps more
than any other, that only the longest hitters will thrive. Tiger Woods,
Ernie Els, Phil Mickelson, Davis Love III: they're the favorites. If
Weir were to listen to the pundits, and to many of the golfers themselves, he might as well leave Augusta. Those Vegas 40-1 odds? Isn't
that called an overlay? Hasn't Weir won twice this year?

CHAPTER SEVEN

Friday

April 11, 2003

Finally, an improving forecast, and golf. Nobody would call this chilly, gray morning pleasant, but sun and moderating temperatures are forecast for later today, as the wedge finally gives up its hold on Augusta. It's doubtful that the field will complete thirty-six holes, but everybody should get in enough golf for the tournament to catch up by the end of Saturday's play.

Mike Weir is nearly ready to go. He's on the extreme left end of the practice area, with Rich Gordin and Brennan Little. Padraig Harrington, attended to by Bob Rotella, is hitting balls beside Weir. Jack Nicklaus is warming up, if that's possible on a brisk morning such as this, when the temperature isn't expected to get beyond fifty degrees Fahrenheit until after noon. He's taking his time for each shot, as he did nearly twenty-two years ago when Weir watched him at Huron Oaks. Weir is doing the same, a few places to Nicklaus's left. They've still not played together in a tournament or practice round. But Nicklaus did notice Weir during one of his attempts at qualifying school, in 1994. Nicklaus was following his son Gary, who was in the same group with Weir. Weir introduced himself to Nicklaus, and reminded him of the letter he'd sent him years before. Nicklaus didn't remember the letter but, after watching Weir that day, he told him he was glad that he hadn't advised him to switch from being a left-handed to a right-handed golfer. He also told him that he was impressed with how he managed his game.

The tournament has started. The first threesome includes the Scottish player Sandy Lyle, who won the 1988 Masters. He hit a memorable nine-iron out of the deep fairway bunker up to the green to ensure his win. Lyle has played poorly in recent years, and has become a devotee of the teaching system called Natural Golf; it's based on the Canadian legend Moe Norman's way of playing, the idea being to take the club back in a straight line from the ball as far as possible without turning one's body, and then repeating the process on the downswing and through the ball. Moe, as everybody knows him – he's one of those first-name golfers, such as Tiger, or Jack, or Arnie – has for years been considered one of the two or three most accurate ball-strikers in the history of the game. He wants no extra moving parts in the swing, so he tries to swing straight back and straight through. "Everybody wants to swing around the course, around the course," Moe says in his usual double-speak manner. "But why, why? You swing through the course, through the course. That's the way to play golf. The ball fits the Moe Norman way, the ball fits the Moe Norman way." But Lyle has been struggling while trying to incorporate Moe's ideas. He has missed the cut in his last three Masters and has finished no higher than twenty-first since he won the tournament.

The British like their golfers to win around the world. They did invent the game as we know it – well, the Scots did, and they prefer to be called Scottish and not British – and the British Open is *the* championship, or so they believe, but one of theirs hasn't won the Masters since Nick Faldo in 1996. Wait, though. There's hope. A writer from a London paper notices that Lyle has parred the 1st hole, while the other two golfers in his group have made bogeys. "We have a British leader," the wag says.

The starting time of 9:20 for Weir, Harrington, and Tom Watson is imminent. Weir leaves the practice green and tiptoes along a sodden path from there to the 1st tee. Watson follows him. "Hi Mike, it's good to see you," he says. Harrington follows. They shake hands.

Weir takes a couple of practice swings with a wedge on the left side of the tee, then puts a driver across the upper part of his back, and stretches. He takes a few hard swings with his driver, and stretches once more. Weir has plenty of rotation in his swing, yet there are no superfluous moving parts. His club looks connected to his body throughout his swing; his arms don't separate from his chest. He has said that his ideal swing is one in which the plane of his downswing matches that of his backswing; there's no rerouting of his club, and, therefore, fewer sources of error. That's the holy grail of the swing for Weir, and he's sensitive to the slightest deviation. He has trained to be that attuned to elements of his swing, and wants to know what's going on so that he can make on-course corrections. That's not always possible, but he means to increase the likelihood of his doing so. He leaves nothing to chance. He may be the only tour golfer to have read *The Physics of Golf*, written by Theodore Jorgensen, Emeritus Professor of Physics at the University of Nebraska. Weir said that he learned a few things from it and that the analysis confirmed some notions he had about the swing. He's always a student.

That's also true of Watson. He knows what he wants to do with the golf swing, and he plays quickly. There's no fooling around in his approach to the game, one reason he has won one U.S. Open, two Masters, and five British Opens. Watson's swing is classic, but he's also aware that many fine players have different methods. "I don't care where you are *here*," he once said while setting his club at the top of his backswing, "and I don't care where you are *here*," placing the club at the end of his follow-through. "But you'd better be *here*," he declared, setting the shaft parallel to the target line in a pre-impact position with his hands leading. He was saying that it makes no difference what a golfer does before or after this powerful position, which would account for the many different looks that produce effective swings, as long as he arrives in the right place at the critical moment. Meanwhile, Watson's swing is conventional, and it's one of the best. Weir prefers a functional, stripped-down swing, which is why he has worked so hard to understand swing mechanics. Add this determination to his increasingly effective technique, and you have a PGA Tour player who sees himself capable of winning majors.

"Fore please, Tom Watson driving." Augusta National member Phil Harison is the voice behind the announcement. Harison is in his late seventies, and has been a club member for fifty-seven years. He has been the starter at the Masters for nearly as long, and his simple way of introducing the players is exactly right for the tournament. There's no "Ladies and gentlemen, Tom Watson, winner of five British Opens, two Masters, one U.S. Open, and thirty-one PGA Tour events." That wouldn't sound the appropriate note should he play with, oh, George Zahringer, whose win in last year's U.S. Mid-Amateur got him into the

Masters. It wouldn't be right to introduce players in a way that would effectively compare their accomplishments.

Watson hits his first drive into the trees to the right. Next is Harrington, who snap-hooks his drive into the trees to the left. "Fore please, Mike Weir next to play," Harison says. Weir puts his ball on the tee, takes one practice swing from behind the ball, lifts his club and aims it down the fairway at right angles to the ground from the same position, sets up over the ball, and then makes his waggle.

The 1st hole at Augusta National sets up well for Weir, whose natural shot is a draw – a left-to-right flight for him. He can aim well away from the yawning bunker on the right side of the 435-yard hole; if his natural shot were a fade the ball would start out nearer to or even toward the bunker, and if it didn't curve, might finish in it. The bunker is 275 yards from the tee; it's an aiming point and, for many players, within reach. The longer hitters can't simply blow their drives over the bunker, as they could before the club moved the tee back, lengthening the hole.

Weir's opening drive in this Masters starts left, heading toward the trees. But it drifts no farther and finishes on the left side of the fairway. He's thirty-five yards short of that bunker on the right side of the fairway. It's uphill to the green from there, the hole is cut on the extreme back-left section of the green, and the wind is into Weir's face. He hits a five-wood at the center of the green. The ball looks good in the air, but rolls through and down a slope.

There's no room to work with from here, so Weir can't loft the ball onto the green. He tries to skip the ball twice into the ground to deaden its momentum, so that it will hit the green exhausted. But the best-laid plans of the best golfers don't always work out when so many variables are involved. His ball hits the green running, and it's all downhill from there. Now Weir has a thirty-five-foot putt for his par.

Mike's brother Jim is watching from the right side of the hole, as is Steve Bennett. So is Nigel Hollidge, the director of operations for the new Taboo Resort, Golf and Conference Centre in Gravenhurst, Ontario, a couple of hours north of Toronto. He's staying in the house that Weir rented. "This is a dream," he says. "It's my first time at the Masters, and I'm a guest of Mike Weir's."

Hollidge approached Weir's agents at IMG on behalf of Taboo the day after he started there. He wanted to see if Weir would be interested in associating himself with the resort, and Weir, after inspecting the course to make sure he liked it, agreed to a five-year arrangement as Taboo's spokesperson, allowing the resort to advertise itself as his home course. Tour pros do move around, so maybe it's not unreasonable to think of Taboo as his home course, even if it's a couple of thousand miles from where he lives in Utah. He gets back for a charity tournament and also to relax with his family in one of the club's chalets, a nice complement to his ski cabin in the Utah mountains.

Weir is also affiliated with Bell Canada, and has been since the fall of 1993. The company was with him from his early days as a professional. John Sheridan, Bell's President and Chief Operating Officer, liked Weir the moment he met him. "He's a genuine, solid man who reflects our company's values. Mike's a quiet, unassuming Canadian who can compete with the best of the best in the world, and who can win. He's a true professional who has a quiet, focused intensity, and on a business level with our customers and employees at special events, he's always delivered."

Little is holding the pin on the first green, and Weir putts. He practiced putting in his hotel room last night. The ball rolls up and over a rise in the green, and then dives into the hole. "That's the way to start a round," Hollidge says. "It just shows up as a par on the card," Bennett adds. "But some par."

The par-five 2nd hole is 575 yards, with woods on both sides of the fairway and a wide, deep bunker out at about three hundred yards. The fairway falls from there to a wide but not very deep green that's protected at the front by two bunkers, with a small opening between them. Until fifty yards were added to the hole, many players could get over the brow of the hill and hit an iron into the green; the shot wasn't easy, since it was from a downhill lie, but most players felt that they would lose a shot to the field if they didn't birdie the hole.

Weir's drive comes up a little farther to the right than he would have liked, short of the bunker, in a messy, muddy area. He gets relief from casual water – water that's pooled in an area – so he can clean his ball; no mudball here. Weir replaces his ball in an area where there's no casual water, but the surface is still slick. He slips during his swing, and loses his balance and control of the ball, which sails well left toward the trees, but continues on through to finish thirty yards left of the green. Weir's scraping the ground with his feet, picking clumps of mud from the soles of his shoes. But there's light in the sky. Maybe the rest of the week will provide better weather.

The pin is on the back of the green, in the middle, so Weir has about twenty yards to use there. His shot lands forty feet short of the hole on his angle, spins a smidgen, and rolls up to within eighteen inches. "Attaboy, Mikey," somebody says. As close as the ball is to the hole, Weir still has to be careful with the putt. He lines up from behind his ball, takes a couple of practice strokes, and holes the putt to make the birdie. He's one-under-par after two holes and hasn't hit the ball as he would like. Course- and self-management have carried him through the first two holes.

Weir is where he wants to be, inside the ropes and playing a tournament, a major. He hits his second shot on the 350-yard par-four 3rd hole twenty feet from the pin, and then makes some practice strokes at the back of the green with his right hand only. He wants to ensure that he continues to accelerate the head of the putter through the ball with this forward hand, no matter how fast the greens become. He two-putts and remains one-under-par.

Rich Weir, who is following his son, moves toward the 3rd hole. He didn't do much in yesterday's lousy weather: a walk, just to get out of the house, then dinner and the playoff game between the Anaheim Mighty Ducks and the Detroit Red Wings on television; Weir's good friend Adam Oates was playing for the Mighty Ducks, while the Weir family has always liked the Red Wings too, since Detroit is only an hour from Sarnia. The game went to triple overtime, but Rich didn't make it that far. He knew it would be a long day today – more of a slog than an easy walk – so he wanted to be well rested. That doesn't mean he won't get a little jumpy out here. This is his son, playing the Masters. His eldest son, Jim, did watch at the house until the game ended, when Paul Kariya scored for Anaheim. "I was one-eyed, but Detroit's my team." Mike made it through the first overtime period, then went to bed. He had some golf to play today.

"I'm nervous, but I enjoy it," Rich says of following his son in the Masters. "I'm pulling for him like crazy." Weir nearly makes his putt, but it coils just right at the hole. Par. Weir, Watson, and Harrington move off the back of the green the few yards to the 4th tee. Heads turn toward the scoreboard to the left of the 3rd green. Tiger Woods, playing a few groups behind, has bogeyed the first hole, by pitching in from forty feet. What does this bogey mean? It means very little. He shot 40 the front nine of the 1997 Masters, his first Masters as a professional. But Woods figured out what he was doing wrong on the way from the 9th green to the 10th tee, and then shot six-under-par 30 on the back nine. He won that Masters by twelve shots. He

could win this Masters by twelve shots. He could win any tournament he plays by twelve shots. Woods won the 2000 U.S. Open by
fifteen shots and a month later won the British Open by eight.

Weir is respectful, but not afraid of Woods, and would love the
opportunity to play with him in the last group come Sunday's final
round. He was surprised to hear Ernie Els, a hugely talented player,
admit that Woods has intimidated him in the past, not by doing anything intimidating other than playing the golf of which he's capable.
Els spoke last year of how he needed to rid himself of what he called
"the little guy on my shoulder," or what Greg Norman has called the
"mental gremlins." Both players were referring to the negative
thoughts and feelings they get sometimes in crucial situations. Els in
particular was thinking about how Woods had affected him.

"It's different coming from Woods than maybe other players,"
Els has said, and this from a two-time U.S. Open champion, which
shows that self-confidence in golf is fragile. But he worked with his
sports psychologist, Jos Vanstiphout, to conquer the little guy on
his shoulder. The Big Easy, as Els is known, beat the little guy and
won last year's British Open.

"I look at Tiger," Weir says, "and obviously, he's an unbelievable
athlete who is doing unbelievable things. But golf's golf. Tiger has an
air about him, and a presence, but you have to combat that and
stand up to that. I relish that, and I think he sees it. He wants the
challenge. Absolutely, he wants the challenge. Great competitors,
athletes like Michael Jordan and Wayne Gretzky, they want the challenges from other players."

The challenges that great players, championships, and championship courses themselves present to players can frighten them, or
can sharpen their attention. Weir has learned to focus in regular tour
events, and a significant part of the challenge for him this week is to
focus here, in a major. "Focus," though, is a nebulous term that

many athletes use too freely. Walking along, Rich Gordin contemplates the word.

"What is focus?" Gordin asks. "What exactly is that space? It's not like you can just decide to get into it and you do. It's something that you learn. It takes lots of repetitions so that a player can make a shot just a shot. It's like Nick Price told Mike. 'You have to make a six-iron shot just a six-iron shot,' whether it's on the 16th at Augusta or playing with your friends at home. Mike has triggers that allow him to do that. He uses audiotapes that train his mind and body to respond to a situation rather than having it control him. You cue in your mind. It has to do with breathing." Gordin and Dr. Lars-Eric Unestahl, a Swedish sports psychologist, produced a program of tapes called "Mental Training for Golf," which Weir has used. They suggest ways for a golfer to enter an "inner mental room," where he is calm, a place where he can learn to control complicated sequences of movement with thoughts and images. Research in sports psychology shows that this can happen. "The possibilities are endless," Gordin claims.

Weir will need to cue in his mind here, because he'll have to wait ten or fifteen minutes before playing the par-three, 205-yard 4th hole. The group ahead, comprising Jack Nicklaus, Hunter Mahan, and K.J. Choi, is leaving the tee as he arrives. Weir gets to work on his backswing. He follows up with some downswing work, checking his position as he starts back to the ball. He's trying to get the feel of the correct positions, because he has not found them yet. Sure, he's one-under-par, but he knows that the course will reveal any flaws unless he corrects them. He might as well use this time to figure things out.

When it's time to play, Weir, up first, hits a shot that lands just to the right and short of the pin, then rolls to the back of the green, about twenty feet beyond the hole. Now *that* was the swing he wants.

He finished in balance, and the ball was on a string. Oh, it had just the slightest hint of a draw, but that's the shape of his shot when his swing is on.

"He's dialed in," Gordin says. "I saw it on the range and the last two days. It's just a feeling that I had from watching him over the years. I can see the patterns."

The round is a learning experience for Gordin, even as his star golf student is the one taking the examination that Augusta National provides. He and Weir are engaged in a long-term process that began that day in his office at Utah State University a few years ago. Although Gordin teaches full-time, he gets out to eight or nine tournaments a year so that he can observe Weir in action. Psychologists call this method of research "naturalistic observation." Nice place to do research.

"I'm trying to add to my repertoire by watching Mike," continues Gordin, a slender one-iron of a man, as he ambles down the left side of the 4th hole to take up a position near the green. "I can tell by his way of walking how he's doing. We also do a fair bit of work on the phone, but I like to see things with my own eyes, too. It's fieldwork. We've just been going over the same things this week that we always do. We're always trying to make this complex game simple."

Weir's ball finishes in the second cut, as Augusta National prefers to call what other courses call secondary rough. But the club's potentates have their own language, and they insist that CBS use it during its telecasts. So, primary rough is the first cut, secondary rough is the second cut, and they prefer that spectators be referred to as patrons. There's no such entity on the CBS telecast as fans, or even a crowd. This is a decorous place, old-time golf, past as present. It does make for a civil atmosphere. You feel guilty when you use the word "crowd." You really do.

Weir putts from the second cut, which only shows that it truly is less "rough" than little more than a brush cut. The putt for birdie slips by the right of the hole. Just right. Weir isn't annoyed, but his pursed lips betray a hint of disappointment. He expects to make putts. What's a putt all about anyway? It's about reading the green, sensing how hard one needs to stroke the putt for a given distance, and going ahead and doing it. Do these things right, and the putts will fall.

Up on the 5th fairway, Weir is over his second shot from the middle of the fairway. Watson, who is fifty-three, still powders the ball, and has driven a few yards past Weir here. Weir's second finishes twenty feet from the hole, not a bad shot, but not a precise one. As he walks up to the green, he stops and swings his putter a couple of times. More self-examination.

Weir's ball has gone just through the green, and picked up a little mud. He can't clean it, because he's off the green. He's only those twenty feet from the hole, but he'll have to be careful with the putt. It could easily get away from him, but it doesn't. Weir pars the hole. One-under through five holes. He's comfortably into his round, although his body language does indicate that he's not sharp. Weir demands a lot of himself. Always has. Always will – as long as he's a golfer. Ever the analyst, ever the assimilator, he does some pencil work on the 6th tee, because there's another wait on the par-three hole. Out comes his yardage book, and he makes a notation or two in it, and then chats with Little. They're both cold, what with the waiting and the chilly weather.

"This is a slow golf course," Watson, a fast player, says to Harrington. Weir is working on his take-away, but not with a club. He's doing what golfers everywhere do, in their kitchens, in their offices, in subways, on the streets. He's making a golf move without a club. At the same time, he's staying loose and trying to keep warm. The wait on the tee becomes ten, now fifteen minutes. David Leadbetter shows up behind the tee, following his young protégés Charles Howell III and Justin Rose. They're playing with Adam Scott. This threesome comprises probably the three finest young players in the world.

Howell, who is from Augusta – his father is a pediatric surgeon here – is twenty-three and has about 6-per-cent body fat, if that; he makes a cable look thick. Howell won his first PGA Tour event last year, and lost that Nissan Open playoff to Weir in February.

Rose was born in Johannesburg but has lived most of his life near London; he's twenty-two, and is best known for holing a fifty-yard shot on the last hole of the 1998 British Open to tie for fourth place there. He was only seventeen, and turned pro the next day. Rose missed the cut in the first twenty-one tournaments he played as a pro, but persisted while working with Leadbetter. He won two European Tour events last year.

Scott, an Australian, is two weeks older than Howell. He works with Woods's coach, Butch Harmon, and his set-up and swing resemble Woods's. Scott won three times on the 2002 European Tour, and tied for ninth last year in his first Masters. He took Woods to extra holes a couple of months ago in the Accenture Match Play Championship, but the world's number-one-ranked player beat him.

Howell, Rose, and Scott are more than promising. They're delivering on their promise, notwithstanding their youth. They make Weir seem like a seasoned warrior, a thirty-two-year-old veteran.

The 6th hole is 180 yards, and it's a picture. The green sits so far below the tee that fans – well, patrons – can plunk themselves down on the hill in front of the tee. They can't see the initial flight of the ball, since they can't see back over the hill. They depend for their initial sense of the ball flight on the way the people horseshoed around the green start to react. When heads around the green turn one way, the heads on the hill follow.

The hole is cut today on the back-right of the green. There's a ledge here, and it's a small one, about as big as a porch on a vintage 1950s bungalow. There might be – might be – just enough room for a man and wife to set out two chairs and read the papers on a summer's night, as long as they don't spread the sections on the ground. Still, there's room enough for a hole location. But how to get there from here, back on the tee? That's the question. The area is so confined that a shot that misses its target by only a little is likely to roll far away. Golf balls that come within as little as a few inches of making it to the ledge often roll back to the front of the green. That's three-putt territory. Or four-putt. Nicklaus just four-putted from down near the bottom-left of the green.

Watson is examining his yardage book while waiting on the tee. So is his long-time caddie, Bruce Edwards. The hole is playing 173 yards today. Players know the exact yardages, although Augusta National's own scorecards only indicate distances in increments of five yards. Even the official tournament program lists this hole as 180 yards. Clifford Roberts wanted it this way, because he felt that there's no point in providing more precise yardages for golfers, and anyway, tee and hole placements change from day to day. The players in the Masters – all pro golfers – demand precision, so they measure off distances such as green depth, the yardage to reach and carry bunkers from specific points, the yardage to ridges. The days of playing by feel alone disappeared long ago. Professional golfers play by the book – the yardage book.

Weir hits a more-than-adequate shot that flies toward the hole, but wanders through the green onto the back fringe. He didn't miss the green to the right, from which the ball would roll down a slope and make for a difficult up and down for par. He didn't miss it short of the ledge, from where he'd face a treacherous first putt, and probably a not-so-pleasant second one either. No, he's on the correct level. Watson also plays an attractive shot that finishes eight feet from the hole.

From the back fringe – again he can't clean his ball because he's off the green – Weir putts down to within a couple of feet from the hole. "Who's this?" a fellow asks. His friend fills him in: "Mike Weir. He's a good golfer." Watson steps up to his ball quickly, but makes a tentative stroke, an I'm-afraid-of-knocking-this-one-a-few-feet-by stroke. He looks up as soon as he makes contact with the ball, because he knows he's not come close to making the putt. Johnny Miller used to ask, with a sense of wonder, "Isn't it amazing how you can hit a putt from sixty feet and you know that it's going to come up one roll short?" Tour golfers know. They just know. Watson taps in for his par, making him two-over for the round, and hands the putter to his caddie. Weir makes his par putt.

To the 7th hole, a par-four of 410 yards. The narrow fairway is lined with trees, and there's not a bunker to be seen in the drive zone. This hole was lengthened by forty-five yards two years ago, so it's now more than a long iron and wedge or driver and lob wedge. The raised green is directly behind three deep bunkers cut into a hill. Two bunkers defend the green at the rear. The green slopes sharply from back to front. Even at 410 yards, the hole is short by modern standards for a par-four. But the average score was 4.2 in the 2002 Masters, which ranked it sixth in difficulty.

Weir's drive splits the fairway. A familiar face looks at him as he walks off the tee, although Weir doesn't see it. It's Joe Carter, who led the Toronto Blue Jays to World Series victories in 1992 and 1993. Carter hit the series-winning home run in 1993, and that night a few hundred thousand Torontonians filled the downtown to celebrate. Carter is retired from baseball and lives near Kansas City. He plays to a five-handicap, coaches school basketball, and is one happy guy to be here at his first Masters. He's wearing a rain jacket with the Masters logo and carrying a Masters umbrella.

"I like Mike's game and his demeanor," Carter says. Asked to compare the act of hitting a baseball to hitting a golf ball, he says, "Hitting a golf ball is tough. It's just sitting there. I'd rather hit a ninety-five-miles-per-hour sinker than a golf ball in front of ten thousand people. I've done it. I played with Frank Sinatra. But I don't know if I could do it in the Masters. I'd be thinking, 'Just let me get it airborne.'"

Weir's second shot finishes three feet above the hole, but he misses the downhill putt. His father notices on the nearby scoreboard that Woods is three-over-par for five holes. "We've heard that before," he says.

After parring the 8th hole, Weir holes a forty-footer on the 9th for birdie. He's two-under for the front nine. It's taken three hours to play the nine holes. This will definitely be a long day's journey into a long evening's golf.

Any golfer who wants to ascend to the highest levels of the game also wants to represent his country in international events. Weir had played for Canada in the World Cup, but an even more important objective for him was to make the 2000 Presidents Cup team. Strictly speaking, he wouldn't be representing Canada in this competition, but a team of "International" players – their Ryder Cup. The Ryder has been going on since 1927. Teams of professionals were drawn, at first, from Great Britain and Ireland on one side and the United States on the other. The United States won eighteen of twenty-two Ryder Cups from 1927 through 1977, with Great Britain and Ireland winning three times, and there was one draw. Jack Nicklaus suggested that European players be added to the 1979 GBI team, given that golfers such as Spaniard Seve Ballesteros and West Germany's Bernhard Langer were making themselves known as top-flight players. Why shouldn't they have the opportunity to compete in the international match-play competition? They and other Europeans were added to the team, and the Ryder Cup then became a highly competitive event. The United States has won six of the eleven Ryder Cups since, Europe has won four, and there's been one draw.

It wasn't long before golfers from outside the United States, Europe, and Great Britain and Ireland were winning championships. In fact, some international players had always succeeded on the world stage. Australian Peter Thomson won five British Opens. South Africa's Gary Player won nine major championships, including each of the four majors at least once. New Zealander Bob Charles became the first, and only, left-hander, to win a major when he took the 1963 British Open. More recently, Greg Norman of Australia, Nick Price of Zimbabwe, Vijay Singh from Fiji, and Ernie Els from South Africa had become some of the world's best players, but they weren't eligible for the Ryder Cup. Like the Europeans before them, they deserved a chance to play in a significant international competition. And so the Presidents Cup was born, for teams of twelve professionals from the United States and twelve drawn internationally, from outside the States, Great Britain, Ireland, and Europe; hence the "International" team. The first Presidents Cup took place in 1994 at the Robert Trent Jones Golf Club in Manassas, Virginia. The United States won.

Weir knew all about the Presidents Cup before he made it to the PGA Tour. His first goal was to reach the PGA Tour, but another important objective for him once he got there was to qualify for the

Presidents Cup team as soon as possible. The first Presidents Cup for which he was eligible occurred in December 1998, but he had only one PGA Tour season to earn enough points to qualify for that team. It wasn't a realistic possibility for him in his rookie season. The next Presidents Cup was in October 2000, and that's where he aimed. Weir increased his chances of making that team after he won the 1999 Air Canada Championship. The International team would consist of the ten international players ranked highest in the world and two captain's picks. Peter Thomson was the captain of the International team for the 2000 Presidents Cup. Thomson had been keeping his eye on Weir, and during a visit to Toronto he said that he hoped that he would make the team. He liked Weir's competitive attitude, and felt he was the kind of golfer who would be an asset to a team.

"The Presidents Cup is a definite goal of mine," Weir said after he won in Vancouver. "It's something I'll really push toward. I'd be the first Canadian to represent Canada there."

To help get there, Weir sought more consistency in his game. Sure, he'd had some highlight-reel moments in 1999, but he was still missing too many cuts. He'd also been working so hard on ingraining his more neutral grip, and on keeping the clubface square going back, rather than shutting it. "I knew in the back of my mind, even when I was playing well, that my grip tended to be way too strong," Weir said of his play in 1999. "I want to weaken it."

By doing so he would also increase his chances of keeping the clubface square. His waggle was part of his plan for more consistency. Mike Wilson wasn't afraid to try out some intriguing ideas on Weir, and Weir wasn't afraid to use them. Wilson knew that, because Weir tended to shut his clubface in the early part of his backswing, he needed to help him build a very different feel. Lee Trevino, the garrulous Mexican-American who won two U.S. Opens, two British Opens, and two PGA Championships, and who had superb ball control, once said, "You can talk to a fade, but you can't talk to a hook," and Weir's bad shot was an uncontrolled hook. He wanted to be able to hit a controlled draw, but found that a difficult assignment. Getting the clubface square would help, so Wilson told Weir during some practice sessions to try to shank the ball. Okay, Weir said, I'll do what you want. But when he tried to hit shanks, he didn't shank at all, because all he had done was square up the clubface. He was building in a feel, and he looked forward to taking it out with him on the 2000 PGA Tour.

All that season, Weir found himself talking and thinking about the Presidents Cup. He was eighth on the International team's standings through the Bay Hill Invitational in March, where he was one shot behind leader Tiger Woods after starting with 70-64, but shot 72-73 on the weekend to tie for seventh. He was in good shape to qualify for the team, but could also slip out of the top-ten automatic choices if he didn't continue to play well. One evening that winter, at dinner, Weir was asked if he feared any golfer. It was one way to gauge how he was feeling about himself, because he was always honest when such questions were posed. His one-word answer told the story of how far he had come since that evening at the Score Awards in 1993 when he said he couldn't yet see himself winning on the PGA Tour. "No," Weir answered.

Working with Mike Wilson one day that winter, he hit shot after shot where the ball flew high and straight. Where was the hook? "We both knew that he was really close to playing some great golf," Wilson said. Canadians were also expecting him to play good golf. He shot two-under-par 70 at the Houston Open in April, but then headed home because Bricia, who had given birth to Lili on Monday of Masters week, was feeling unwell. Some Canadians reacted in ways that indicated just how closely they were watching him. They were querulous: What's he thinking, leaving a tournament after shooting two-under in the first round? Weir found the questions too personal for his taste, but didn't pay much attention to them. His brother Jim was also hearing all sorts of things from Weir's fans. "I'm getting it from all sides," he said. "Women are saying that it's great that he's a family man and that he would come home when he could play for so much money. Some guys are asking what he's doing coming home. It's amazing."

Weir addressed the intense scrutiny he was under, but only when he was asked about it. "I think I have a good perspective on things," he said. "When I get older, I won't regret missing a tournament. Anyway, I definitely feel more support than anything from Canadians. Earlier in my career I interpreted it as pressure, but now I look at their interest as support." He did wonder why people would be interested in his personal life and habits: what he and Bricia enjoyed eating, what cars he liked. He was a golfer and he had no interest in being considered a celebrity. Weir didn't think of himself that way. He was a golfer, and that was it.

Weir played in the U.S. Open in June 2000 at the Pebble Beach Golf Links. A year after his first U.S. Open, he was no longer nervous about playing in the championship, or in a major. The 1999 U.S. Open had been his first major, and Pebble Beach was his favorite course; he'd played it some twenty times, and had tied for seventh in the AT&T National Pro-Am earlier in the year, when he closed with a 66. Back then, at the AT&T, in the winter, Pebble Beach played softer than it would in June, and the rough wasn't high, as at the U.S. Open. Richard Zokol played a practice round with Weir at Pebble the day before the first round of the U.S. Open and was impressed.

"Mike's on the cusp of being a top-twenty guy in the world," Zokol said. "He has a great, pure attitude about him, he doesn't carry bad thoughts about anyone, and that's very empowering. He's managed to deal very well with the few negative shots he's taken from people in Canada, mostly due to the times he hasn't finished particularly well, and that's a learning process, too. It takes five or six years to grow skin thick enough not to let any of that stuff bother you."

But the 2000 U.S. Open would not be Weir's week. He shot 76 the first round, when he didn't make a putt, in one of those "so goes golf" days. When the second round was suspended due to darkness, he had two holes left, and he was right around the cut line. Weir made the cut, but finished at nine-over-par 293 for the tournament, twenty-one shots behind Woods. Nobody had ever won a U.S. Open by Woods's margin of fifteen shots, and maybe nobody ever will again. Weir figured it was just a bad putting week for him, and looked forward to the British Open the next month at the Old Course in St. Andrews. "I feel like I'm right on the verge of something good happening," he said. "Maybe it'll happen at the British Open. I think my short game and imagination might be suited to the Old Course."

Weir arrived in St. Andrews the Sunday before the week of the tournament, and went over to Carnoustie to play the 1999 British Open course just for fun. He played with his father and his brothers, Jim and Craig. A second group included his hockey-playing friend Adam Oates, Brennan Little, Mike Wilson, and *Toronto Star* columnist Dave Perkins, an overseas member at Carnoustie who organized the games. Club members were pleased that Weir would return to the course for a casual round, and, as is his thoughtful way, he presented a framed photograph that Toronto photographer Doug Ball had taken of him and the late Payne Stewart during the 1999 British Open. Weir was reminded on the 1st tee that he hadn't paid his green fee, and, after taking care of that with a smile on his face, he ripped his drive down the 1st fairway. Just as he had felt when he first set sights on Monifieth fifty-three weeks before to try to qualify for the British Open, he enjoyed links golf. He was coming over to St. Andrews to put his appreciation for this type of golf to the test on golf's most venerated links.

But Weir did have some problems. He was still concerned about Bricia's health, and he didn't think his game was as sharp as he would have liked coming into the Open. He showed this the first round, when he shot 75, again making very few putts. He lipped out of the hole nine times. He changed putters for the second round and shot 68 to make the cut. Still, he did miss many birdie putts of the length a golfer usually makes when he's going to contend for a championship, or any tournament. A 70 and a 75 over the weekend dragged him back in the field, as Woods won another major. Of Woods, Weir said, "It's down to us all to improve our games and make inroads into his undoubted superiority." The next major up for Weir: the 2000 PGA Championship, at the Valhalla Golf Club in Louisville, Kentucky.

But he didn't contend there, after opening with 76, and then shooting 69-68-71 – respectable, but not what he had planned, and fourteen shots behind Tiger Woods's winning score. However, his thirtieth-place tie ensured he would qualify for the Presidents Cup. The qualification period ended with the PGA Championship, and Weir was in seventh place, easily making the list of ten automatic spots. That was the good news. The not-so-good news was that he had opened with high scores in each of the 2000 majors: 75 at the Masters; 76 at the U.S. Open; 75 at the British Open; 76 in the PGA Championship. He called this, "just a coincidence. It's nothing to worry about. I just have to keep playing golf. It won't last like that." There was no reason to believe it would.

At the Air Canada Championship, where he was the defending champion, Weir got within two shots of the lead early in the third round, but tied for thirty-eighth place. Then, at the Bell Canadian Open the next week, Weir finally made his first cut in the championship in ten tries. He was hardly a player who set his goals on making cuts, but he was relieved to make it in his own country's championship. He had never pretended to like the Glen Abbey Golf Club, where he had played every Canadian Open of his career except in 1997, when the tournament was at Royal Montreal's Blue course. "I think it's just visual for me," he said prior to the tournament at Glen Abbey. "I like to have very specific targets, and for some reason they're not in the right spot where I want to hit certain shots."

Tiger Woods was in the field, so Glen Abbey was buzzing. Woods had won the last three majors, and he went ahead and won at Glen Abbey after hitting a memorable 216-yard six-iron from a bunker on the last hole just over the green. Woods at the time was a shot ahead of New Zealander Grant Waite, with whom he was playing, and figured he would need a birdie to maintain the lead. Waite was in the fairway and was likely to hit the green with his second shot, maybe even make an eagle. Woods pushed his shot a bit, but it was still a tremendous shot under the circumstances. He won the tournament, matching Waite's birdie. Weir finished at two-over-par 290.

The Presidents Cup loomed, but first Weir got into a playoff for the Michelob Championship in Kingsmill, Virginia, by making a ten-foot birdie putt on the last hole. David Toms won the playoff, but Weir had put himself into contention again, shot 64 the last round, and had come up just short.

Captain Peter Thomson at the Presidents Cup introduced Weir as "our team mascot," during a festive dinner to open the competition. Over the years, many people had referred to Weir as "diminutive," and "small," but nobody had introduced him quite like that. Then again, this was his first time at such a big international event, one where U.S. president Bill Clinton attended the gala dinner. Weir's teammates included stars such as Nick Price, Greg Norman, Vijay Singh, and South Africans Ernie Els and Retief Goosen. Goosen, like Weir, was a Presidents Cup rookie. The United States side included Tiger Woods, Phil Mickelson, Davis Love III, and David Duval, and was heavily favored on home turf, although the International side had soundly defeated the American side two years before in Melbourne. Weir was pumped to be a member of the International side, and enjoyed spending time with his teammates and getting to know them. He even relished the impression others had of him being the mascot. He'd just play his golf, and probably show the followers of the competition that a fighting spirit can go a long way.

The role of favorite accorded the U.S. side was well-placed, notwithstanding the fine players on the International side. The U.S. team trounced the International side by ten points. But Weir won three out of a possible five points, while playing every match, and was the top player on the International team. Along the way, he and Price defeated Duval and Mickelson five and four in a better-ball match. He hit a bunker shot that U.S. captain Ken Venturi said was the best he'd ever seen; the shot was from a downhill, sidehill lie in a bunker, which had to carry some sixty feet, land in deep rough to kill its speed, and then bounce and run the forty feet to the hole. Weir, who normally doesn't get too excited, or at least show much emotion on the course, ran toward the hole as his ball landed in the rough, seemed to stop, but then kept going and finished a foot from the hole. This and other fine shots that he hit were small consolations to Weir, who would have preferred that his side win. However, he did continue to gain confidence in his ability to rise to the big occasions, because the successful shots he hit under pressure were multiplying: the four-iron shot with which he nearly aced the 16th hole in the last round of the 1997 qualifying school, just when he needed something special; the putt to make the cut in the 1999 British Open; the 64-64 finish to win in Vancouver, culminating in the shot he holed from the fairway on the 14th hole and the long lag putt he hit beside the hole on the final green; and now, leading his team in his first Presidents Cup. Weir was banking positive experiences, and, with Rich Gordin's help, had learned to cope with disappointments along the way. The veteran Johnny Miller, who holds strong opinions, called Weir a "superstar in the making" after watching him at the Presidents Cup. He also called him "a ball-striking son-of-a-gun," just the words that Weir enjoys hearing from a fellow who was one of the best ball-strikers himself – and a U.S. and British Open champion.

Weir had worked his way into consideration as one of golf's most improved players as the 2000 season was ending. By making the Presidents Cup team, he had also become eligible for the American Express Championship in Sotogrande, Spain, in November. The tournament site was the Valderrama Golf Club, where the Europeans had defeated the Americans in the 1997 Ryder Cup.

Weir started well, shooting four-under 68, but his second-round 75 was disappointing. He went to the practice range and worked on his posture, then shot 65 on a windy Saturday in the third round to move within one shot of the lead. In the final round, he had a two-shot lead while waiting on the tee of the par-five 17th hole, and it was on that hole that he hit one of the most impressive greenside shots of his career – every bit as good as the bunker shot that impressed Venturi at the Presidents Cup – and more critical, in that it determined the tournament's outcome. The shot was a little chip and run from behind one of golf's most outrageous greens. There's a pond short of the green, which is tilted so steeply from back to front that even a ball hit well into the green from the usual tight lie in the fairway can spin back into the water. Seve Ballesteros redid this green, and he must have had the Marquis de Sade in mind when he did. Price was in contention when he hit two balls into the water while making a triple-bogey eight on the hole. Woods was in contention, but he found the water and double-bogeyed the hole. Weir himself triple-bogeyed the hole in the second round. "It's probably the worst green I've ever seen in my life," Price said.

This time, Weir took any possibility of going into the water out of play. He hit his shot well beyond the hole, which was cut on the bottom level of the green near the water, and the ball went just over the green. He had six feet to the edge of the green, and that's just about as far as he wanted to carry the ball. Any farther and it could roll all the way into the water. His shot came off perfectly, landed on the edge of the green, and rolled and rolled, four feet past the hole. He made the putt and went on to win the tournament. Weir has said that this was one of the best shots of his career. It showed tremendous control both of his golf club and of his nerves. It was a championship shot. Weir won the tournament, a million dollars, and moved from twenty-seventh on the PGA Tour's money list to sixth. But money wasn't motivating him.

"I can honestly say that I never think about money when I'm playing," Weir said. He didn't think about money when he didn't have any, and he wasn't thinking about it when he did. "I'm just trying to get better and put myself into position next year to win a major," he said. He also was looking forward to making some changes in his waggle, the rehearsal by which many people identified him from across a fairway. That, he was confident, was an important step to take if he were to advance even further in the game.

·‿

Tenth hole, first round, on this long Friday at the 2003 Masters. Weir drives well, and follows the shot with a solid second that finishes thirty feet short and slightly right of the hole. Weir tosses some blades of grass in the air, as if to say that the wind fooled him or changed direction. He two-putts for par, comes up just short on his approach to the 11th green, but makes a six-footer for par after his chip shot doesn't release to the hole. Tiger Woods hates a bogey. Mike Weir hates a bogey. That's the way to approach the game.

Nicklaus, in the group ahead, has already finished playing the 12th hole. He trudges to the 13th tee back in a corner of the course, up against the adjacent Augusta Country Club. Nicklaus shot 45 on the front side, an unheard-of score for him. Scott Tolley, who works for him, leans against the front of the bleachers behind the 12th tee and gazes across at the solitary man on the other side of Rae's Creek down here in the far southeast reaches of Augusta National. "It's tough to watch," Tolley says, "especially when he was feeling so good. The putter betrayed him, and it's been all over since."

Nicklaus was considered the one golfer whom you would want to try a putt if your life depended on it; nobody was better from ten feet in when a putt mattered, and he always seemed able to make even longer putts on the final hole of a round or tournament, as if he wanted to give his fans something to remember. But he's sixty-three now, and he isn't making the putts he used to make; who does, at that age – or even younger? Watson is ten years younger than Nicklaus, and he used to make every short putt he looked at, but no more. The hole closes up all too often, but Watson deals with this well. "I've made more than my share," he says.

Weir, thirty years younger than Nicklaus and twenty years younger than Watson, is nowhere near that stage yet. He tries to make every putt and, if his ball runs a few feet by the hole, well, that's fine; he has the confidence to make it coming back, as did Watson when he was younger. Weir played twice with Canadian LPGA Tour golfer Lorie Kane in an alternate-shot event in Florida called the J.C. Penney Classic. Before their first effort in this team tournament, Weir's caddie Brennan Little asked Kane if she minded five-foot putts. "If he's hitting it that close, great," she answered. "No, I mean for the second putt," Little came back, meaning that Weir, when it was his turn to hit the first putt on a green, would likely knock it a few feet by if he missed it. Kane didn't mind that approach, and said she could use more of the self-confidence in herself on the greens that Weir had in himself.

The hole is cut behind the right side of the bunker in front of the 12th green. Rae's Creek is in front of the green on this 155-yard hole; it curves and winds off the property behind the green. Weir aims left of the hole, because the green narrows considerably to the right and falls away toward the water, and his shot finishes thirty feet left. His putt looks in all the way, and he sinks halfway to the ground as it nears the hole, trying to urge it in. But the ball just misses the hole. Watson makes a twelve-foot putt for birdie from behind the hole. He's comfortable anywhere outside about ten feet, the range where golfers don't expect to make many putts. Perversely, some of those go in.

Weir's on the 13th tee. This is one of the holes for which he has practiced hitting a fade. It didn't take many rounds at Augusta National for him to realize that, if he were going to contend for the

Masters, he'd need to move the ball right to left. That, for Weir, is a fade. This isn't a course where a player can get away with one ball flight, and one ball flight only. Lee Trevino's standard shot is a low fade, and he had a hard time adding a draw to his repertoire. Eventually he managed, but he couldn't increase the height of his shots; he'd grown up in Texas, and had learned to hit the ball low to control it in the constant winds. Bruce Lietzke's only shot is a high fade, and he never tried to change it. Lietzke has always maintained that he has seen many a golfer lose his way while trying to change his natural swing and ball flight. Both Trevino and Lietzke have had excellent careers sticking with what they have. Trevino has won six majors, but no green jackets. In twenty Masters, he had no top-five finishes and only two top-tens. Lietzke, in fourteen Masters, had a similar record: no top-fives and only two top-tens. The underlying truth, the most basic fact, about Augusta National is that anybody who hopes to contend in the Masters, let alone win, must move the ball all ways, right to left, left to right, low and high.

This probably accounts for why Canadian golfer George Knudson, one of the sport's finest shot-makers, loved Augusta National and felt he'd play well in the Masters. He thrived on moving the ball in whatever manner was required, and knew that Augusta National rewarded such play. Knudson played in seven Masters between 1965 and 1973. He tied for second in 1969, for sixth in 1966, and was tenth in 1965. Knudson never did win the Masters, but that wasn't because he couldn't hit the shots that the course demanded. He didn't win because he wasn't an effective enough putter. To win the Masters, a player needs to hit the ball every way possible in the air, and to roll it with precision and touch on the greens. Knudson had the air game, but not the ground game on the greens.

Weir has progressed in learning the shots he needs to contend in majors. From tee to green, he has been working toward becoming a complete player – a player with all the shots and the ability to manage his game. He hit a sweeping hook with his driver during his early years as a tour pro. Eventually the hook turned into a manageable draw. He can still hit a sweeping hook, but it's by choice, not because it's all he has. He used to hit the ball low with his driver and his longer irons, which meant that he could sometimes run out of fairway as the ball rolled and that he couldn't get to pins tucked on firm greens behind bunkers. With the help of his teacher, Wilson, he has learned to hit the ball higher. His distance control with his short irons wasn't PGA Tour caliber, and certainly not major-championship quality, so he learned as he tightened his swing to keep the ball within a smaller range with these clubs. Earlier this year he said that he felt that he had a good chance of holing shots with short irons. That's how confident he was of being able to control the distance with them. Around the greens, meanwhile, he developed a wide variety of shots – that shot on the 71st hole at Valderrama was a prime example.

While it's easier to hit a full shot than a delicate shot such as the one he had at Valderrama, it's still a difficult assignment to add a shot with an opposite ball flight to one's standard repertoire. Weir started thinking about hitting a fade at Augusta the November prior to the Masters, and he felt good about the shot coming into the Masters. He had hit a fade on the tenth, and it came off well. Now he wants an even sharper fade on the 13th, and he hits this shot.

But Weir chooses not to go for the green, because the hole is cut on the extreme front-left. There's very little margin for error, because the stream is only a few feet away at that point. The penalty for missing the green could be severe. Weir lays up, and then displays his distance control with the short irons, from seventy yards. He hits a low one that stops three feet from the hole. After making the putt he's three-under-par.

On the 440-yard 14th hole, Weir faces a second shot to a hole that's located on the right-center of the green. This is one of those Augusta greens on which to miss a shot by a little is to miss by a lot, because the ball can go rolling away off one of the massive contours. "Okay, Weirsy, stick it," Nigel Hollidge, of Taboo, says. "Have you ever seen a green that's so big but that plays like it's so small?" Weir's shot is right over the flag, and goes just through the green. "He's playing tidy golf," Hollidge observes. He's left with six feet of fringe and fifteen feet of green. Watson's ball is three feet in front of Weir's, and just to the right of his line. He doesn't ask Watson to mark it. Weir knows that he won't mis-hit his putt by that margin. But he does hit it too hard, and the ball rolls six feet by the hole. Weir grimaces, tosses his ball to Little for cleaning, and shakes his head. He takes his yardage book out and makes a note. Weir's already got his doctorate in golf. He's doing post-doctoral work here. His research will continue until the end of his career.

The par putt goes in, dead center of the hole. Steve Bennett notes, "That's the difference, the make-or-break putts."

Weir, Watson, and Harrington make their way to the tee at the par-five 15th hole. It's only 500 yards. Only. Drive the ball in the fairway and then hit the green, probably with an iron. Sounds elementary, except that the drive has to be no farther left than the left-center of the fairway, because of a huge tree whose limbs overhang it. The golfer who does find the fairway will likely have some sort of a hanging lie. The large pond in front of the green is the major hazard.

As usual, there's a wait on the 15th tee, because the players ahead who want to go for the green have to wait for it to clear. Weir knew it was going to be a long day, but did he think it would be this long? He told himself last night to be ready for it, and that his challenge would be to stay focused. He's on the 15th tee and has been out here for four and a half hours. Still, Rich Gordin has worked with Weir to help him prepare mentally for at least two long, slow days on the course. That was always going to happen after the Thursday round was canceled.

Gordin is leaning on the big tree to the left of the 15th fairway, waiting for Weir to hit his drive. He's quite happy to discuss how much waiting there is in golf.

"I equate golf to shot putters, or track-and-field competitions. If you're a shot putter, you go out and you throw, then you wait for the rest of the guys to throw. Then you get to throw again after twelve guys take their turns. Then, if you make it to the finals based on what you've done, you wait again, and so on. Golf's the same. You wait to perform, just like here on the tee. They're waiting a long time. A player's biggest ally is a routine, so that he feels in control. Still, you only have so much control, because eventually you'll have to wait. Feeling in control is good for all of us. The idea is to take the interference and deal with it."

The suggestion is made to Gordin that he and Weir are working to reduce to a minimum the chaos that a golf tournament can bring – chaos on the course and in a player's mind. Weir has said that all kinds of thoughts come into his mind during a round, not as many as in his earlier years, but they're constant. There's so much dead time in golf. "Tennis players have a similar problem," Gordin says. "What do they do between points? This is very important. You have to shift momentum."

He's saying that a player can't focus on only the upcoming shot. Weir and Little talk about sports, or other subjects that come to mind. Then Weir switches back to his shot when it's his time to play. He has backed off shots and started all over again when he has been distracted, unlike Doug Sanders on the last green in the 1970 British Open at St. Andrews.

Weir finally plays his shot after a fourteen-minute wait, but finds the left rough. The bottom third of his ball is hidden from view, and the trees block his view of the green. He plays back to the fairway, his third finishes on the back of the green, and he two-putts for his par. The group started at 9:20, has been out for five hours, and still has three holes left. He pars the 16th with two putts from the back fringe, pars the 17th after hitting the green, and then hits a long drive on the par-four, 465-yard 18th hole. It might as well be 500 yards, it's playing so long. Weir and Harrington are joking with each other as they walk off the tee. Lunch is only a few hundred yards and a few minutes away. Weir hits a three-iron to the front of the green, some sixty feet below the hole on the back-right. His first putt runs five feet by, but he misses the comebacker to make his first bogey of the round on the last hole. There's applause. He tips his cap, signs his scorecard in the hut behind the green, and walks toward the clubhouse for lunch.

"Too bad he finished like that, but he'll be all right," somebody says to Gordin. "Oh yeah," Gordin says, with conviction. Gordin shakes Weir's hand, and accompanies him into the clubhouse. He has forty minutes before he'll start his second round, on the 10th tee.

Els shot 79 this morning, and missed only two fairways. Harrington had trouble picking the right club on a few occasions, and 77 was the best he could do. Woods had to save par on the last hole to shoot 76, and did. Nicklaus shot 85, his worst score in forty-three years on the PGA Tour – that means 2,235 rounds. No excuses, though. Palmer shot 83, a terrific score for a seventy-three-year-old man playing such a long course. The British Amateur champion, Larrazabal, shot 82. The U.S. Mid-Amateur champion, Zahringer, also shot 82. Darren Clarke, who likes a cigar or two or three while he plays, and who always looks like he's relaxing on a river while fly-fishing rather than playing a golf tournament, shot 66, the low score for the first round. U.S. Amateur champion Ricky Barnes, playing only his second professional tournament, shot 69 while playing with Woods.

"He made me feel relaxed," Barnes said. "He told me to enjoy myself and things will go my way." Golfers: they're all philosophers.

It's late Friday afternoon, which would normally mean that the second round in a tournament is winding down. But this has not been a normal Friday, so Weir is only beginning his second round. With half the field, he starts from the back nine in breezy and partly sunny – yes, sunny – conditions, because the officials went to a split-tee configuration for the day to get as many players around as many holes as possible. After an opening par, Weir misses a six-footer for par on the 11th, pars the 12th, birdies the 13th, and then chips in from just over the green on the next hole to get to one-under for the second round and three-under for the tournament. He's on the leaderboard.

Woods, after his 76 this morning, is making a move. He has also started on the back nine, and birdies the 13th hole with a twenty-foot putt after opening with three pars. It's his first birdie of the tournament, which elicits a chuckle from the world's number-one player. He's patient, and doesn't think he's out of the tournament. The conditions are tough, so he'll just try to keep from making mistakes and pick up a few birdies along the way. He could squirm his way forward in this manner.

Weir birdies the 15th, lipping in a five-footer. It's his third consecutive birdie. He's playing disciplined golf, hitting fairways and greens, and continues this way through the 18th hole, his ninth of the second round, and his twenty-seventh of the day.

Weir is playing smart, strategic golf. His play impresses CBS's Jim Nantz and Lanny Wadkins; Wadkins mentions that Weir seems comfortable and in control. Nantz says that he doesn't have any loose parts, mentally or physically, and that he doesn't make mistakes. Well, no mental mistakes anyway. A player can control that part of the game. The physical part, the golf swing, isn't as readily controlled.

Weir rips a long drive down the 2nd fairway, and makes an eight-foot putt to birdie the hole. He'll probably get one more hole in before play is called due to darkness. His tee shot on the 3rd is in the left side of the fairway when the horn blows to suspend play at 7:26, but a player can choose to finish a hole that he has started. Weir wants to keep going, and hits his approach right at the flag and six feet short. He's calm as he waits on the green for his turn, and makes the birdie putt to get to six-under-par for the thirty holes he has played. He has a two-shot lead over the field as play ends today. But this doesn't mean that he has a two-shot lead after two rounds, which would normally be the case after Friday's play ends. He still has six holes to play to finish his second round, and will start at 8:15 tomorrow morning. There are forty-two holes left in the Masters for him. He's leading, but he won't get excited about that yet.

"It would have been nice to finish," Weir says outside the media center as darkness closes in over the course. "But I'm glad that we got in as many holes as we could. I thought that we'd get twenty-seven in, but we got thirty. The maintenance crew did an outstanding job out there."

They did, inside the ropes anyway. It's not easy walking outside the ropes. Sloppy doesn't begin to describe the conditions. It's a bog, a "sloppyfest," as Els predicted it would be.

Weir is pleased with how he played. He put himself in the right places most of the time off the tee, and gave himself favorable angles into the hole locations. He also made the six-footers that a player needs to keep a round going.

"The talk has been that this would be a bomber's week," Weir says. "But I felt that, if you're consistent, and if you have a good putter in your hands, these are the equalizers."

This is Weir's first trip to the press room in the Masters. He has watched the press conferences the last few years from his room in a hotel or rental house. Now, as he says about being in here, "It's a dream," a dream that he had, and that he has now fulfilled. But he wants to be in here after play concludes on Sunday.

Somebody asks him if he's a different player than the one who went up against Tiger Woods in the last round of the 1999 PGA Championship, "I'm a lot different. I'm much more experienced and my game's a lot different. I think it's more well rounded. Back then I said that I was coming out of the Q-school that year and there I was in the final group of a major. I was probably a little out of my element. I wasn't prepared to handle it. But I learned from that and hopefully I can use that somehow this week."

He'll see. We'll see.

CHAPTER EIGHT

Saturday

April 12, 2003

The most important day in Martha Burk's efforts to compel Augusta National to admit a female member has arrived: it's protest day for Burk in a field a few hundred yards from the golf club, far from where patrons enter the club and as distant from Magnolia Lane as a battered old Chevy is from a Mercedes. There's lots of golf to be played today as the players try to complete their second and third rounds. Play will start at 8:45, and the weather has returned to normal conditions for Augusta in April – sunny and milds with little humidity; there's high pressure over Augusta National. An hour before the golf starts, and more than three hours before the scheduled demonstrations, a fair number of people are already gathered at the protest site. But nearly all of these people are police officers. A trailer from the Columbia County Sheriff's Office dominates the grassy field just in front of the Savannah West Apartments, a series of low-slung buildings on the north side of

Washington Road. Thirty police cars are parked around the five-acre field, while officers lean on their vehicles, sipping coffee and chatting.

"I don't know nuthin'," one officer says, though nobody asked him a question. "I'm just standing here."

So is Todd Manzi, a forty-one-year-old former advertising executive and real-estate salesman who had a revelation last fall while driving from Orlando to his home in Tampa. He happened to hear Burk on the radio, and something clicked – or snapped, depending on one's point of view. Manzi decided he needed to oppose Burk's initiative on behalf of anybody who felt she was wrong, and so he started a Web site called <theburkstopshere.com>. Manzi isn't a golfer, but he's a man who cares about doing what's right, or what he thinks is right. A friendly sort, he wants to have a chat in the field with folks from the media. He introduces himself to a reporter: "Hello, Todd Manzi. I don't know if we've met. I'll give you my card." Manzi, who is unemployed, will announce later today that he's seeking a job in the private sector as of tonight.

It's important to take the imminent protest seriously, because it's hard to understand why a golf club would exclude women from membership. It's also reasonable to assert that discrimination on the basis of gender is no different from discrimination because of race. Ralph Morrell, a seventy-four-year-old man from Atlanta, took a bus with fellow protesters from there to Augusta this morning. He was in Washington when Martin Luther King, Jr., delivered his famous, ringing "I have a dream" speech in 1963, and he feels that there's no difference between fighting for civil rights or for women getting in as members at Augusta National. The *Augusta Chronicle* newspaper quotes him as saying, "Discrimination is discrimination, regardless of where it lands."

Over at the course, on a gorgeous, brisk early morning, the golfers are taking up the positions where they finished last night.

Woods is walking alone up the first fairway, his hands in his pockets. He'll start on the 2nd hole, while Weir will begin on the 4th hole to finish his second round with Tom Watson and Padraig Harrington. The club is quiet this gentle morning as play gets under way. Woods reaches the 2nd tee, while his mother, Tida, is a couple of hundred yards up the right side of the hole with baseball player Ken Griffey, Jr., one of her son's close friends.

Woods was reminded earlier this week that he asked in a national advertising campaign when he turned professional, "Are you ready for me?" He also said as part of this campaign that there were clubs in America where he couldn't play and where he still can't play because of his color. Woods was asked if he's as passionate about issues of discrimination now as then. "I am," he said. That was all he offered. "Thank you," the fellow asking the question said, after which a nervous, collective chuckle filled the press room. Woods is a golfer, not a civil-rights advocate. He has never pretended to be a social activist. Maybe it's enough that he be a golfing genius and nothing more. Or maybe he'll grow into taking a more active role off the course as he matures.

Weir is getting ready to play. Rich Gordin went back with him to the hotel last night, as he has done every night this week. They come out to the course and leave together every day. Neither has returned to the house that Weir has rented since Tuesday night. They reviewed yesterday's thirty holes, ordered dinner from room service, and parted company. There wasn't much to discuss, because Weir had played so well. "He hit good shots all day, even the misses," Gordin says. "If he was a little long, they were in places he could play from." What's that observation? "It's the quality of your misses that count in golf." Yes, that's it.

The horn goes off, signaling the players to start. Weir has to wait, because the Nicklaus group ahead is also on the 4th tee. Weir waits. Brennan Little waits. Gordin waits. Rich and Jim Weir wait. Steve Bennett waits.

First shot. Weir misses left, into the bunker. His head is down for a moment after the shot. This is no way to start. In disappointment, he sweeps the grass with the blade of his club. The hole is cut on the left side of the green, so Weir has short-sided himself; the lip on the bunker is high, so he'll have to spank the sand with some speed to get it out of there with enough height to carry the lip. That's task number one. But meeting this primary demand will mean he won't be able to stop the ball very near the hole. He hits a first-class shot, but the ball rolls six feet by. It's not what he wants to start his day, a six-footer for par. He works on his stroke, while Watson putts and misses from twenty feet. Weir puts his ball down, lines the putt up from behind, sets in, and makes it. Up and down. Well done. He remains six-under-par for the tournament.

On the 5th, Weir's drive finishes a yard into the right rough. It's enough that he won't be able to control the ball properly. He hits a crisp shot that lands on the left front of the green, then catches an upslope and comes back off the green. The hole is on a knuckle-like bump, past a depression in the green. Weir putts from short of the green, but his ball zips twelve feet by the hole. He tosses the ball to Little with a bit of heat on it, and misses his par putt a moment or two later. Back to five-under-par. The bogey resulted from a chain of events: a drive into the rough, which meant he didn't have a clean lie, which led to his ball coming up short, which led to a difficult putt that he rolled well by the hole. Still, as Jim says, looking at his brother on the 6th tee, "He's one shot at a time, one shot at a time. I would think there's a little excitement in Canada now."

It's okay for Weir's brother to have such thoughts, but Weir is playing only his thirty-third hole of the tournament, which isn't halfway over. Then again, it is Saturday, so it feels like the third round. The Canadians following him are constantly reminding themselves of this fact. Still, he is leading the tournament. That's another fact.

The pin is back-left on the 6th green. Weir's shot comes up thirty feet short, a smart play, because there's little room behind the hole or to the left. The green falls off only three feet to the left of the hole. A miss on that side would send the ball scuttling away. Watson has hit his shot past the hole onto the back fringe. He has to putt through the first and second cuts back to the green, and play a twenty-foot break. Watson is four-over-par, right on the cut line. He has missed the cut in four of the last five Masters, and would like to make it, as much for his caddie Bruce Edwards as for himself. He and Bruce have worked together since 1973, except for a brief spell after Watson advised him to caddie for Greg Norman. Watson's career on the PGA Tour was winding down, and Norman was one of the game's best players. But Edwards and Norman didn't click; the magic that Edwards and Watson had and their ways of being with each other that made the relationship work, weren't there. Edwards returned to Watson. They're a team.

Edwards loves it out here between the ropes. He could have gone to university, and he did get his real-estate license. But the only real estate he wants to be spending time on is a golf course. Sadly, he'll have to take leave of the golf courses of the world far too soon. He was diagnosed last January with ALS, amyotrophic lateral sclerosis. The progressive neuromuscular affliction is also known as Lou Gehrig's disease, because it took the famous New York Yankees ballplayer's life. The disease causes motor-nerve cells in the brain and spinal cord to degenerate, and Edwards has been told he has one to three years to live.

All through this Masters, Edwards has simply been doing his job – checking yardages, consulting with Watson, attending the pin.

He has chatted with Weir, Harrington, and their caddies, yukked it up from time to time when there's been a break in the play. Watson has often looked at him from a few yards away while Edwards was doing something, and the concern and affection he feels for his friend are apparent.

Walking outside the ropes on one hole while Watson is back on the tee, Edwards notices a few friends. "Hey, buddy, how you doing?" one of Edwards's friends inquires. "I'm doing well," he answers. But his voice is slurred because of the disease. "I sound like I'm drunk, but that's the way I am, after eight o'clock, anyway."

That's not true. Edwards has been a responsible caddie in all ways. He continues talking to his friends, while digging into Watson's golf bag. "Wait till you see what I'm about to have for lunch," he says, smiling, and pulls out a pillbox. He takes more than a hundred vitamins and other pills daily. He then walks back onto the fairway to get over to Watson's drive.

Edwards wasn't on Watson's bag when his man won the 1977 and 1981 Masters. But Watson was at Edwards's side last January in Hawaii, as his best man. Edwards married Marsha Moore, a woman he had met nearly thirty years ago at the Byron Nelson Classic in Dallas. He and Marsha stayed in touch, and were married during a Champions Tour event that week in Hawaii. Every player in the tournament attended the ceremony.

"I live the way I caddie," Edwards says. "My thoughts are simple: to carry on. If you have a bad hole, forget it, go to the next tee, and try to get better."

Here, on the 6th green, Watson has one of those bad holes. He doesn't hit his putt quite hard enough from the second cut, and by the time it reaches the first cut it's running out of speed. The ball dives left when it rolls on the green, and now he has twenty feet left for par. Weir has thirty-five feet for birdie, but his putt stays to the right of the hole, finishing four feet away. He's surprised, and chats with Little while Watson works on his par putt. Watson rolls his putt three feet by, putts again, and misses again. He taps in for a double-bogey. He has four-putted and fallen to six-over-par. Weir makes his par putt, dying it in the hole.

On the 7th, Weir's drive goes left. He's staring over there and isn't sure where his ball has finished. A young fellow watching Weir says, "He's a very good golfer. He has a good chance this weekend. From what I can see, he has a very good fan base, not only in Canada but in the U.S."

Weir is one-over-par for the three holes he has played today, and isn't hitting the ball particularly well. He could easily bogey this hole, because trees block his way to the elevated green that's behind the three bunkers cut into a rise in the ground. "If you can't get it airborne here you have no chance," Steve Bennett says. Weir can't get it airborne because of the trees, not airborne enough, anyway. He hits a low burner into a front bunker. The hole is on a shelf, eighteen feet into the green. He's so comfortable in the bunkers, and his shot is a beauty. It comes out without much spin, as he wanted, and rolls forward, finishing three feet short of the hole. The green is so fast, and so sharply downhill, from back to front, that Weir marks his ball as soon after it settles as possible. While Harrington putts, Weir works on his set-up and posture. Now it's his turn, and he makes yet another par putt. "He sure keeps a round going," his brother Jim says.

Weir is in the right rough on the par-five 8th hole after two shots, and hits a pinpoint shot that lands on the green and stops near the hole. Bennett is impressed, but not surprised. He remembers those long practice sessions back at Huron Oaks. "We hit so many of those shots on the range, one-bouncers and then stop. He's so creative with those shots. That's all he ever did, practice out there. He was dinking around. All he ever did was dink around and work on his game while the other kids were inside eating french fries."

The birdie putt goes down to get Weir back to six-under-par for the tournament. Earlier, when they were all talking about the big hitters having an advantage here, Weir told Bennett, "Well, it all comes down to putting, doesn't it?"

One hole to go in his second round. Dan Cimoroni, who works for IMG in Toronto and takes care of Weir's day-to-day business affairs, is looking forward to Monday there, when the plan for some time has been to launch Weir Golf Accessories. "But it could be about other things too." He doesn't want to say this out loud, but he's thinking about the celebration that could ensue should Weir win the Masters. Cimoroni used to be in the music business, and he has an eye for a good party. But maybe Cimoroni and the rest of the Canadian contingent should consult Rich Gordin, because they're getting ahead of themselves. Time to slow down. Weir pars the 9th hole, two-putting from a few feet off the right side of the green, pin-high. He didn't have his best stuff this morning, but he's played scrappy, tough-minded golf. After rounds of 70-68, he's four shots ahead of Darren Clarke, who shot 76 in the second round after his opening 66.

"He can win this thing," says Jaime Diaz, one of the most perceptive golf writers working today, while Weir checks and signs his scorecard. "I think he'll win a U.S. Open eventually, but he could win here, too. They say it takes a long hitter, but I don't know about that."

CBS wants to interview Weir. Another film crew is also after him. His presence is required in the media center. The guy's leading the Masters. He's in demand, and speaks to the point and only to the point, whatever he's asked. This is a man without frills, so his answers are direct, and his comments are like his golf swing, stripped of excess. Weir doesn't waste words.

"My putter's been hot. I made my par putts. A nice six-footer on 4, a good putt on 6, and another on 8. I was a little indifferent with my swing. I'm glad to get in where I am. The putter held me in there. Now I'll have time to rest and practice and try to establish a good rhythm.

"That was a nasty putt on 5, but you're going to have some hiccups here and there and I'm prepared to handle them. There's a long way to go, thirty-six holes.

"I can't overpower this course, so I have to play to my strengths. The talk was all about power, but I still feel that a medium-length hitter can do well. You rely on your wedge. The great thing about golf is that there are lots of ways to do it.

"There's no question about whether I can do it. We'll see on Sunday. But I feel good about it."

What are the greens like? Can anybody who isn't playing understand their difficulty?

"I don't think anybody can appreciate how slick and treacherous those greens are until they're out there on them. That six-footer right-to-left and downhill that I had on 4 to start, I could breathe on it and get it going.

"I'm not thinking about numbers. Not at all. I'll just keep grinding. I'll warm up the same way for this afternoon and do some stretching. I felt a little tight."

Jack Nicklaus has shot 77 in his second round and missed the cut by fourteen shots. He's in the middle of a large ring of media on the lawn, and talking about the course. "This will not yield to good golf unless you're long," Nicklaus says. "I don't know if anybody who isn't a long hitter has a good enough short game to sustain it over seventy-two holes. I'm just not sure what you can do when you're hitting to the hood of a car and the ball is going away from you all the time. The issue that I have is that, sure, guys who are medium-length can play well with a good short game. But can they do it over seventy-two holes? I don't think so."

Somebody asks Nicklaus how he can account for Weir's four-shot lead, since he's not a long hitter.

"Good for him," Nicklaus says. "He's medium-length. He'll have to remain totally on his game to get there in the end. But I always enjoyed sleeping on a lead. The harder you work, the easier you sleep on it."

Woods is finishing his second round on the 9th green a few yards away. He's five-over-par and has hit his second shot from the left trees into the front-left bunker. The cut has moved to five-over, so Woods has to get up and down. He has lots of green to work with, and hits his bunker shot three feet behind the hole. It's a downhill ski slope from there. If Woods misses the hole, his ball will go off the green and down the hill into the fairway. But he doesn't miss, burying the ball in the middle, and he makes the cut right on the number. Woods is eleven shots behind Weir, but at least he'll be playing the last two rounds.

A call from Canada comes through to the media room, from a concerned Weir watcher. He wanted to see Woods play the last two rounds, but he also didn't want to see him play; the guy's conflicted. "If Tiger's out of the picture, it's a beautiful thing," he says. "The other guys make mistakes down the stretch. The Tiger we've come to know doesn't make mistakes. I'm still worried about Tiger, even if he is eleven shots back."

The official statistics indicate that Weir took forty-eight putts in the first two rounds. But this is misleading, because he hit about ten fringes and putted each time. Players count it as a putt whenever they have a putter in their hands. The key statistic is that Weir has made just about every short putt he's had. He has missed only one putt inside eight feet, the one for par on the 18th hole the first round. But, as he says, he's not thinking about numbers. He's thinking about getting some rest, and then preparing for his round this afternoon. It's just after eleven. He'll start his third round in a few hours with Darren Clarke.

·⤳

The protests today didn't attract many people, once they did get started. Burk arrived by eleven-thirty, and spoke to a crowd that consisted mostly of reporters. There were a few other speeches, and that was it. Burk was asked what she thought of the Ladies' Golf Club of Toronto, the one women-only golf club in North America; Canadian golf star Ada Mackenzie founded the club in 1925, because many clubs made it difficult for women to play except at certain times. Burk wouldn't comment on the club, she said, because it's not in the United States. She was directing her protest at the Augusta National Golf Club only.

As the proceedings, such as they were, ended, Nicklaus was saying about the patrons at Augusta National, "Do you think these people really care about what's going on outside the gates? They're here to see a sporting event." He didn't comment on whether it was a good or bad thing that the folks from the outside – the public who visit Augusta National during the Masters, now gathered in the sunshine on the inside – didn't care about what was going on beyond the gates.

·⤳

The most important aspect of Mike Weir's winning the 2000 American Express Championship wasn't that he picked up a million dollars. It wasn't that he was soon after named Canada's male athlete of the year, the first golfer to win this award since Sandy Somerville, who won the 1932 United States Amateur, was honored that year. It wasn't that he moved up into the top-ten on the PGA Tour's money list. More than anything, it was that he had won over the golfers who are there at the end in majors: Vijay Singh, Nick Price, Tiger Woods, and Sergio Garcia were all in the mix on the back nine at Valderrama in Spain. Weir's win inched him that much more forward in the confidence department.

Still, looking back, he didn't fool himself about his year. He didn't contend in any tournaments until toward the end of the season, and he found that frustrating. He had played in all four majors in a season for the first time, but hadn't contended in any. Wins in each of 1999 and 2000 were satisfying, but Weir wanted more chances to win. A couple of top-ten finishes during the West Coast swing in the winter of 2001 were encouraging, but again, he hadn't contended into the final rounds. When he arrived in Florida to play a few tournaments in the run-up to the 2001 Masters, he was intent on doing just that, and shot a ten-under-par 62 in the first round of the Doral tournament in Miami to take the lead; he shot 29 the front nine, when he made two eagles. Weir was still leading at the start of the final round in blustery conditions, but shot 71, as Joe Durant came in with a 65 to win. Weir finished second.

Still, Weir demonstrated to himself that he was getting closer to winning again. There was something even more important, as he showed that he wouldn't let anything distract him from giving himself the best chance of playing to his ability. That meant striving for distraction-free golf, something he had worked on with Rich Gordin. And an incident occurred on the 10th tee during his first round at Doral that indicated the extent to which Weir had developed an automatic response to distraction.

Weir was over the ball on the tee at the par-five when he was distracted by a couple of carts in the area. He stepped away from the ball and put the headcover back on his club. He wasn't waiting for the noise of the moving carts to abate; he could have done that while standing over the ball. The idea was to start his routine over. If there has been one factor in Weir's approach to golf that has helped him improve since his early days as a professional, it's that he understands the value of routine. The more he makes every situation resemble every other situation, the better he's able to lock himself into the state of mind he wants. He started all over on another shot that week as well, when he was playing his second shot to the par-five 12th hole in the last round. There he was ready to start his swing when a leaf blew over the top of his ball. He backed off and started again. A leaf blew over his ball a second time, and he stepped away a second time. Finally, he wasn't distracted by anything, and hit the shot. People watching were scratching their heads, wondering why he didn't just go ahead and hit his shot the first time. Surely a tour pro could concentrate well enough to let a leaf blow by without stepping away. But that's amateur thinking, something Weir wanted to avoid.

"You can't hit a shot until you're ready and I'm not going to hit a shot until I'm ready," he said after his round. "That's why I put the club back in the bag." Asked if it bothered him when spectators thought he was being finicky, he answered, "I don't care. I'm not going to hit it until I'm ready. I'll do it again. I'll do it five times. I'm not hitting a shot until my mind is in the right place."

Gordin liked what he was seeing, and he, like Brennan Little, Mike Wilson, and others in Weir's circle, could sense that he was becoming one of the tougher players in the game. In late March, at the Players Championship, he said that he was mentally much stronger than in previous years, and that nothing much bothered him in the game. Bad weather? Just another challenge. It had snowed a few times when he played in Ontario high-school championships. Looking back, he realized that had been a helpful experience. Maybe it wasn't such a detriment for a pro golfer to grow up in a northern climate. Nicklaus grew up in Columbus, Ohio, and went to Ohio State, after all. Weir kept turning negatives into positives, kept finding solutions for problems. If he wasn't swinging well, he could rely on his mind and determination now, and turn a 75 into a 70. Asked about his waggle – and he was asked about it frequently – he found new ways of discussing it. He enjoyed talking about his swing more than anything else, so why not let himself be engaged when journalists prodded him on the matter?

"It's to stop a bit of lateral movement that I had in my swing," he said during the week of the Players Championship. "It keeps my right arm against my chest and I set the clubface open with my right hand. I cut my right wrist, which gets the clubface a bit more open, and I try to maintain that in my backswing. It's a technical thought, but it gives me a feel for what I want to do in my swing and sets the club on plane."

Another time, Weir found himself in a discussion of the changes Tiger Woods had made to his swing. Woods was heavily criticized in 1998 for tearing apart and rebuilding the swing with which he had won the 1997 Masters by twelve shots. But he wasn't satisfied with his ball-striking that week. It was good enough, obviously, but Woods's putting is what truly won him the Masters; he didn't three-putt for seventy-two holes on greens that PGA Tour player Jesper Parnevik says can make a player crazy with fear. Woods went to work with his coach, Butch Harmon, and won only once on the 1998 PGA Tour while he was assimilating the changes. Weir watched what Woods was doing, and noticed that it wasn't all that different from what he was trying to accomplish himself. Woods, Weir observed, also had a problem with a shut clubface.

"Once Tiger changed his clubface from a very shut position to square, he became that much more confident," Weir said. "Every part of his game became sound. He's so in control of his game." Weir sought a similar degree of control, and he was getting there.

His ball control tended to show up most noticeably in rough weather, particularly when the wind was up. Wind won't affect a solidly struck shot nearly as much as it will a shot hit even slightly off-center. So it was no surprise that Weir didn't mind wind and even cold; he also had the happy memory of playing the last ten holes of the 1999 Air Canada Championship in high winds, and hitting one solid shot after another.

Weir was also eight shots from the lead after two rounds of the BellSouth Classic in Atlanta in April 2001, when the field was forced to play thirty-six holes the last day. The forecast was for cold, brutish weather, which only meant that Weir had a better chance of catching the leaders if he could stay patient and play his game. He shortened up his swing for control, as he does in such circumstances, and shot 73-67 that last day to finish in second place. He could have offered a lesson in golf psychology at the time. Lesson number one he learned from the American Express Championship, in which he started the weekend eight shots from the lead: "You're never out of the tournament starting the weekend if you're in the tournament." Lesson number two: "Accept whatever conditions you find, and enjoy the challenge."

After the BellSouth, Weir tied for twenty-seventh in the 2001 Masters – not what he expected, because he'd been playing well. He took three weeks off and didn't touch a club, while he and his family moved into a new home. The house was only a couple of blocks from where they'd been living, but the move came during the third week of his time away from competition. His life, he said, was disorganized then, and he would have preferred to get some practice in that third week rather than dealing with a move. The move was supposed to occur during the week after the Masters, but the house wasn't ready. "It's definitely going to be my last move," he said. "It's too much." Too much particularly for somebody who craves routine, who needs routine.

Meanwhile, Weir had been working with TaylorMade on a new set of irons. He had only one club contract to this point in his career, with the Wilson Sporting Goods Company, and had tried a variety of irons. He was using irons from the Ben Hogan Company in 2001, but was committed to TaylorMade for the long run, although the company knew he wouldn't put a set in his bag for tournament play until he was completely satisfied with them. And, as always, he was thinking about his golf swing as he returned to competition in New Orleans after the Masters.

"I feel like I'm getting closer to having the club where I want it on the downswing," Weir said that week in New Orleans. "I'm a little rusty, but Mike [Wilson]'s been out here and it's starting to feel good. The way I see it, it's the same as when Hogan figured out his swing. He didn't have to practice as much or as hard as before. I'm finding that with my game. Before, when I took this much time off, I'd be sloppy with my swing. But now I can pinpoint things and figure it out faster when I come out. I'm out here each week thinking that I have a chance to win."

But he didn't come close to winning in New Orleans, starting and finishing the tournament with a 68 but shooting 74 in the second and third rounds. A final-round 75 at the Memorial

Tournament two weeks before the U.S. Open cost him a chance at a good finish there. At the U.S. Open he putted well but tied for nineteenth, nine shots behind his Presidents Cup partner, Retief Goosen, who won in a playoff over Mark Brooks. Then, out of nowhere, and proving that there's no telling what a week's golf will bring, he missed the cut in the British Open at the Royal Lytham & St. Annes Golf Club in St. Annes, England. Suddenly Weir was in a golfing funk. A sixteenth-place tie in the PGA Championship in August was okay, but he finished twelve shots behind winner David Toms. Another season of majors had passed, and Weir hadn't contended in one. Two weeks later, he missed the cut in the Air Canada Championship – the tournament he had won in 1999.

In the meantime, Weir had visited Toronto briefly, where he spoke at a dinner during the Canadian Amateur championship. Ranked tenth in the world then, he was an example of the value of persistence to the young golfers gathered, and spoke of amateur golf as the arena in which he cultivated his dreams. "I wasn't a dominating amateur at all," he said. "I had a few wins, but I had a dream of getting better and going further. I felt that, if I just kept making progress, I would realize my dream. There were lots of soul-searching times when I wondered what it would take, but the point is that I had a dream. To you guys, I'd say that it's a great accomplishment that you're here, and that you should keep your dreams alive." He added, "The biggest thing that I've learned on tour is to play my own game. Just take what got you there and make small improvements. I don't try to be anybody but who I am."

But as the end of the 2001 season approached, Weir hadn't won a tournament. He made the cut at the Canadian Open in Montreal, but wasn't a factor. The American Express Championship that he had won the year before was called off due to the September 11 attacks. In November, he played in the season-ending Tour

Championship in Houston, to which the top-thirty money-winners of the year were invited. Starting the final round two shots behind leader Scott Verplank, he kept making six- to twelve-foot putts to save par the last round, scrambled during an afternoon in which he wasn't swinging his best, and shot 68 to get into a playoff with Ernie Els, Sergio Garcia, and David Toms.

The playoff took only one hole – one long hole. A few minutes passed while Garcia got a ruling. Another few minutes passed until it was Weir's turn to play, but he and Little talked about college sports to pass the time, and then he hit a wedge five feet from the hole. Weir had the putt to win, and made it. He had again won the last tournament of the season, and moved up to eleventh on the money list. The U.S. weekly *Golf World* called Weir Mr. November, referring to the fact that he had won the 1998 qualifying school in November, the American Express Championship in November, and now the Tour Championship in November. He had also won the Air Canada Championship in the latter part of the season. It was widely thought that there was something about the way he played the game that allowed him to win tournaments later in the season; he had won each of his three college tournaments after a winter layoff as well. Weir kept saying it was coincidence, but the world loves a trend, and had found one.

The day after the 2001 Tour Championship, Weir began to review his season. He was pleased that he had won again, but he hadn't met his objective of contending in the majors. "I would rather play not as well in regular events and play better in the majors," he said. "Maybe I was just trying to do too much. Maybe I was trying to make my swing too perfect." At the same time, he looked forward to spending a couple of weeks in Palm Springs with Mike Wilson during the off-season and continuing to refine his swing. Meanwhile, in the latter part of 2001, he had played a few tournaments without his waggle, or rehearsal swing, and that had given him something to think about.

"Down the road, I think I will increase my swing speed by not doing it," Weir had told PGA Tour *Partners* magazine. "The routine of doing that is kind of a static, deliberate move, which, physiologically, kind of slows my swing down, because I do it very slowly and specifically. When I get into my swing, my nerves are telling me to do something slow. If I get rid of doing that, I think my swing speed will pick up and I'll be able to hit the ball a little farther."

Having tied for twelfth and thirty-sixth in two fall events without his waggle, he acknowledged that the results were mixed at best. He had what he described as "one really good day" at the first tournament, the Michelob Championship in Williamsburg, Virginia, and a "struggle" at the Disney in Orlando. He put the waggle back in for his win in the Tour Championship, but still believed that it would help in the long term if he played without it. That would help move him in the direction of a no-frills swing, so he reasoned that it made sense to remove it.

•ᴗ

Weir and Darren Clarke are the only two golfers left on the practice green, a few minutes before they'll start their third round of the 2003 Masters. Now it feels like Masters Saturday, because two rounds are done. Halfway to Butler Cabin and the green jacket. For somebody. For Weir? For Clarke? For Woods? Come on. He's eleven shots behind Weir.

Weir, up first, stripes his tee shot down the middle. Clarke, a long hitter, hits his tee shot forty yards by Weir's, on the right side of the fairway. Weir's second comes up ten feet off the front of the green. The pin is on the front-left, and there's a slope between his ball and the hole. He pitches his ball two-thirds of the way to the hole rather than running it all the way. The ball checks and stops a foot from the hole. Short game matters.

Note from Bobby Jones in the spectator guide: "Contestants playing in their first Masters Tournament are sometimes discouraged by the finesse required around the greens and the extra putts required." Weir is in his fourth Masters, and has never been discouraged by the finesse required around the greens. Challenged, but never discouraged.

Up ahead, Phil Mickelson is playing. He started the third round at one-under-par 143, five shots behind Weir. Earlier this week, a reporter asked Mickelson whom he believed would be the next left-hander to win a major. "I can't tell if you're being facetious or if you want me to really answer that," Mickelson responded. When the fellow told him he was serious, the left-hander said, "I'm going to leave that one unanswered. I think we all know the answer to that."

T.R. Reinman, who until a couple of years ago wrote on golf for the *San Diego Union-Tribune*, works for Mickelson now and is following him. He's aware of how well Weir has been playing and of the focus on Mickelson, who was winning tournaments on the PGA Tour while Weir was playing in Australia, Asia, and on the Canadian Tour. Yet they were contemporaries in college, and are the same age. Mickelson won the 1990 U.S. Amateur, and the next year won the Northern Telecom Open on the PGA Tour as an amateur. He has won twenty-one PGA Tour events, while Weir has won five, and has played in forty-two majors without winning one; he has finished third in three Masters, including the last two. Mickelson is constantly reminded that he's the best player in the world not to have won a major. The subject comes up major after major, and will come up major after major until he wins one. He's a favorite this week, of course. CBS, in a pre-tournament release, led its list of tournament contenders with Woods, while putting Mickelson next. It listed thirty-seven golfers who were playing in "America's most prestigious gathering of international professional and amateur golfers," including a group of "international stars" such as Els, Garcia, Price, Colin Montgomerie, Shigeki Maruyama, and others. Weir wasn't on the list.

"If Mike wins," Reinman says, "it will be the biggest thing since the Ice Age to hit Canada."

Weir hits the 2nd green with his second shot, and then two-putts from seventy feet for birdie to get to seven-under. Clarke bogeys the hole after driving into the left trees, and drops to one-under. Weir leads by six shots. He's out there alone, and people are beginning to think it's his tournament to win. Or lose. Michael Healey, a Toronto playwright, has come down for the day on a corporate junket run by Standard Broadcasting, which owns radio stations across Canada. Mirvish Productions buys airtime on Standard's flagship station, CFRB in Toronto, and its head producer, Brian Sewell, was provided with a ticket that he couldn't use. Sewell offered his ticket to Healey, who would have hitchhiked to Augusta with a ticket to the Masters, never mind flown in a private plane. "There was lots of buzz on the plane because of Mike," says Healey, who appreciates well-played golf.

Weir's on the 5th hole now, after pars on the 3rd and 4th. But he drives into the right rough, misses the green, and has one of those troublesome shots around the green that Jones felt could discourage players. He pitches up over a high, peaked mound on the green, but the ball kicks left and runs eight feet by.

Studying the green, Weir waves his putter across the line between his ball and the hole. He's done this from time to time so far, and it's not without a reason. Weir is trying to find the exact spot on the green where he thinks that the putt will start to run out of speed and begin to break, and then sense the speed from there to the hole. The idea came to him during the week, and he's been using the approach whenever the subtle breaks at Augusta suggest it to him.

But here, Weir misses his second such shortish putt of the week. Back to six-under, after which he follows a par on 6 with a birdie on seven, where his approach finishes a couple of feet from the hole. When the putt falls on 7, a guy in a bright yellow shirt, who is smoking a cigar and sitting beside Healey, screams. Somebody says, "Calm down. It's only Saturday," to which the happy fellow responds, "You don't understand! I've got ten thousand dollars on Mike Weir at 25-1." Maybe he does.

Weir pars the 8th and, after driving into the left rough on the 9th, has some tree problems. He drills a low cut shot to the front-right of the green. The hole is sixty feet away, and Weir's putt comes up five feet to the right. He misses the par putt. He has bogeyed the 5th and 9th holes, and has missed a couple of those must-make putts. But maybe it's too early to say that they're must-make putts. He still has twenty-seven holes to play. It wouldn't be sound self-management to put that sort of pressure on himself.

"Mike's a very grounded individual," Rich Gordin says. "He studies himself and what he needs to do – and what he doesn't need to do." What he doesn't need to do is fret over a couple of missed putts.

Clarke has shot two-over-par 38 on the front side, and has fallen six shots behind Weir. The amateur Ricky Barnes is playing well, and is second, four shots behind Weir. Woods started on the back nine, and birdied the 11th, 13th, and 15th holes. He birdied the second hole to get to four-under for the round and one-over for the tournament. Woods is seven shots behind Weir, and charging.

After a par on the 10th, Weir hits a poor iron for his second shot on the 11th hole. He loses concentration for a moment, when his eyes wander away from the safe, right side of the green and toward the pin to the left. The idea at the 11th is to play well away from the pond that's situated left of and short of the green. Weir's ball is left all the way, though, and slams into the bank between the water and the green. It's inside the hazard line and barely visible. Little wants him to take a one-shot penalty and go back to the drop area, then try to get up and down from there for a bogey. But Weir thinks that he can get the ball out of the bank and onto the green; if he does, he'll have a putt for a par.

"You *think* you can get it out?" Little asks Weir. "I want to hear that you *know* you can get it out." Weir tells him that he knows he can get the ball out, and chooses a pitching wedge rather than a sand or lob wedge for the shot, because of its sharper leading edge.

His calculations there: "I just kept thinking that, if it's soft enough in the bank for the ball to plug so deep that I could only see the top of the ball, only a few dimples, then I figured it must be pretty soft behind and underneath. So if I hit the pitching wedge with its sharper leading edge, and dig the heel into the ground, and really make sure I follow through the shot, not stop, then I thought I could knock the ball into the bunker (on the other side of the green). Even if it wasn't as soft as I thought it was, in the worst-case scenario, I'm still probably going to get it in that bunker. But I really thought it should come out fairly soft, as much as it's buried in that slope."

Weir takes a mighty slash at the ball, digging the heel of the clubhead into the pulpy soil. The face of the club opens a little, and the ball pops out to the left, fifteen feet from the hole. Weir's laughing, and almost makes the putt for par. He hates bogeys, but in this case Weir knows that he's made what golfers call a "good" bogey. It could have been worse.

At the 12th, Weir's eight-iron shot flies just over the green. The pin is on the front-right, so he wasn't going anywhere near it, not

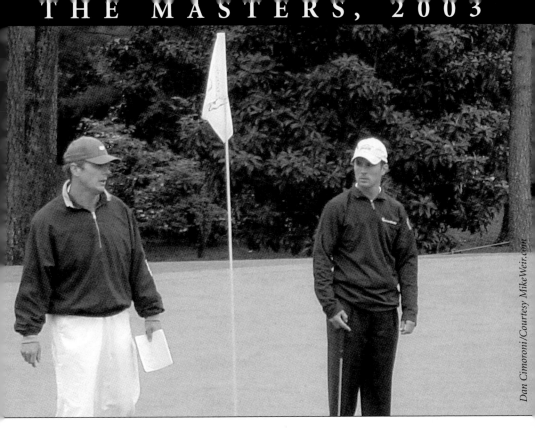

Dan Cimoroni/Courtesy MikeWeir.com

Brennan Little and Mike Weir preparing at Augusta National.

Dan Cimoroni/Courtesy MikeWeir.com

Mike Wilson and Rich Gordin on the range at Augusta National, as Mike Weir practices behind them.

Opposite, top: Mike Weir practices putting on the 14th green.

Opposite, bottom: Lining up a shot: Part of the routine.

Above: Brennan and Mike walk onto the 13th green during practice.

Dan Cimoroni/MikeWeir.com

Mike drives off the 18th tee.

Opposite: Mike's reaction after holing the putt to get into the playoff

Bricia Weir on
the 10th green,
congratulating Mike.

Mike and his
dad, Rich, on
the 10th green

Opposite: Mike's
reaction after
tapping in to win

No caption required.

with the creek so close there. But his ball picks up a big glob of mud, exactly where he'll make contact with it. It's hard to predict how the ball will come off the face of the putter, but it comes off nicely and rolls down the green. And rolls and rolls, six feet by. Weir grits his teeth, studies the putt, and rolls in the right-to-left uphiller for his par. A terrific par. He's still five-under-par. Jeff Maggert, three holes ahead, misses a five-footer for birdie that would have taken him to three-under-par for the tournament. Maggert started the round seven shots behind Weir, but he shot two-under on the front side and, even with a double-bogey on the 11th hole, is one-under on the back nine.

Woods is continuing to advance. His forty-foot putt for birdie on the 6th (his 15th hole of the day) is moving fast, so fast that it could go off the green. But nearing the hole, it looks as if it could catch the middle. Woods starts moving to his right, in a golfer's anticipation of something good happening. The ball slams into the middle of the hole and drops. Fist-pump. Woods is five-under for the third round and even for the tournament. It's always been his goal to get back to even-par. A guy can play from there, win from there. He's six shots behind Weir, suddenly tied for fifth. Woods started the third round today tied for forty-third, in last place.

Things feel condensed out on the course now. There's Woods, back on the front side, finishing. Here's Weir, on the 13th hole, playing along all right but not making any birdies. There's Maggert on the 16th, holing a ten-footer for birdie to move to three-under-par.

Weir has 215 yards to the hole on the 13th, from the right edge of the fairway. He has a sidehill, downhill lie, and chooses a three-iron. The wind is right-to-left, the lie is perfect. The only real issue is that there's a bit of mud on his ball, but Weir doesn't figure it will affect the shot. He's committed to the shot he wants to play, and looks for the ball to slide right to left off the lie and find the middle of the green. His swing here is a good one, the contact is solid, and the ball is flying toward the middle of the green when it veers to the right in the last twenty-five yards. Did the wind affect the flight? He thinks so. The ball plops into the creek, and he bogeys the hole. He's two-over for the back nine and the round, four-under for the tournament. Weir finishes the round at three-under for the tournament after a birdie on the 15th and bogeys on the 16th and 17th. Meanwhile, Maggert birdies the 16th and 17th to shoot 32 on the back nine, 66 for the day. Woods shoots the same score. Maggert picks up nine shots on Weir, as does Woods. Maggert leads after three rounds at five-under-par 211, Weir is at 213 after his 75, and Woods is at 215.

Somebody standing beside the last green as Weir finishes says, "He had it." But he hasn't lost it. He acknowledges the ovation the crowd gives him by taking off his cap. He knows that he's still in the tournament. Two shots off the lead after three rounds? Perfect. Another spectator says to a friend, "He's okay. He's tough."

CBS's Peter Kostis interviews Weir behind the green after he signs his scorecard. "Obviously, I'm not real happy, but I still have a chance to win," he says. "I have to look at it like that. That was my bad round, I hope." A cart whisks Weir off to the media center.

"When you take chances like that you've got to live and die with them," Weir says of his second shot at the 13th. He speaks of the challenges involved in shooting 65 and the challenges involved in shooting 75. "I had a bunch of those [challenges] today and you just know going into it that it's not going to be easy."

Weir didn't show any nervousness on the course, and it was impossible to believe that he wouldn't face any major challenges here. He spoke earlier of having a few hiccups during the tournament. He has hiccupped, yet he's only two shots out of the lead, and he'll play in the last twosome on Masters Sunday.

Weir and Gordin soon leave the club and head back to the hotel, where they review the round. "Are your legs tired?" Gordin, who walked every hole today, asks Weir. "Mine sure are." Weir says that his legs are indeed tired. It was wet out on the course, even in the drying, sunny conditions. There are lots of hills at Augusta National, and Weir played thirty holes yesterday and twenty-four today.

"Let's put our feet up," Gordin says. "We need to rest our legs." They do so, order in some food, and remind themselves that the game is on. Weir had a bit of a struggle on the last ten holes, where he made five bogeys. But as he told Little, "What can you do? This is Augusta National."

Weir soaks his feet later, while taking a long bath, and then sleeps for ten hours. He's trying to make this night like every other night. There's one round to go, and he's in contention to win the Masters. Where else would a professional golfer like to be on this Saturday night, even if he'd prefer not to think about his situation too much? He's a man of routine, and he means to stick to his plan .

CHAPTER NINE

Sunday

April 13, 2003, Pre-Round

He has taken all the steps and faced all the obstacles ahead of him, and now it's time to learn whether he'll handle whatever he comes up against today. But Weir doesn't want to think about what was, or what might be. There's only this round, with tens of thousands of people at Augusta National, now gleaming under an early morning sun. There's only Weir, in contention to win his first major championship.

"Everything's a stepping stone." That's been his credo. Now, in his sixteenth major championship, and five wins after he stepped onto the PGA Tour, Weir is two shots behind Jeff Maggert. They'll start their final rounds at 2:50. Brennan Little will be at Weir's side, and he and Maggert will accompany each other, but he'll really be alone. A golf course is such a vast landscape that it's easy to pick out the golfer, walking along by himself. Even when he's talking to his caddie, acknowledging spectators, and chatting with fellow players, he's on his own. There's that moment of being over the ball, of drawing the club back, of ultimate trust – or distrust – in oneself. Which would it be, today at 2:50, and on into the evening as the 2003 Masters winds down?

·~

Nearly two million Canadians are planning their day around the Masters telecast. The season hasn't started across most of the country, so the Masters arrives at the ideal time. No wonder it's called a rite of spring. The National Golf Club of Canada in Woodbridge, Ontario, is holding its opening cocktail party this afternoon and members will be spending more time in front of the television than in front of the bar.

Weir's friend Rob Roxborough, the director of golf at the Magna Golf Club in Aurora, Ontario, will watch the Masters there with some sixty members. Five years and a few months after he saw Weir through the 1997 qualifying school as his caddie, Dan Keogh will watch with his father in Las Vegas. Weir invited Keogh to spend the week at the Masters in the rented house, but Keogh had planned some time ago to take his father to Vegas to celebrate his seventieth birthday. He knew he would see Weir the day after the Masters in Toronto.

Meanwhile, George Knudson's widow, Shirley, will watch from her home in Toronto, as will their son Paul, a golf professional. She presented Weir with the George Knudson Memorial Trophy when he won the 1997 Canadian Masters. Weir is constantly being compared to Knudson, but he hasn't cared to speculate whether he's better than Knudson, and isn't even interested in the comparison. Weir is interested only in getting the best out of himself.

"I know that's what people want," Weir said a few weeks prior to the Masters when asked about any thoughts he might have regarding his status compared to Knudson's. "But I don't think about comparing myself to him. Unfortunately, I never got the chance to play with George. I feel bad about that. From everything I've heard and from his record, I know that he was a great player and a great guy." Weir would say no more. This was not a discussion into which he wanted to be drawn. Better to allow his golf to speak for him. Anyway, it's impossible to compare golfers across eras. Bobby Jones had said that a player can only beat the players in his own era, so it's silly to try to make comparisons. His logic is unassailable.

Shirley Knudson wasn't interested in the comparisons either. Her husband did win eight times on the PGA Tour. Knudson died in 1989, at the age of fifty-one, so he didn't have a chance to play the Senior PGA Tour, now called the Champions Tour. Had he lived to see this day, he would have watched every shot of this last round at Augusta. Knudson had fallen for Augusta National and the Masters when he first played the tournament. He was always proud of any Canadian who played well, anywhere, and he would have enjoyed the way Weir had learned to manipulate the golf ball, to hit all sorts of shots. Knudson liked to follow consummate golfers, and Weir is becoming a consummate golfer.

Peter Mansbridge, the host of CBC's nightly newscast, *The National*, has been aware of Weir's progress. He knew that Weir was exactly where he deserved to be, in the final twosome on Masters Sunday. Mansbridge had written a column about Weir in the April 14 issue of *Maclean's* magazine, the Canadian newsweekly.

"Weir is having a great year on the pro circuit – one of the best ever for a Canadian – but winning one of the four annual majors is what separates the great from the *really* great," Mansbridge wrote. "Weir knows that, but also feels he's ready to join the elite golfing class." He reflected back on Weir's appearance in the 1998 Canadian

Export "A" Skins Game at the Links at Crowbush Cove in Prince Edward Island – the first time he was invited to the event – where he playfully hit a drive 250 yards, right-handed.

"The Masters at Augusta is a long way from the Skins Game at Crowbush Cove in P.E.I.," Mansbridge wrote. "The stakes are a lot higher, and the pressure has made some of the best golfers in this game's history crumble. So don't expect any left-handed/right-handed tricks as on that day in 1998 – but *do* expect a classy performance, whatever the result." Mansbridge plans to settle himself in front of his television at home in Stratford, Ontario, so that he can watch the classy performance he expects; he'll watch with his three-and-a half-year-old son, Willy, while his wife, actress and singer Cynthia Dale, in Toronto this evening rehearsing for a series of concerts, will receive updates by phone.

Everywhere, it seems, people are attached to their televisions. Singer Michael Burgess, a keen golfer, intends to watch the Masters until the last putt drops. He has an engagement tonight at Toronto's St. Lawrence Centre, but that shouldn't interfere with his following the last round. Tomorrow night he'll sing the national anthem at the Toronto Maple Leafs–Philadelphia Flyers playoff game at the Air Canada Centre. Should Weir win, he'll no doubt sing "O Canada" with an extra burst of pride.

Across Ontario, to the west, everybody in Sarnia is also ready to watch their favorite golfer. The clubhouse at Huron Oaks will fill up. Former Ontario premier Bob Rae, who, like Weir – like all golfers – knows that the game is often enjoyed best alone in the early morning, with a bag of clubs slung over one's shoulders and an empty course ahead, looks forward to the last round. One fellow who watched Canada win the gold-medal Olympic hockey game in the winter of 2002 plans to follow the last round from a pub, with other interested Ontarians. Something is building in the province and, indeed, across the country. The last round of the Masters is becoming a national happening.

Weir-watchers in Ontario will be joined by people across Canada on this final day of the Masters. In British Columbia, Bob Zimmerman, the president of the National Association of Left-Handed Golfers, in Cobble Hill, is thrilled at the possibility of a left-handed, Canadian major champion. Meanwhile, Norman Embree and Bruce Cook have played an old-timers hockey game in Vancouver, and are returning to their homes in Salmon Arm. They don't want to miss the tournament's conclusion. But they know they'll be in trouble, because their schedule will put them on the Coquihalla Highway at about the time Weir is starting the back nine. The tournament isn't being broadcast on radio. What will these guys do?

Canadian golf professionals feel a bond with Weir too. They're connected to him by virtue of being Canadian, and because they know how difficult it is to reach golf's highest levels. And here he is, with an opportunity to become the first Canadian male to win a professional major championship. Richard Zokol, who played the 1992 Masters, will watch; he'll drop his twin boys, Conor and Garrett, at a Canadian Junior Golf Association event in Surrey, where Weir won the 1999 Air Canada Championship, and then spend the afternoon with his wife, Joanie, and his parents watching the Masters at their home in White Rock, south of Vancouver. Stan Leonard, who played in twelve Masters and finished in the top ten six times, including a tie for third in 1958 and a tie for fourth in 1959, plans to watch from his winter home in Rancho Mirage, California. Leonard and Arnold Palmer were tied for the lead after three rounds of the 1959 Masters, but Leonard's 75 pushed him back to a fourth-place finish. Palmer was leading the tournament by three shots with seven holes to play, but hit his tee shot into Rae's Creek on the par-three 12th and triple-bogeyed. He got the lead back with a birdie on the 15th, but missed birdie putts of three and four feet on the 17th and 18th holes. Art Wall, Jr., birdied five of the last six holes to win. Cary Middlecoff finished second by a shot, and Palmer was another shot back. Things happen on the back nine on Masters Sunday, where, Leonard says, "the pressure is really unbelievable."

Three thousand miles from where Leonard will watch today's last round, Lorie Kane, Canada's top player on the LPGA Tour, looks forward to following Weir from her Titusville, Florida, home. There's no way Kane would miss this last round of the Masters with Weir in contention.

This is true also for Jack Nicklaus and Jesper Parnevik. Nicklaus, perhaps, now has a special interest in Weir, since he's been reminded of their correspondence nearly twenty years before. He can't remember any youngster to whom he's sent a letter of encouragement going on to win a major championship. Nicklaus rarely, if ever, watches golf tournaments on television, but he followed the third round from his home in North Palm Beach, Florida, and will watch the last round.

Parnevik, five years older than Weir, knows what it is like to come close in a major. He was leading the 1994 British Open at Turnberry in Ayrshire, Scotland, with a few holes to go. Nick Price, playing ahead of him, finished birdie, eagle, par, to take the lead. Parnevik didn't study the scoreboard and thought he needed to birdie the final hole to get into a playoff, although that wasn't so. He aimed for the hole, which was cut hard against the left-front side of the green, near high rough just beyond. He missed the green, bogeyed the hole, and lost to Price. Then, in 1997, Parnevik retreated on the back nine at Royal Troon, not far from Turnberry, and lost the Open to Justin Leonard. He, like all PGA Tour players, is aware that

Weir has become one of the finest golfers in the game. Parnevik will watch today's events from his home in Jupiter, Florida, to see how Weir will perform under the pressure of Masters Sunday. As Sweden's top male professional, Parnevik has some sense of what it's like to represent a country, as Weir does Canada.

"Augusta is very special," Parnevik says. "I very rarely watch golf, but you have to watch the finish at Augusta. It's even more fun if you've played there, because you can see what the problems are. I can understand how tough a shot is. At Augusta you really need to produce a lot of shots. It tests all your game."

Meanwhile, Wayne Gretzky, Weir's amateur partner in the AT&T National Pro-Am at the Pebble Beach Golf Links two months prior to the Masters, also plans to park himself beside the television to watch the last round. Gretzky had offered those encouraging words to Weir after the 1999 PGA Championship, and they've become friends. Gretzky knows that Weir is facing an ultimate round in his career, perhaps a defining round.

Far from Canada, and far from the United States, other people are also anticipating the last round. Claude Burul is a surgeon working in Abu Dhabi for a hospital that Canadians started and run; he has followed Weir since his Canadian Tour days, but had been one of the many Canadians who found fault with Weir's 2002 season. He questioned his desire and work ethic. Weir's two PGA Tour wins before the Masters had indicated to Burul that he might be wrong. But could he win a major? Burul intends to watch the final round in his home, although the telecast won't start until eleven at night local time.

In Palm Desert, California, Mike Wilson, who went home after working with Weir earlier in the week, has been watching the Masters since it started. He kept his lesson tee open so that he could follow Weir's progress. Wilson is accustomed to going on-line to catch up with what Weir is doing at various tournaments around the world, while taking breaks from his teaching. But the Masters is too important to follow on-line, so he has watched the telecast since the first round. He has a good feeling about Weir's final round, but he's still anxious. Anxious and eager.

Butch Harmon is having breakfast with Adam Scott in the grill-room at Augusta National. Scott is at seven-over-par 223 through fifty-four holes, and will start his last round at 11:30 with fellow Australian Robert Allenby. Today he's playing to acquire more experience at Augusta National. There's no reason why he shouldn't win the tournament some time. There's always next week in pro golf. When Weir was twenty-two he was a rookie professional whose first Masters was eight years away. Scott, now twenty-two, is moving along nicely in his career. What better place to continue his development than during the last round of a Masters, even one in which he's not a factor for the green jacket?

Scott leaves for his pre-round warm-up. The round is under way. Kenny Perry teed off at 11:00, in the second group of the day. Perry has won four times on the PGA Tour, and this week has made the cut in the Masters for only the second time in the six tournaments he has played. Perry and Weir played the first two rounds in the Ford Championship at the Doral Resort & Spa in Miami five weeks ago. Weir shot 70-67 in those rounds, without his best stuff. Perry spoke later of what he'd observed while playing with Weir.

"He plays like such a veteran," Perry said. "I noticed his course management and his thinking. He sure can maneuver himself around a golf course. Mike's on his way to being a superstar. I imagine Canada's out of control when it comes to interest in him.

"He'll definitely win a major," Perry added. "He has the will to win. He could win any of the majors. He has a great shot at winning the Masters. I think he can win it this year. Augusta National is a second-shot course, and he hits those pinpoint irons. Then he's deadly with that putter."

Phil Mickelson's manager, Steve Loy, is spending some quality time around the huge oak tree on the lawn outside the clubhouse this dreamy morning. His best-known client has shot 73-70-72 for a three-round total of one-under-par 215, and is four shots behind Maggert's lead, and two behind Weir. Mickelson is in the fourth-last twosome this afternoon, playing with Jim Furyk.

Somebody says to Loy, "Hey, we have two lefties in there. Let's have a playoff." "Amen," Loy responds, and adds, to nobody in particular, "Where's the drama in golf? Is it mental?"

Certainly players will feel the pressure later, which makes the drama both mental and emotional. But at the same time, errors in the mind have their way of finding expression in the swing. The sounder the mind, the more likely the player can swing properly. But the sounder the swing and the more confident the player in his mechanics, the more likely he can trust himself at the critical moments. Weir has worked for years to make his swing into a finely honed, repetitive motion. He won't blame his swing for the four bogeys he made over the last ten holes in the third round yesterday, when he went from four shots in the lead to two behind Maggert. He was tired, simple as that, and his legs gave way.

Out on the range, Fred Couples, a feel player if ever there was one, isn't ignoring mechanics. He's working with Harmon, who is inspecting his grip. Couples points to the fingers on his left hand, while Harmon takes a club from his bag to demonstrate a grip refinement. Tour players are artists. Everything must feel right, and they like to know why something feels right or why it feels wrong. Knowledge is indeed power. During the 1990 British Open at the Old Course in St. Andrews, Nick Faldo worked for a few hours with

David Leadbetter, making a minute adjustment to his grip on the range. Minor changes can lead to major developments, good and bad. Players and teachers need to be careful. Careful and vigilant.

"Can you see yourself winning? That's the first question?" This is the sports psychologist Bob Rotella talking, near the practice green. He speaks of the importance of feeling comfortable at a major. "You'll be more relaxed then. You'll feel you're where you're supposed to be. You need to be able to deal with all kinds of silly, funny, crazy things during a major, so the ability to accept anything that happens is huge. If you have any flaws, if you're loaded with fear, if the conditions get severe and you're indecisive, these flaws will show up."

•⁀

Weir's starting time is drawing nearer. It's an hour and a half before he'll start, and he likes to begin his pre-round warm-up about fifty minutes to an hour in advance of his tee time. Members of his support group are already at the club. Rich Gordin is chatting with Brennan Little on the road in front of the clubhouse. Gordin visited Weir in his hotel room this morning. They chatted about Weir's post-Masters plans, and then Gordin raised the subject of today's round. "You know what, Rich?" Weir said. "I'm fine. Let's just stop here. I don't want to over-analyze anything. I just want to go out there and play." Gordin said, "Beautiful, I'll see you at the ceremony."

Now Gordin goes into the locker room to see Weir, while Little walks the twenty yards to the caddie area on the west side of the clubhouse to get some towels, leaving Weir's bag on a walkway. He returns to the bag, sits down, and chats for a moment with a couple of writers. The fourth round, the crucible, is imminent. Little has been on Weir's bag for all his majors, and he's ideally suited for the role of his caddie in these high-pressure situations. For one thing, Little is by nature calm; nothing seems to faze him. It doesn't hurt the partnership that Little, as a pro golfer, understands what Parnevik calls the insanity of the game. Little can still play, too, although he claims he's no better than a four-handicap now. Still, it wasn't that long ago when players on the practice tee at the La Costa Resort & Spa in Carlsbad, California, goaded him into hitting some drivers. There he was, with some of the finest players in the game, at the Accenture Match Play Championship, and he hadn't hit a shot in some time. Little grabbed a driver and ripped some long, straight shots far to the end of the range, said nothing, and replaced the club in the bag. This past winter, Little participated in a long-drive competition during a practice round. Without a practice swing, he hit his shot farther than the caddies and the pros. The guy can play. The guy can caddie. He hasn't been late once in the more than four years he has been caddying for Weir. Little is a professional all the way, and he also knows how to have a good time. Weir's a buttoned-down guy on the course and during a tournament, and golf fans don't get to see the fellow who enjoys a beer or two with his friends, who can kick back as well as anybody. But if a person can be known by the company he keeps, well, Weir keeps company with friends who enjoy their lives: Little, Dan Keogh, Rob Roxborough, Dan Cimoroni, his boyhood chum Dave McKinlay, and other pals are regular guys.

On the course, Little has the knack of knowing what to say to Weir, and when to say it. He likes most sports, and so might mention the Dallas Mavericks basketball team on one hole – Little lives in Dallas now. Or he might get into the World Cup of soccer on another hole, if it's World Cup time; or he might chat about bullfighting – he went to the bullfights with writer Dave Perkins during golf's 2002 World Cup in Mexico; or maybe there's some stock-car racing or wrestling on the week's sporting agenda. This week the Stanley Cup playoffs are available to break up the tension as conversational fodder. The chit-chat is part of the game, even in a major – especially in a major.

"Once you're out there, even in a major, you're out there," Little says. "A major is more fun than a regular tournament, though. I'll have to make sure that I stay level-headed for Mike. He'll be a little riled up inside, I'm sure. Regardless of the outcome, I'll be very surprised if he doesn't play well. His attitude is great and his short game is great. Any time he has to use his imagination, he gets into it, like at the British Open. It's fun. You're always thinking. It's not like you stand up on every hole and just beat on a driver."

Some of Weir's family and friends are gathering in an ever-increasing but tightening circle near the range. IMG Canada's Kevin Albrecht flew in this morning for the last round. He mentions that Weir's play this week has been front-page news in Canada. Albrecht spoke with Weir this morning, and says, "He's feeling great. He's so positive." Albrecht is excited, although he's trying to contain himself. Looking ahead to the best of all possible outcomes, he says, "Can you imagine if Mike won today and they asked him to drop the puck tomorrow night in Toronto?" He's referring to the National Hockey League playoff game in Toronto. "Can you imagine the ovation he'd get?"

Weir emerges from the clubhouse, fifty-five minutes prior to teeing it up. He's wearing all black, head to toe. People are making comparisons between "little" Mike Weir and "little" Gary Player (who also often wore all black). Player is five-foot-seven and just under 150 pounds. Weir is five-foot-nine and 155 pounds. They're both wiry and fit. Player has prided himself on his fitness, which has allowed him to travel millions of miles, playing golf around the world, for nearly fifty years. Weir is also a fit athlete, every workout meticulously calibrated to help him get the most out of himself, to prepare himself for a test such as he'll face today. Johnny Miller has said that the golfer who looks after every aspect of his game and his life away from the game – swing, physical fitness, mental fitness, nutrition, taking care of off-course business, looking after his family – has a much better chance of performing at his best. It's as if the golfer will believe that, because he has worked hard and intelligently on all the right things, he deserves to play well.

Still, a player needs perspective. Weir inserted a photograph of his wife, Bricia, in his yardage book while playing the PGA Tour qualifying school one year, so he could remind himself of what's really important in life. Nicklaus and his wife, Barbara, had their first child, Jack, Jr., when he was twenty-one, and five children by the time he was thirty-three; he always knew there was more to life than golf, which, paradoxically, allowed him to concentrate fully on the game when he was playing it. He was able to get away from golf because he had a life besides golf. Tiger Woods isn't married, and he seems consumed by golf and golf alone. But he has had a girlfriend for most of his professional career. His current girlfriend, Elin Nordegren, a Swede who was working as a nanny for Jesper Parnevik when Woods was introduced to her, and his mother, Tida, often follow him at tournaments, especially the majors. Woods's father, Earl, was behind the 18th green when his son won his first Masters in 1997. They embraced immediately after Woods came off the green. Golf is such a private game, and players feel this so intensely, that it's important for them to realize that how they play doesn't define who they are. Weir has learned this over the years. Bricia flew into Augusta today from Salt Lake City to be with him as he goes after his first green jacket. Noticing her in the gallery will help relax him, should he need to calm himself down. He has done this all week when he has noticed his father, Rich, his brother Jim, and the friends who have come to the Masters. Then, when it's his turn to play, Weir gets right into the shot.

Weir takes up a spot on the left side of the range. David Toms, who won his first major at the 2001 PGA Championship, is to his right. Woods is another spot over. This is quiet time, quiet warm-up time. Weir is hitting the ball where he's aiming. By the time he reaches his driver, he knows that he's ready. He's sharp, and hits only three drivers before heading to the practice green. He hits his first driver dead straight, aiming for a pole three hundred yards away and hitting it. Now he hits a draw, aiming for the same pole, and misses it by inches. His third shot is a fade, and he misses it by only a few inches again. "Okay, I'm ready," he tells himself.

Now he's on the putting green, as is Maggert. After a session there, he walks the few yards between well-wishers to the first tee, and gets a big hand. He gives the scorecard to Little, takes an iron out of his golf bag and swings it a few times, and then pulls out his driver. Brennan is checking his yardage book. Weir swings his driver back and forth, and puts it back in his bag, so that he can go through his pre-shot routine when it's his time to play. He ties his shoelaces, and stretches all the way down to the ground without bending his knees. It's 2:50, time to start this last round. Inside the ropes on the golf course that people around the world know so well, Weir is alone. The ultimate moment is here, when Weir is over the ball, about to make his first swing on Masters Sunday.

CHAPTER TEN

Sunday

April 13, 2003, Last Round

K en Dryden in *The Game*, his insightful dissection of his years as goalie for the Montreal Canadiens, observes, "Because the demands on a goalie are mental, it means that, for a goalie, the biggest enemy is himself." In golf, a player's *only* enemy is himself. Nobody but himself can prevent Weir from playing well today. Somebody could come in with a lower score and win the Masters no matter what Weir does today, but there's nothing that Weir can do about that. His task, as in every round, is to play the best golf of which he is capable. The on-course situation could change during the round, especially on the back nine, demanding a response to what another player is doing or has done. Still, another golfer won't be able to bodycheck him into the boards, as in hockey, or block a shot he makes from under the basket, as in basketball, or strike him out, as in baseball. He will be alone on the course, playing the course and himself. He will be the sole arbiter of his result today. These fundamental tenets of the "onliest" game are never more evident than during the last round of a major, when everything a golfer has done before will somehow be expressed in the result.

"Fore, please, Jeff Maggert now driving." And so the last twosome begins its round on a gleaming afternoon that helps everybody forget the bitter weather that lasted until midday Friday. There's an obvious symmetry here, because Maggert and Weir played nine holes during a practice round on Tuesday, and also played the Par 3 Contest together. Now here they are, each seeking his first major championship. Maggert's drive is down the left-center of the fairway, in excellent position.

Now it's Weir's turn. Bob Rotella has called a player's routine his "rod and staff." He elaborates: "The foundation of consistency is a sound preshot routine." It's something a player does every time, no matter the situation. Rich Gordin and Mike Wilson have helped Weir ingrain his routine, which hasn't varied from his opening tee shot through the last shot he hit in the third round yesterday. It's unlikely that it will vary today. If it does, this could indicate a problem, such as nerves, indecisiveness, or confusion.

"Fore please, Mike Weir now driving." Weir stands behind the ball, looking down the fairway. He puts his right hand on the club first, a couple of inches down the grip, and points the clubshaft down the fairway. Then he slides his right hand up to accommodate his left hand below it. He's over the ball, waggles his club as he always does, puts it back behind the ball, and swings. The drive is ideal, and finishes just behind Maggert's ball. The hole is cut on the right-center of the green, in a bowl. Weir's approach finishes left of the hole, and thirty-five feet long, while Maggert misses the green to the right by fifteen yards. Maggert plays a neat little shot, one-hopping his ball through the fringe and onto the green. It runs on and catches the left lip of the hole, hard, leaping eight feet by. He'll have a difficult putt for par to begin his round.

Plenty of people are following Maggert and Weir, but not nearly as many as are with Tiger Woods and José Maria Olazabal, two groups ahead, or with Phil Mickelson and Jim Furyk, three two-somes forward. Almost everybody expects Woods to make a move on the leaders. IMG's Kevin Albrecht and Dan Cimoroni are walking along, as are Steve Bennett, Rich and Jim Weir, and Bricia. Paul Coffey, a retired National Hockey League player, and a friend of Weir's, is also here, and so is Eddie Heinen, a friend from college. Rich Gordin is out for a Sunday walk at the Masters. They're on the right side of the 1st hole, up near the green, as Weir putts.

He has a tricky putt, because his ball will go slightly uphill before crossing a ridge in the green. It will then pick up speed, lots of speed, on its way downhill from there. Weir hits the putt firmly, and it crosses the ridge easily enough. The putt looks good. The ball slides three feet by the hole. Weir marks his ball, after which Maggert holes his par putt. That's saving a shot after a second-shot error. Weir holes his putt for par, and they move on to the 2nd hole.

Both Maggert and Weir hit good drives, left of the fairway bunker on the right side, and short of it. Bricia says that she found it harder watching at home in Draper, Utah, than being out here, where she can read her husband's body language and talk with family and friends. She thought he looked calm this morning, and told him, "Honey, just another day at the office." Weir said, "I'm just happy I'm here, in the last group at Augusta."

"He's not usually like that," Bricia says. "He's usually more intense." Everybody around him has noticed the same things this morning: his calmness, his readiness. He has said of majors, "I just want to have a ready, powerful feeling," and he appears to have that.

The air is fresh this mid-afternoon, too; it's felt grimy all week, what with the humidity and the persistent rain. It's still difficult to walk outside the ropes, where mud doesn't provide much of a platform, but the sky is blue and it's warm. Bricia feels happy to be outdoors. She spoke last night with Rosalie, Weir's mother, and said that it was too bad she didn't live on the way to Augusta so that the plane could pick her up. But Rosalie said she couldn't have come in anyway, because of her fractured foot.

Weir and Maggert lay up short of the green with their second shots. Weir and his brother Jim spent an hour together this morning in Weir's hotel. "He was in a real good mood," Jim reports. "Walking in, I wasn't sure what I would find. But he was feeling so good, very positive."

Weir's third shot on the par-five is right at the hole, and spins behind and around it, nearly going in. He soon taps in for birdie to get to four-under-par for the tournament. Maggert pars the hole, to remain five-under-par. This is exactly the start that Weir wanted, and it might even allay some of his brother's anxiety. "I have to admit I had trouble getting some food down this morning," Jim says. "It was a fun feeling."

The 3rd hole at Augusta National is a cunning, short par-four. It's only 350 yards, and it's straightaway, but it's full of mystery and, sometimes, misery. At this length, and with the fairway getting firmer as it dries in the sun, and with some slopes that propel a ball forward, the hole might tempt longer hitters to try to drive the green. This is the shortest par-four on the course, and has changed hardly at all over the years. There was no reason to change it, because it was always meant to test a player's thinking and strategy more, much more, than his ability to hit the ball a long way. And if he does choose to hit it a long way, he had better hit it straight.

Tiger Woods decided to go for the green a few moments ago. He had parred the first and birdied the second hole, so was two-under-par for the tournament and only three shots behind Maggert at that point. He consulted with his caddie, Steve Williams, on the 3rd tee as to what shot he should play. Williams thought that this was the right time to gamble, and that Woods ought to try to get as near the green as possible, because the hole was cut in the front-left. Williams figured that, if Woods hit just the shot required, he could then chip or pitch the ball closer to the hole than if he had a short iron in from the fairway. Woods hadn't hit his driver off the 3rd tee in any of the earlier rounds, but took Williams's suggestion.

Trouble. Woods's tee shot soared to the right and finished in the azaleas. A shrub blocked his access to the ball, preventing him from swinging right-handed. He turned the head of a short iron around and made a left-handed swing. The ball skittered up the fairway, finishing near the green on the tightly mown fairway. Woods then skulled his third shot right through the green. What was going on? Tiger Woods doesn't make such errors. But he's human, and had compounded one error with another. After his thin, third shot, he hit his fourth shot fat onto the green, but well away from the hole. Two putts later, Woods had double-bogeyed this peach of a short par-four that is called, appropriately enough, Flowering Peach. "Tiger made double on 3?" Jim Weir asks as his brother walks up the 3rd fairway after laying up perfectly, to the right of the deep bunkers to the left. He's looking at the scoreboard to the left of the third hole as Woods's double-bogey is posted. "That's the fun of the Masters, scoreboard-watching," Jim observes.

Maggert isn't having any fun on the 3rd hole. His tee shot finds sand, and there's a high lip a few feet ahead. Still, he has only a short iron to the green. The shot isn't overly difficult, except for this being the last round of the Masters, except for the fact that he hasn't come into the tournament feeling too confident, and except for the fact that there's no margin of error on the shot. Hit it a little fat and the ball might stay in the bunker or plop out a few yards forward. Hit it a little thin and – well, it's not helpful to think along these lines. Better just to assess the shot, pick out the target, and swing away. Maggert has one of the most reliable swings in the game. He finishes the same way every time, in impeccable balance as he holds his finish while watching the flight of the ball.

That's how he finishes after his sand shot, but the ball doesn't emerge from the bunker. Maggert has caught it slightly thin, just enough that it doesn't carry the lip. The ball ricochets off the hard, raised edge of the bunker and snaps back toward him. Like a baseball hitter frozen at the plate while a high, hard one comes right at his head, Maggert doesn't have time to react. He stands there in place, in balance, as the ball hits his chest. Maggert comes out of the bunker and points to his chest, informing Weir of what has transpired. He waits to advise a rules official of the situation, and then plays from the bunker under penalty of two shots. Maggert is suddenly playing his fifth shot on the hole.

Rule 19-2B in golf's official rules code applies: "If a competitor's ball is accidentally deflected or stopped by himself, his partner, or either of their caddies or equipment, the competitor shall incur a penalty of two strokes." Maggert's fifth shot reaches the back of the green. Now it's Weir's turn to play. He has waited about ten minutes to play his next shot, while Maggert resolved his unfortunate situation. It's a test for Weir, part of Sunday at the Masters.

Weir is over the ball in the 3rd fairway. He takes the left side of the hole out of play, hitting his second intentionally long and to the right. Weir's playing controlled golf so far. After Maggert rolls his long putt ten feet by the hole, Weir merely touches his putt and watches it stagger down the slick green to four inches short of the hole, dead center. "Way to go, Mike," some people say. And also, inevitably, "Go, Canada." Maggert holes his ten-footer for a triple-bogey. Woods went from two-under to even-par on this hole a few minutes ago. Maggert has gone from five-under and the lead to two-under. Weir remains at four-under, and is leading the Masters again.

"You have to feel for Jeff," Bricia says. Tom McCarthy, a member at Toronto's Rosedale Golf Club, who flew down this morning from Toronto with his son Peter and forty other people, says, "Our boy, he's tough, and he's going to be tough to beat." *Tough.* The word keeps coming up with reference to Weir.

He demonstrates his fortitude again on the par-three 4th hole. After hitting his tee shot onto the apron of the green, thirty-five feet from the hole, he runs his first putt eight feet by. But then he makes his par putt. On the next hole, he makes an unforced error, driving into the deep pit of a bunker to the left of the 5th fairway. This is the same bunker that Weir visited during his early practice round a couple of weeks ago. It's the one place he wanted to avoid.

Fortunately, Weir's ball has come back into the middle of the bunker. Still, not even the top of his head is visible to the spectators on the right side of the fairway, perhaps forty yards away. The ball comes up and over the high lip of the bunker – it's the first thing they see after the spray of sand – and finishes just short of the green, on the right side. It's there or thereabouts, as British golf commentators like to say.

The hole is cut on a higher portion of ground than where Weir's ball lies, and a ridge runs diagonally to him along the direct line to the hole. He has two choices: He can flop the ball onto the higher point and hope it stops quickly, or he can play a chip-and-run well out to the right so that the ball will take the slope and slide back to the hole. Leslie Schon, in his book *The Psychology of Golf*, written in 1923, calls this a "just not" shot, a shot just not on the green, "a nerve-twisting, score-spoiling, match-losing shot, for the simplest of all reasons, that it can be played and played well in one-and-twenty different ways, and played badly in a hundred."

Steve Bennett, chewing feverishly on a cigar, says, "I guarantee you he is going to wedge it." But Weir fools Steve when he plays a clever chip-and-run. He chooses to use the ground rather than throw the ball up in the air. It runs up along a line ten feet right of the hole, climbs and slithers up the ridge, then takes a sharp left turn and finishes three feet from the hole. Maggert, having parred the 4th hole by getting up and down from sand, holes from thirty feet for birdie here. He's three-under-par. Weir holes his par putt. Despite his triple-bogey on the 4th hole, Maggert is still only a shot behind Weir. As for Woods, his name has been removed from the leader-board. He's no longer a factor. His run at a third consecutive Masters is over.

Sunday pins are part of the fun during the last round of the Masters. Experienced players are all but certain of where the Tee and Cup Committee will put the holes for the final round, and plan their strategy accordingly. The location on the 180-yard 6th hole is on a knob on the extreme upper right of the green. The hole is here every second Sunday in April in every final round of the Masters, and it's inaccessible to anything but the most precise shot. Weir's shot elicits a reaction that builds as the ball flies toward the hole. The ball soars over the heads of the people on the hillside below and seems suspended in the air, as is always the case when a shot comes from an elevated tee. It hangs there, and the spectators around the green stare up at it. Their eyes lower as the ball plummets, and what started as a collective hum crests to a rousing finale. Weir's ball digs into the green a couple of feet to the right of the hole, and settles there.

Back on the tee, Weir pumps his left arm – mildly. Brennan Little acknowledges his fine shot. "Thank you," Weir says, and then walks down the hill with him. They hear a huge roar from the 16th green to the right. Bob Estes has nearly made a hole-in-one. Weir smiles as he looks over at the green. He's having fun. A few minutes later, more fun – but for Weir this time, who holes his short birdie putt to go to two-under for the day, and five-under for the tournament.

But one perfectly played hole does not necessarily lead to another. Weir hooks his drive into the goop right of the fairway on the 410-yard 7th hole. Thinking about his tee shot here on Saturday night, Weir decided he'd been fading the ball nicely and would go with that flight today. But, standing over the ball, he didn't commit to the shot, and said to himself, "Okay, let's just hit it straight." Weir made a thinking mistake, and the result was his worst swing of the day, and one of his worst swings all week.

His ball is plugged, so that only its top is visible. He waits for a ruling, and it's a complicated one. Charles Lanzette, a rules official for the PGA of America, makes his way over. Given that golf is played over a vast landscape subject to weather and ground conditions, it's not surprising that many unusual situations occur. In this case, Rule 25, which addresses what are called "Abnormal Ground Conditions," applies. Rule 25-1 in particular is applicable to Weir's situation. "Interference by abnormal ground conditions occurs," it declares, "when a ball lies in or touches the condition or when such a condition interferes with the player's stance or the area of his intended swing." Weir gets relief from the mud, but has no shot to the green. Trees block his direct route there. There's an opening back to the fairway, so he'll make sure he gets back there first and then try to hook the ball hard so that it will scoot up the fairway toward the green – and, he hopes, into one of the bunkers in front of the elevated green. Objective one: Get out of the trees and back into a decent spot. Objective two: Reach the front bunkers.

"I need you back just a little bit, guys," Weir advises the people gathered to his right, so that he can clearly see his path out of the trees. Cameramen kneel behind him. He hits the shot he wants, and it runs up into the sand short of the green. The hole is cut on the front of the green, not that far from where he'll play his third shot. It's a sweet one, and finishes ten inches from the hole. These par saves keep a round going. He's demonstrating the tenacity that Weir-watchers have noticed. Richard Zokol mentioned this morning that he thought it was helpful that Weir was a couple of shots out of the lead starting the final round, because he had won each of his five PGA Tour events coming from behind. "His tenacity will show up," Zokol predicted.

Weir's tenacity is one of his trademarks, and it shows up again on the par-five 8th hole, where, after a good drive, Weir finds mud on his ball, and so aims well right. He hits what he thinks is a good enough shot, but his ball squirts left, just into the rough, from which he has no angle to the pin on the back-left of the long green. Tree limbs and then high mounds intervene between him and the hole. The overhanging limbs mean he can't hit the ball in the air, and the mounds that roll every which way make it risky for him to try to hit the ball hard along the ground and up and over them. He takes the prudent route to the right, chipping his ball low and planning to run it up the right side of the green. But the ball doesn't reach the green. Weir now has a twenty-yard shot back to the pin. He can see only the top half of the flagstick, because the hole is cut behind a steep rise.

No problem, because Weir's a craftsman. The situation demands a shot lofted all the way over the upslope short of the hole. His father, Rich, watches from the right side of the fairway near the green as Weir uses what amounts to almost an underhanded swing to get the ball up quickly. He judges the distance so well that the ball nearly goes in the hole. Somebody says, "He's playing with our nerves. He's scrambling, but he's hitting phenomenal shots." IMG's Albrecht adds, "I think he's having fun. This is what you work so hard for."

Weir makes his par, which means he has made two consecutive scrambling pars. Weir has said all week that he'll try to do whatever he has to do to get the ball in the hole, and that he'll accept all challenges. He's staying true to his commitment. A conventional par follows on the 9th hole, where Weir takes two putts from fifteen feet. Steve Bennett, Weir's pro from the Huron Oaks days, looks slightly more at ease than he did while Weir was making those two unconventional pars on the 7th and 8th holes, and lights another cigar.

The tension is increasing as Weir and Maggert move into the back nine. Weir has said for years that he wants only to be in contention heading into these last nine holes. He's in contention all right. He's leading the Masters, still five-under for the tournament.

Meanwhile, Len Mattiace, who started the last round at even-par, is playing flawlessly. He's four-under for the day and tournament through twelve holes, and only a shot behind Weir.

Walking along, Weir sometimes looks into the gallery. He spots Bricia, and his father. He's getting ardent support from the Canadians here, and also from other visitors who appreciate well-played golf and an exciting competition. Weir's a finely tuned athlete, which means he knows when to focus on the task at hand and when to take a reflective moment. When he notices his dad, he sees calmness, and feels calmed himself.

It's a good thing that Weir can't see inside his father's nervous system. Rich is munching on his lips, and his mouth is dry. Jim refers to his father's state on the way to the 10th tee. "My dad's not being rude if he walks right by you and doesn't say anything," he tells a friend. "It's just that he can't stand still."

This is also true of Steve Bennett. He's trudging through the mud right of the 10th fairway after Weir has hit his drive down the middle. Albrecht observes how quickly Bennett is moving, and that he's off to the side by himself. "He's dying," Albrecht says of Bennett. "He's living every shot. I told him not to ruin the celebration if Mike wins by making us to go a funeral in Brights Grove."

Clearly, some of Weir's supporters are becoming unglued. They're feeling the pressure. Is Weir? Albrecht, walking with Jim and Bricia, doesn't think it's getting to him, at least not to the point where it's affecting his shots. If anything, he's hitting the ball better and longer, because he's into the flow of the tournament. Weir has learned to maintain his rhythm while contending for a tournament, and he has demonstrated – so far – that he can do this while leading a major on the last day.

"Look how long he hit this drive," Albrecht says. "He's pumped. I think he's just having fun." That word again. *Fun.* "Kurt Browning was the best I ever saw at this," Albrecht elaborates, referring to the former Canadian figure-skating Olympic gold-medal winner. "Guys are throwing up in the locker room, and he's asking, 'Why? This is where I want to be.' He was always two steps ahead of everybody. The good ones are. At the World Championships, he's laughing in the locker room. He's calm."

Weir pars the 10th hole, and moves into the feared stretch called Amen Corner – the 11th, 12th, and 13th holes. In 1958, the writer Herbert Warren Wind named this area after a blues song by Mezz

Mezzrow called "Shoutin' in That Amen Corner." Until Wind appropriated the felicitous phrase, members called this area the "water loop." The par-four 11th turns right to left from a tee deep in the woods to the left of the 10th fairway, then sweeps downhill to a green that's protected by a pond that begins at the front left and works its way around to the rear. The par-three 12th across Rae's Creek plays to a wide-but-shallow green, and players often get confused trying to read the wind here. The par-five 13th is short, at 510 yards, and players can reach the green in two, especially if they turn their drives around the corner on the dogleg-left hole; but a stream coils in front of and to the right of the green, and has drowned the hopes of more than a few Masters contenders. The player who makes two pars and then a birdie at Amen Corner is shoutin' all right; he's shoutin' good golf. But it's also possible to make larger numbers. Ray Floyd hit his second shot into the water at the 11th during his 1990 playoff against Nick Faldo, who won the Masters on that green. Tom Weiskopf made a thirteen on the 12th in the first round in 1980; his first shot found Rae's Creek, after which he hit four shots with a sand wedge from the drop area. Weiskopf kept trying to hit the shot near the hole behind the bunker, but hit one shot after another into the water. He stood in place, shot after shot, putting his hand out so that his caddie, Leroy Schultz, could hand him another ball. And in 2002, Ernie Els drove into the woods where the fairway turns left on the 13th hole – exactly where he had told himself not to venture, or even come near – made a triple-bogey eight, and lost any chance to catch Tiger Woods and win the Masters.

Len Mattiace hasn't been having any problems in Amen Corner, although there was plenty of shoutin' – from the thousands of people gathered in the region. He's eagled the 13th hole and is six-under-par for the tournament. He now leads Weir by a shot, who pars the 11th hole after an excellent drive and a well-played iron right of the hole, which was cut near the water to the left; Weir learned his lesson after the way he played his second shot on the 11th in the third round. He gets an impressive ovation when he walks onto the 12th tee, just twenty yards to the right of the 11th green. A stand behind the tee is full of people, and ahead, all the way to the green, there's nothing but golf course.

Spectators can't get there from here, so the players, after hitting their tee shots, are alone with their caddies as they walk into the secluded corner. Nobody but players, their caddies, and officials go there. It's the heart of Amen Corner, a lonely place. The same is true of the 13th tee and the walk back to the 13th fairway. The players and their caddies appear almost as silhouettes from the vantage point behind the 12th tee. They're cast in sharp relief, lone figures against a massive, green landscape.

As always, the Sunday pin placement on the 12th is in the far-right segment of the green. Rae's Creek squeezes nearer the green here than on the left side. Most players consider this pin position inaccessible, and play well to the left, away from the hole. But golfers find it difficult to focus their attention away from the pin. Fred Couples said in 1992 that he meant to play to the left of the hole in the last round, but that his attention drifted to the flagstick at the last moment. His ball followed his eyes, but it came up short. Couples got a break that was equivalent to a Masters miracle, because the ball hung up on the bank just above the creek. He parred the hole and went on to win that Masters.

At the 12th, Maggert, now four-under for the tournament, hits his tee shot long and into the back bunker. Weir aims just over the left of the center of the front bunker, but pushes his shot eight yards left, his worst shot into a green today. His ball settles on the far, far left of the green. Jim says, "You can play from there. It's on the green." Tom McCarthy, the Rosedale Golf Club member who flew down today, moves on. "This is exciting. Good luck the rest of the way, Bricia," he tells Weir's wife.

Weir is farther from the hole than Maggert, so it's his turn to play. The ball moves slowly down the green, picking up speed as it approaches the hole. For a second, Weir thinks the ball will drop. He lunges forward from eighty feet away, in anticipation, but the ball wanders by. And wanders by some more, until he's left with six feet for par. He marks his ball. It's Maggert's shot, from a dicey lie in the bunker. The area hasn't been raked properly, so Maggert can't be confident that the ball will come out softly.

It comes out low and running – through the green to his left and into Rae's Creek. Disaster. He walks across the bridge on that side of the green, all the way to the drop area about fifty yards away on the opposite side of the water. After taking a one-shot penalty for finding the water, he hits his fourth shot back into the creek. This is another grotesque development for Maggert. Amen Corner is silent. There's no shoutin'. Maggert plays his sixth shot to the green. Weir waits. Maggert doesn't change expression.

"Poor Jeff," Bricia says. "He has the fight in him," she adds, knowing that he won't quit. She says that she and her husband have a beautiful painting of this hole at their home. It was given to the golfers who played in the 2000 Masters, Weir's first. Right about now, Maggert would have a problem seeing any beauty in the work of art.

Maggert's troubles elicit some untoward comments. "Goodbye," a fellow barks of his chances in the Masters now. "That's rude," Bricia says. Weir is over his par putt on the 12th green, while Bricia notes Mattiace's play today. "How about Len Mattiace? What a round he's pulling off."

Weir makes his par putt. He's making every putt today. All those drills at home in his basement; the days and nights and weeks and months spent on the Huron Oaks practice green; practice until sunset after rounds in Australia and on the Canadian Tour; the putting work in his basement in Draper, where he had a hole cut into the foundation of the home when it was being built – they're adding up to this round, today, Sunday at the Masters.

Weir's college buddy Eddie Heinen offers a resounding "Yes" when the par putt goes down on the 12th green. Heinen won his second consecutive California Amateur last June. The tournament is held every June at Pebble Beach Golf Links. Heinen was one up playing the last hole in every one of his last four matches, then parred the par-five 18th at Pebble Beach to maintain that margin. He knows his golf, and he likes what he's seeing in Weir today. When Weir played the Canadian Tour, Heinen, who lives in Las Vegas and likes a little golf action, brought him down to play matches against a couple of guys. They knew that Weir was a tour pro, and were keen to play the Heinen-Weir team in better-ball matches. Weir recalls that they played twice on back-to-back days. He walked away with a few hundred dollars at a time when he needed the dough.

Mattiace isn't giving any ground to Weir today. He didn't win on the PGA Tour until his 220th event, in 2002, and then he won again the same year. Now he's leading the Masters while playing the round of his life. Mattiace retooled his swing under the eye of noted instructor Jim McLean. It's a long, graceful swing, and he's hitting one sharp shot after another. He's just birdied the par-five 15th hole to get to seven-under, two shots up on Weir, who is playing the 13th.

Weir's drive on the 13th is too far left, but does find the fairway. Overhanging limbs from a tree interfere with his direct line to the green so that he has to fade his shot some thirty yards, aiming at the part of the stream that runs up beside the right edge of the green. He chooses a four-iron, but overcuts the shot. Weir sees the ball hit

the green, watches it roll to the left, and assumes that it has gone just
through the left side and onto the fringe. By now every shot is critical; Mattiace is looming as Weir's sole opponent down the back
nine, posting low numbers and making it imperative that Weir not
lose a shot. He's playing so well that Weir has to make up some
ground, but his four-iron onto the 13th green didn't stay on the
edge of the green, it rolled into a hollow. The hole is cut on the front-
right of the green, not far from the creek. The green slopes away
from Weir and toward the water.

"Okay, Michael," Bob Weeks, editor of the Canadian magazine
SCOREGolf, says. The May issue is ready to go to press, but a Weir win
here will force Weeks to tear it up and redo it to allow for a new
Masters section – a problem he and his associates would love to have.

Weir is facing the most difficult putt he has had all week. The
problems are complex. First, the ball has settled into a small groove
in a section of turf that resembles resodded grass; he'll also have to
go down and after the ball, which is slightly below him. The ball will
jump out of the groove with topspin as soon as Weir makes his
stroke. He putts, and the ball climbs the few feet of ground before the
green, then starts rolling and curling, rolling and curling. Here it
comes, from well to the left of the hole, down a slope, and on toward
the hole. But wait. It's picking up speed and it could go all the way
into the water. That way lies disaster and, surely, the end of Weir's
chances. But the ball slows and stays on the edge of the green, fifteen
feet from the hole.

"We need to get this thing in here," Weir tells Little. He's looked
at a leaderboard and noticed that Mattiace has birdied the 16th hole
to get to eight-under-par. Weir, at five-under, can't let this birdie
chance slip.

Golf's a game of vision, as Rich Gordin has impressed upon
Weir. A player has to use his eyes, to look out to the target, out

there. Weir looks, really *looks*, at the right edge of the hole. He focuses his eyes on the right edge, not allowing them to wander to the center or any other spot, or on any other possible outcome. He does this, and makes the putt. Left-hand fist-pump. Weir is six-under-par. Hearts race. Eddie Heinen asks of somebody, anybody, "Do you know where the pin is on 14?"

Weir has passed through Amen Corner in par, par, and birdie – just what was required. But he can do nothing about how well Mattiace is playing. He's not in the same twosome with him, for one thing, so can apply only indirect pressure by playing mistake-free golf, and, perhaps, picking up a birdie or two on the way in.

Weir's drive on the 14th hole is in good shape, up the left side of this par-four whose green is wild, wild, wild, with more humps and bumps than a wave on the sea when the surf's up. The pin is back-left, twelve feet from the edge of the green and fifteen feet over one of the humps, which are often referred to as elephant burial grounds.

Weir's second shot lands thirty feet right of the hole, then rolls farther right, before stopping forty feet away, still on the top side of the green. That's good news. His putt comes up four feet short, not what he wants. But he goes right to work. It's another must-make putt, because he's two shots behind Mattiace. He makes the putt.

The 15th hole is another par-five that Weir can reach in two. He's looking for a big drive that will leave him something like a four-iron into the green, which is on the other side of a pond. Memorable things have happened here. Gene Sarazen holed a four-wood in the 1935 Masters to erase in one stroke the three-shot lead that Craig Wood held over him, then went on to win their playoff. Jack Nicklaus eagled the hole on his way to playing the last ten holes in seven-under-par to win the 1986 Masters; just behind him, then-leader Seve Ballesteros hit a weak four-iron into the water from the center of the fairway, ending his chances of winning that year.

The variety of things that can happen on the 15th hole makes it one of golf's most compelling back-nine holes. If the Masters doesn't truly begin until the back nine on Sunday, the tension that players, spectators, and people watching on television feel truly begins to build here. This is because a score from three to seven, or even more, is possible. Most holes – the 14th, to cite one – generate a range of scores in which the lowest – a birdie – is two shots lower than the highest – a bogey. Sure, a player could make an eagle here, but he'd have to hole his second shot. At the par-five 15th, though, a golfer can go from an eagle to a double-bogey – a difference of four shots – with only one swing. The Masters often turns on this hole.

Weir gets ahead of the ball and pushes it toward the left rough. The ball lands in the fairway but runs too far. It nestles into the rough – and this is genuine rough, now three inches long, because the course crew hasn't been able to cut it this week; there's been too much rain. Weir is only a few feet into the rough, but that's enough. There's the depth to which his ball has sunk, and there's a tall tree about sixty yards ahead, which blocks his direct line to the green. He's 240 yards from the green, and he would have to hit a big slice – two o'clock to ten o'clock – to get there; this would be a challenge, even if his ball weren't sitting down in the rough. He doesn't have much choice but to lay up his second shot and rely on his wedge to get him near the hole. Weir needs to birdie the hole to inch a little closer to Mattiace.

He purses his lips as he approaches his ball in the rough, and shakes his head. He has his hands on his hips, and offers a bit of a snort. Then he chats with Little in the fairway before coming over to inspect his lie more closely. He says to the people gathered nearby, "It's Augusta National. They're not supposed to have any rough."

Weir wouldn't have made this lighthearted comment a year ago: he would have grimaced at the lie, and, perhaps, put pressure on himself to hit a perfect shot. Maybe he would have even taken an ill-advised gamble and gone for the green. But he's put in the time on his short game so that he can depend on a layup short of the pond and a wedge to have a good chance to birdie the hole. Weir has the recent memories of birdieing holes with wedges in his hands to win the Bob Hope Chrysler Classic and the Nissan Open.

Weir wastes no time after deciding to lay up. He hits an eight-iron that rises over the tree straight ahead. The ball finishes ninety-one yards from the hole. He's gone a little farther than he wanted – precisely four yards too far. Players talk about "having a good number" for a shot, by which they mean a yardage that allows them to hit a full shot. It's easier to make a full swing, especially in pressure-laden circumstances, than to make a three-quarter or half swing. But Weir is too far from the hole to use a full sand wedge, and so has to take a little off the shot to make sure that the ball will skip forward, rather than spin, when it hits the green. The shot will call for a little sand wedge, and touch and control – just when the circumstances are conspiring to make it difficult to swing with this finesse.

Weir has practiced for this moment by hitting all sorts of little shots. He enjoys taking something off a shot, or dialing in a little extra speed. There was a late afternoon during the Honda Classic near Ft. Lauderdale, Florida, when he hit nothing but fifty-yard shots for an entire bag of practice balls. Asked what he was trying to do, he said, "I'm trying to turn my upper body and keep the club in front of me, then do the same back to the ball." There was no extra movement. The clubface was stable all the way back and through, moving only with the gentle motion of his upper body as he stabilized himself with his legs.

Weir settles over his third shot on the 15th hole. The hole is in the back-right of the green. From behind, Weir makes what looks like a perfect swing; it's an exact copy of the shot he hit beside that practice green at the Honda tournament, except that his backswing is longer, because the shot is longer. The plane of his swing is the same going back as through, which is what he's been looking for while working on his swing. There's no clubface rotation. The swing is simple. He's made the complex simple, to use Rich Gordin's apt phrase.

The ball flies right at the hole and finishes two feet away. Weir's brother Jim is near tears. He's not the only one. "That's awesome," he whispers.

Weir walks along a pathway left of the water in front of the green, and just to the right of the spectator stands. He's given a standing ovation. His shot was elegant, and he's conducting himself with class. No extravagant gestures. A tip of the cap. A gentle wave. That's Weir. Modest. A boy from small-town Ontario whose roots remain solidly there.

A gasp that cascades into a roar surges from the people gathered in the bleachers around the 15th green, from which they can see a nearby scoreboard. Mattiace has bogeyed the 18th hole to fall back to seven-under, and his score has just been posted. Weir is six-under with a short putt to tie Mattiace. He's the only player left on the course with a chance to win the Masters. Only. Lonely. To what degree do the roars penetrate? To what degree is he locked into his game? Is he in a bubble, the "inner mental room" of which Rich Gordin speaks? It will take close to an hour for Weir to finish the 15th hole and then play the last three holes. Tour players say that the hardest way to finish a tournament is when somebody has posted a score so that golfers still in contention know a mistake can cost them the tournament, but that they need a birdie to win or force a playoff. Just when the player would like to play an aggressive shot, he has to caution himself about the potential for error. The margin of error diminishes to a vanishing point, especially hitting into Augusta National's greens. The golfer remains his own enemy, as Ken Dryden said of the goalie in hockey, but the new score already posted has become his enemy as well.

"Seven's the number," Albrecht declares, meaning that's where Mattiace has finished and that's what Weir must have for a playoff. Weir makes his birdie putt, so he's seven-under-par. Three pars and he'll be in a playoff. One birdie and two pars and he'll win the Masters. One bogey and two pars and he'll finish second. The mathematics are brutal. So is the task.

.-

In Toronto, Bob Rae is on the edge of his chair while Weir plays the back nine. His wife, Arlene, a non-golfer, watches, "glued to the set and cheering him on with great gusto," Rae says. In Stratford, Peter Mansbridge provides his son, Willy, with relevant history of the Masters – the old saw that the Masters doesn't begin until the back nine on Sunday. Mansbridge is nervous, but not Willy, who keeps saying, "Don't worry, Dad, Mike Weir is going to win." Willy is so sure of this that he heads to his Lego set after the 15th hole. Mansbridge implores his son to watch the last few holes. "Willy, come here. You have to sit on my knee. This is history. You'll be able to tell your kids and your grandkids that you saw this." Willy obliges his dad.

A couple of hours away, the Brantford Golf and Country Club is holding a Masters Sunday party for the first time. In Aurora, David Kaufman, a pro golfer and the executive director of the Magna Golf Club there, is having anxiety attacks, along with Rob Roxborough and their members. "I wonder if Mike Weir is as nervous when he putts as I am when he putts," Kaufman exclaims as Weir stands over yet another must-make putt, and then there's silence. The tension in the room explodes when he holes it. Nobody budges from his or her seat; everybody becomes superstitious, and

Roxborough won't get up from the couch where he's sitting, even to use the bathroom. His more urgent need is to watch the golfer he played against when they were juniors in southern Ontario, an age group behind him, the kid he remembers as "a scrapper. "He was always going to get it done," Roxborough tells anybody who will listen. "When you finished your round, you looked to see what Mike was doing." The kid from a younger age group often came in with scores lower than the older golfers.

Across the top of Toronto from Magna, members of the National, long settled in front of a huge television screen after noshing on sushi and shrimp, groan with every putt that Weir leaves himself for par. They high-five one another after every putt he makes, and shed tears too, although they know he has plenty of work to do. But there's a feeling in the room of something enormous unfolding. Emotion streams across Canada, a national river of feeling that swells as the afternoon wears on. In British Columbia, Norman Embree and Bruce Cook, the fellows returning from their old-timers hockey game in Vancouver, are approaching Merritt on the Coquihalla Highway. Each is wondering if the other would mind stopping to spend a couple of hours in a roadside pub to watch the conclusion to the Masters. Each mentions the idea at just about the same time.

The fellows notice a sign for a pub, pull off the highway, and tear into the place, where they find a giant television screen with the sound turned way up, one waitress on duty, and the pub filled with senior hockey players who, like them, have stopped to watch the Masters. They're returning home from hockey tournaments around the province. The parking lot, Embree reports, started to look like the pits at the Le Mans racetrack.

In Abu Dhabi, Claude Burul is still watching the last round, although it's three in the morning, local time, on Monday. At the

Newtonmore Golf Club in the Scottish Highlands, members are cheering Weir on because he plays left-handed; Newtonmore has a higher percentage of left-handed golfers – at least 35 per cent – than any club in the world; locals believe this is because the first sport a youngster plays here, shinty, is usually played left-handed, with an instrument called a caman. When kids take up golf, they naturally play it left-handed, or, as they say in Scotland, cack-handed or corrie-fisted. And when they stick with golf in this area, they join Newtonmore. The members are ready to welcome Weir should he win the Masters. "We can certainly promise him a real Highland welcome and a game of golf in real Highland scenery," Robin Cattanach, the secretary of the Scottish Left-Handers Golf Association, and a Newtonmore member, tells Bob Shields of the *Scottish Daily Record*. "And I reckon we've got one or two players here who will give him a good run for his money."

Meanwhile, Canadian prime minister Jean Chrétien is watching today's round with his wife, Aline, and aides in the Dominican Republic, where he's attending a trade meeting. In Pinehurst, North Carolina, Tom Stewart, a golf professional who owns a golf-memorabilia store, watches because he has become enamored of Weir's creativity around the course, and of his modesty. Jeff Neuman, an editor in New York City, is taken by Weir's "nerveless putting." Dan Keogh and his dad have a 7:00 p.m. flight out of Las Vegas, and had to check out of their hotel earlier in the day. They watch the telecast in the Bellagio's sports-book room. Rick Gibson, Weir's World Cup partner, watches in Manila, where he lives.

And back in southern Ontario, in the city of Cambridge, Bill Leigh, a Scotsman who moved with his wife, Betty, to Canada in 1967, watches from his hospital bed. Leigh is seventy-four, and was diagnosed with lung cancer a short time ago. In 1989, he lost his right leg to osteomyelitis. Leigh became active in amputee golf, and helped organize the Canadian Amputee Golf Championships. He's followed tournament golf and, particularly, Weir. He's been in the hospital for a month, and knows that he doesn't have much time left. Leigh and his wife are watching the final round in his room. He sleeps through much of the telecast, but he's aware of what's happening. He knows that Weir could win the Masters.

·⌣

Nick Price has finished his round while Weir is playing the last few holes. Price's respect for Weir has been growing year by year. He saw in Weir a young man who would work and work and work, as he himself had. Eventually Weir and Price met, became colleagues and friends, and played matches together during the 2000 Presidents Cup. Weir sometimes thinks of what he calls "Nick Priceisms," such as, "Just make a shot a shot, whether it's for fun or for the Masters," and "Keep chipping away at your tendencies and improve little by little every year."

Price was sitting on the deck of the MacArthur Golf Club in Hobe Sound, Florida, a week before the 2003 Masters. He spoke of Weir, and what it takes to win a major.

"When you're in control of your golf swing and you're not hitting these maverick shots, these wild shots," Price says, "the game is so much fun. You go out there and you wonder how deep in the 60s you'll go."

Asked to assess Weir's game and chances of winning a major, Price said, "If Mike doesn't win a major, I'll be surprised. He has his ducks in a row, and he has at least nine or ten more years of four chances each year to win one. He has so much game. I think he's still learning, too. He's also not such a short hitter, although people think that he is." He adds, "I'm happy to see that he's come out of his lean patch last year and is doing all the right things. It's just a matter of finessing what he has now. Mike has a wonderful ten years ahead of him."

The par-three 16th hole is 170 yards over water from tee to green and along the left side of the green, which appears to emerge from a hall of mirrors. There's no point in playing directly at the hole most of the time, because of the green's complicated slopes. It tilts hard from right to left, too. Today the hole is cut to the back-left of the green, the traditional placement on Masters Sunday; anywhere short of and to the left of the hole is to be avoided, because the right-to-left slope of the green will move the ball left and probably into the water. A shot pin-high but to the left will likely roll into a deep bunker. Weir's shot is ideal, and finishes ten feet right of the hole. He'll take the lead if he makes the putt, but he could also easily three-putt. There's a couple of feet of break in the putt; it's rare to find that much break in a ten-foot putt, but this is Augusta National.

Weir receives another warm ovation that starts a hundred yards from the green as he walks there. He raises his putter, waves, and tips the bill of his cap to the crowd. Maggert also gets an appreciative welcome. He's parred the 13th and birdied the 14th and 15th after his debacle on the 12th hole. Here he's first to putt, from twenty feet away, and makes his third consecutive birdie. Maggert's having a strange round.

Weir can't go aggressively at his putt, and it runs out of speed and just misses. Par. On to the 17th hole, 425 yards, and playing down a chute between trees. The landing area is invisible from the tee, because it's on a higher piece of ground. Both Maggert and Weir hit their drives into ideal spots. While walking up the 17th fairway, Little, the master of casual conversation, asks Weir if he has heard that "Rowdy" Roddy Piper might be returning to professional wrestling. He and Weir chat for a moment. Then it's back to work.

The hole is directly behind the deep bunker at the front-right of the green. There's no room for error on a line toward the hole, so Weir, who has 147 yards to the hole, will surely play left. There's no margin for error there, either, because a shot coming in too short in that direction will kick off a sharp slope down to the front of the green. It would be nearly impossible to get close to the hole from there, because of the intervening bunker.

Not surprisingly, Weir comes up thirty-five feet left of the hole and beyond it. He marks his ball, and then tosses it to Little for cleaning. His putt drips three feet by the hole. Here's another treacherous little par putt, but he holes it, center cut. "No chicken there," somebody says. Thirty-five million people are watching the last round on U.S. television, and a couple of million are watching in Canada. They let themselves breathe for a moment, and then tense up again as Weir walks to the 18th tee.

"Hey, Brennan, if somebody had told us that, if we make birdie on 18, we win the Masters, that would have been pretty cool, right?" Weir says as they make their way to the tee. "Let's hit a good drive here," Brennan tells Weir, "and go from there." Birdie to win. Par for a playoff. Four hundred and sixty-five yards of golf hole, the 18th shoots uphill so steeply that television viewers can't see the elevation change. Massive bunkers gleaming with white sand soar, seeming to reach into the sky. The golfer must thread his drive through a narrow chute, with tall pines on either side. One drive left.

Patrons are jamming the left side of the fairway, where they can walk – but gingerly, in the drying but still shifting dirt. Spectators surround the green, and people are massed all the way back to the clubhouse. The media stand left of the green is full. Weir is over the ball on the 18th tee, makes his swing, looks for a second down the fairway, and bends to retrieve his tee in a golfer's reflex action after hitting a good drive. The ball lands on the left side of the fairway and finishes thirty-five yards short of the deep bunker there that's three hundred yards from the tee.

Weir walks up the fairway side by side with Little. Choruses of "Let's go, Mike" resound in the early evening. Weir offers a slight wave of his hand, and walks ten yards past Maggert's ball to his own. He has 199 yards to the hole, which is cut on the rear portion of the green, on a second, higher tier. Should he fly his ball all the way to the flag, Weir's likely to face a scary downhill putt. Should the ball finish short of the rise in the green, he'll have to putt over the slope and risk either coming up short and leaving himself with a par putt of some length, or going past and having a slick downhill putt for par. The possibilities might befuddle a less mentally tough golfer. For Weir, it's a matter of computing the yardage to the front of the green, figuring out the yardage from there to the ridge and the hole, choosing a club, and making his swing.

Weir pulls out his four-iron. Brennan steps away to the left. Weir's trying to land his ball on the front third of the green, intending that the upslope kill its forward momentum so that it won't go beyond the hole.

The ball's in the air, and prompts a mixed response from high up the hill around the green. At first the sound rises, as the ball hits the green and rolls toward the hole. Will it get up the hill? The sound changes and becomes constricted. The hill killed the speed all right, but so much so that the ball didn't make it up the slope. It's rolled back to near where it landed. Weir has forty-five feet to the hole. He takes his putter out of the bag a hundred yards from the green, doffs his cap as the spectators applaud, then puts it on as he walks onto the green.

Maggert is putting from a few feet farther away than Weir, on a similar but not identical line. He comes up short, though he hit the putt firmly. It's Weir's turn. Little is holding the flag while he is over the ball, and then removes it as the ball starts rolling. It's coming up short, well short. Weir has seven feet to get into the playoff.

Here is a career-defining putt.

Many Canadians turn away from their television sets. Others shield their eyes, or turn off the sound. Michael Burgess had to leave his post by the television set to get to his engagement at the St. Lawrence Centre for the Arts in Toronto, but has found a black-and-white set there so he can watch the conclusion to the Masters.

Weir studies the line of his putt from behind the hole, from the right, and, after replacing his ball, from behind it. He then stands over the ball, looks at the hole, and takes two practice strokes – routine, routine. Mattiace is on the practice green between the ninth green and 10th tee, waiting to see if he'll be in a playoff in a moment or if he'll be the Masters champion. Weir makes his stroke. The ball darts for the hole and dives in the middle. It's the best putt he has hit all day, on a day when he hit nothing but wonderful putts. It's the best putt that he has hit in his life, considering the circumstances. Weir takes off his cap again, and congratulates Maggert on his play, on a day when he played through a triple-bogey and a quintuple-bogey. The British writer Bernard Darwin once said, "It's a hard world and golf is a hard game." Today golf was a hard game for Maggert. Today Weir, who has shot a four-under-par 68, was harder than the game. So far. His sudden-death playoff against Mattiace will begin in a moment on the 10th hole.

People tear back down toward the 10th fairway and green to watch the playoff, traversing dangerous, slippery ground. At the pub off the Coquihalla Highway in British Columbia, the senior hockey players are on their cellphones, telling their wives they'll be a little late because of what's happening across the continent in Augusta,

Georgia. In her husband's hospital room in Cambridge, Ontario, Betty Leigh is watching her husband and the telecast.

Mattiace, up first, drives well down the fairway, left-center. Weir swings, and bends down quickly again to pick up his tee – that sign of a fine shot. The two golfers remaining in the tournament are three feet apart in the fairway. The hole is on the back-left of the green. Mattiace is first to play as the shadows lengthen over this downhill hole that sits on a lower part of the course; there's a ninety-foot drop in elevation from tee to green. Weir walks forward ten yards to step off the distance to the hole from a marker, and makes a notation in his yardage book. Mattiace takes a couple of practice swings, steps back from the ball, and settles over it. He steps back one more time before assuming his stance again. He's trying to play right of the hole, because the green isn't far from the left edge of the green, which falls away into shrubs, trees, and pine straw. But he comes over the top of his shot and the ball flies left as soon as it leaves his clubface. It bounds down into the treed area. Advantage Weir.

Weir is behind his ball. He takes a practice swing and looks down the line from behind before running his fingers along the clubface to clear it of any grass clippings or moisture. Now he's over the ball, takes his waggle, and swings. The ball flies toward the hole, coming up forty feet short. It's a good shot, just what he needed, although he wouldn't have minded the ball getting up nearer the hole.

"How's your pulse?" somebody asks Tom McCarthy, one of the Weir-watchers in from Toronto. "My mother's in heaven and I'm praying to her," he answers. At the Magna Golf Club, Rob Roxborough notices that his pant legs around his thighs are soaked from the sweat that's been pouring from the palms of his hands.

Mattiace can't play toward the hole, because a tree blocks his way, so he aims to the right and pitches up to the green over a rise in the ground. He didn't have much of a chance to get near the hole on that angle, and his ball runs twenty-five feet by the hole. Weir goes through his routine and watches as his ball comes up to the hole. Might it go in? The ball rolls six feet by.

Mattiace is on his haunches, studying his par putt. Weir is on the opposite side of the hole from his own putt, and waits while Mattiace putts. Mattiace loses the speed of the putt, and his ball shoots eighteen feet beyond the hole, and nearly off the green. He misses this bogey putt as well. Weir has two putts to win the Masters. His first putt rolls just by. Weir says later he likes to think he would have made it if he needed to. He taps in his bogey putt – he didn't make a bogey for the round itself – and wins the Masters. Betty Leigh tells her husband, Bill, that Weir has won. He gives her a thumbs-up and smiles at her, a gesture that, after he dies a week later, she says she'll never forget.

Weir raises his hands and head after he taps in to win. He and Brennan Little embrace one another; they've traveled a long road together. Brennan takes the flag as a souvenir. Exultant, family and friends race onto the green: Bricia, tightly hugging her husband, the new Masters champion; Rich, embracing his son, both in tears; brother Jim; manager Dan Cimoroni. The road to the Masters ends here. Who knows what lies ahead?